Language and control

Other books by the same authors

By Roger Fowler

Introduction to Transformational Syntax
Understanding Language: An Introduction to Linguistics
A Dictionary of Modern Critical Terms (as editor)

By Gunther Kress and Bob Hodge

Language as Ideology

Language
and control

Roger Fowler · Bob Hodge ·
Gunther Kress · Tony Trew

Routledge & Kegan Paul
LONDON, BOSTON AND HENLEY

First published in 1979
by Routledge & Kegan Paul Ltd

39 Store Street, London WC1E 7DD
Broadway House, Newtown Road,
Henley-on-Thames, Oxon RG9 1EN and
9 Park Street, Boston, Mass. 02108, USA

Set in 11/12 Monotype Ehrhardt 453
and printed and bound in Great Britain at
The Camelot Press Ltd, Southampton

British Library Cataloguing in Publication Data

Language and control
    1. Sociolinguistics
    I. Fowler, Roger
    301.2'1   P40   79-40662

    ISBN 0 7100 0288 2

Contents

Preface

This book explores three related propositions about the way language functions in social and political practice. First, the language which we use and which is directed to us embodies specific views – or 'theories' – of reality. This thesis has been developed in the writings of the linguists Edward Sapir and Benjamin Lee Whorf. Whorf applies it to whole languages: any speaker of Hopi (an American Indian language) views the world differently from any speaker of English, he maintains, because the structures of the two languages cut up the world in radically different ways. We show how this works in varying choices of words and constructions *within* one language. Different styles of speech and writing express contrasting analyses and assessments in specific areas of experience: not total world-views, but specialized systems of ideas relevant to events such as political demonstrations, to processes such as employment and bargaining, to objects such as material possessions and physical environment.

Second, variation in types of discourse is inseparable from social and economic factors. Different social strata and groups have different varieties of language available to them. The same is true of institutions and media. So the discourse of managers is different from that of workers; the language of television news reporting contrasts with that of pub or club conversation. These variations are regular and, once this characteristic of language has been understood, quite recognizable. Linguistic variations reflect and, what is more, actively *express* the structured social differences which give rise to them. They express social meanings. Among these social meanings are, importantly, the systems of ideas mentioned in the first paragraph.

Third, language usage is not merely an effect or reflex of social organization and processes, it is a *part* of social process. It constitutes social meanings and thus social practices. Necessarily, we speak and write and listen and read within actual social and interpersonal contexts. If our discourse articulates social meanings, then the act of articulation in context affects the situations and relationships which formed these meanings in the first place. Very often the effect is to reaffirm and consolidate existing social structures. A good example of this conservative reinforcement is provided by interviews. In typical interviews, there are marked differences between the speech of interviewers and interviewees. These differences express the socially ascribed status of the interviewer, and allow him or her to manipulate the behaviour of the interviewee. There are both practical and ritual (ultimately practical also) functions in these interactions. In practical terms, the interview is a mechanism of *control* of one individual by another; the 'ritual' function is the reaffirmation of the interviewer's right to control the interviewee, and this ritual is part of the legitimation of the roles of 'more powerful' and 'less powerful' which society has ascribed to the participants. Language with its strong encoding of social meanings is then both a mediator of interpersonal relationships and a force in the perpetuation of the social relationships which underpin them.

Interviews are from our point of view not simply a random example of the role of language in social practice. Their embodiment of inequality of power and their use as an instrument of control make them a *typical* example. A major function of sociolinguistic mechanisms is to play a part in the control of members of subordinate groups by members of dominant groups. This control is effected both by regulation and by constitution: by explicit manipulation and by the creation of an apparent 'natural world' in which inequitable relations and processes are presented as given and inevitable. Power differential provides the underlying semantic for the systems of ideas encoded in language structure. The provocativeness of this fact is hardly noticed by the practitioners of sociolinguistics, the academic discipline devoted to the study of language in society. Sociolinguists are, therefore, at best naïve in accepting the social structures they describe as neutral, while at worst they collude in a view of existing social structures as unchangeable. Our book was designed not as yet another academic study in sociolinguistics so much as a contribution to the unveiling of linguistic practices which are instruments in social inequality and the concealment of truth.

This concern with language and control explains the inclusion of our first essay, on George Orwell. Orwell recognized some of the connections between language, ideas and social structure which are at the centre of our argument, and in his novel *1984* he explored the notion that language-structure could be mobilized to control or limit thought. His concepts of 'doublethink', 'newspeak' and 'duckspeak' rest on recognizable principles of language-patterning. However, a broader range of linguistic devices, and, above all, the syntax of a language, needs to be studied for a more comprehensive analysis of the language of control. In the chapters which make up the bulk of the work we attempt to describe the social, interpersonal and ideological functions of a much wider range of linguistic constructions than Orwell refers to.

Our materials are all samples of real language drawn from a wide variety of discourse contexts: newspapers, printed rules and regulations, three different kinds of interview, a child's spoken response to a story in a picture-book, even the minimal language of greetings cards, birth registration certificates and newspaper birth announcements. We show how linguistic structures are used to explore, systematize, transform, and often obscure, analyses of reality; to regulate the ideas and behaviour of others; to classify and rank people, events and objects; to assert institutional or personal status. Many of the processes mentioned here happen automatically, eluding the consciousness of source and recipient. If they were generally subject to conscious scrutiny, they would be less effective. Since we regard many of the effects as undesirable, one of our practical goals is to expose these processes to open examination. This requires some quite searching linguistic analysis, but not an enormously complicated linguistic methodology.

The linguistic apparatus we have used is a composite of a number of sources. The natural basis for this kind of work is a 'functional' model, that is to say a theory of language which proposes that the structures of language have developed in response to the communicative needs that language is called upon to serve rather than a linguistic model which assumes that structures are natural, universal properties of the human mind and so unaffected by social function. We have chosen the most fully developed of contemporary functional theories, that of M. A. K. Halliday, whose recent work is very compatible with our aims in insisting that the functions of linguistic structures are based in social structure. Halliday's linguistic model is still in the process of development, and we have freely selected from it and adapted it to our purposes. We have also supplemented it with concepts from other linguistic models: for instance, we have used transformational descriptions of syntax where appropriate, and have also taken concepts from speech act theory. We must emphasize

3

that we are not offering a full and definitive model, but a mode of analysis which is still being refined and systematized, and which at this stage aims at practical applicability rather than theoretical neatness.

We believe that the apparatus is simple and consistent enough to be applied by non-linguists in a 'do-it-yourself' critical linguistics of texts which interest them professionally or personally. The fact that discourse is social as well as linguistic, and provides so much of the material used in sociological investigation, should make these methods useful as a means for extracting more from such materials than linguistic theory has hitherto made possible.

We began writing this book when all four authors were teaching at the University of East Anglia, Norwich, around 1975. Much of the material has been discussed in our undergraduate seminars and lectures, and we owe much to our students of that period for enriching and correcting our analyses. The linguistic theory emerged through many valuable experiences of team-teaching shared by various pairings of the authors, and many hours of less structured discussions which also helped us realize and develop our common intellectual and practical aims.

The book was devised, planned and revised in a co-operative mode; and we are all in general agreement about its contents and claims. The individual chapters were written by the people to whom they are attributed in the list of contents, but all were submitted to the other authors for criticism, and most were extensively revised as a result. There remain minor inconsistencies, but that is a consequence of the provisional nature of the linguistic theory. Some differences in the area of social theory will also be evident. But this book does not aim or claim to be a final, agreed, synthesis. It is a demonstration of work in progress towards what we regard as an original, critical and practical theory of language in society.

Our thanks go to Susan Hoffman, and to Isobel Durrant and Bod Wright, for recording, transcribing and discussing in essays the interviews used in chapter 4; and to Gareth Jones for making available to us his research texts, on which chapter 5 is based, for contributing to the writing of that chapter and for reading and commenting on much of the other material from a sociologist's perspective.

A note on further reading

Language and control discusses questions which are the concern of linguistics, sociolinguistics, sociology and political theory. However, our approach does not fall within any of those disciplines as they are traditionally conceived. In fact, it is strongly critical of the dominant currents within the disciplines as they are presently constituted, especially linguistics and sociolinguistics. Existing work which is to some extent compatible with our approach is not completely so, or not immediately so. For this reason we have decided not to select a list of books recommended for supporting reading. However, we have of course drawn many specific analytic concepts and terms from the available theories, and our sources are given in the notes. These references are not intended merely for documentation or authority, and readers are strongly recommended to follow them up, guided by the discussion in the particular points of our text where they are introduced. Together, these references constitute our list of recommended reading.

1 · Orwellian linguistics

BOB HODGE and ROGER FOWLER

The Government have concluded that this section (section 2 of the Official Secrets Act 1911) should be replaced by an Official Information Act.

(Merlyn Rees, British Home Secretary, Statement in House of Commons, 22 November 1976)

Our response to this statement contains simultaneously outrage and a sense of its ordinariness. We habitually accept such perversions of language from government officers and agencies, yet there is still a sense of shock at the precision and openness of the lie, the naked insanity of its logic. There is a word in English for this sort of thing: Orwell's 'doublethink', from his great political novel *1984*. Short, blunt and unerring, the word gives a liberating sense of control over the phenomenon. Rees's Act, of course, recalls *1984* unusually closely. The 'Official Information Act' is designed to suppress rather than publish information, just as Oceania's Ministry of Truth in *1984* is devoted to the falsification of historical records. Orwell's novel is now part of our culture's understanding of itself, and even people who have not read it can project its terms onto the Westminster and Whitehall of the decade before 1984. But like Winston Smith, the hero of the novel, we find the term is not so simple after all. We think we know that Merlyn Rees must know it is a lie to call 'secrets' 'information', and we know that, even knowing this, we will adopt the usage when the Act becomes law. We are sure – almost – that Mr Rees must realize that the whole process conjures up the world of *1984*, yet he can still get away with it, and like Winston Smith we continue to accept an Oceanic regime.

But for a novel which has had such an impact on our general consciousness about the language of politics, *1984*'s analysis of this topic is curiously underestimated. It is as if the talismanic words 'Newspeak', 'reality control' and 'doublethink' have passed too quickly into the English language. They have been so memorable that they make the novel seem redundant. As Orwell said of New-

6

speak, the extreme compression of the language eliminates the complex of ideas in the full concept, which is neutralized and replaced by something much simpler. But there are other reasons why Orwell has proved difficult to interpret. One is the confusedly partisan criticism that his work has received, and invites by its own partisanship and contradictions. So *Animal Farm*, as a satire on Soviet Russia, was seized on with delight by cold-war intellectuals of the right, but Orwell claimed he really meant it to expose the betrayers of the revolution, which would make it ultra-left rather than reactionary. *1984* has a similar ambiguity. Was he really predicting a horrific totalitarian society growing out of the rule of the post-war Labour government ('Ingsoc' from 'English socialism')? But the terms of his materialist analysis of the language and society of *Oceania* come from a lifelong, if ambivalent, involvement in left-wing politics and thought.

Another difficulty in interpreting Orwell's significance as a thinker on language comes from the fact that his major contribution has the form of a novel. He wrote a number of essays on the subject, but these are brief, informal and insubstantial. On the basis of these essays Orwell might seem like just another product of Eton, denouncing the decay of the English language from the columns of the *Daily Telegraph*. In his essays 'Politics and the English Language' (*Collected Essays*, vol. IV, pp. 156–70)[1] and 'The English Language' (*Collected Essays*, vol. III, pp. 40–6) he complains that English is 'in a bad way' and in a state of 'temporary decadence', and protests against such 'abuses' as dead metaphors, pretentious and foreign diction, vacuous words, euphemisms, ready-made phrases, etc.:

> modern writing . . . consists in gumming together long strips of words which have already been set in order by someone else, and making the results presentable by sheer humbug ('Politics and the English Language', ed. cit., p. 163).

> Except for the useful abbreviations 'i.e.', 'e.g.', and 'etc.' there is no real need for any of the hundreds of foreign phrases now current in English (ibid., pp. 160–1)

> American is a bad influence and has already had a debasing effect ('The English Language', ed. cit., p. 45).

Such statements as these, articulated with Orwell's usual unrelenting anger, sound as if they belong to a familiar conservative, purist and chauvinistic tradition which stretches back to Sir John Cheke's condemnation of 'inkhorn terms' in the sixteenth century. Orwell's patriotism and his pessimism lead to these negative and apparently reactionary judgments. But his real affiliation is with a line of sceptical, critical thinking about the misuses of language which overlaps confusingly with the reactionary, conservationist line in that both share a similar list of alleged abuses. For the conservationist, the threat is that the cultural values impregnated in English will be superseded, weakened or obscured by misuse or tainting of the language. For the critical thinker, the danger is that slovenly language will inhibit thought and turn us into helpless victims of the manipulators who currently hold power. On this point, Orwell's ideas have affinities with, and in some cases are influenced by, the arguments of such people as C. K. Ogden, I. A. Richards, Count Korzybski and Stuart Chase.[2] Chase, for instance, passionately warns us that words are not things, that a great deal of the language to which we are exposed delivers no content but mere valueless abstractions: political and commercial language is often mendacious, pretending to deliver the goods but actually just giving vent to noise (cf. 'Duckspeak', below). One reason Ogden used to justify basic English is that it

gives us a chance of getting free from the strange power which words have had over us from the earliest times; a chance of getting clear about the processes by which our ideas become fixed forms of behaviour before we ourselves are conscious of what history and society are making us say.[3]

Orwell's list of linguistic abuses given in 'Politics and the English Language' contains examples of most of the misuses of language that have become the favourites of indignant letter-writers of any persuasion. Of dead metaphors like 'ring the changes on', 'take up the cudgels for', he says 'many of these are used without knowledge of their meaning'. Pretentious words – his examples include 'phenomenon', 'categorical', 'virtual' – 'are used to dress up simple statements and given an air of scientific impartiality to biased judgments' and to 'dignify the sordid processes of international politics'. He cites 'strictly meaningless' words in art criticism, and worse still, political words like 'democracy', 'socialism', 'freedom' which are 'often used in a consciously dishonest way' and 'with intent to deceive'. Summing up, he refers to 'this catalogue of swindles and perversions'. This seems a vague and emotive judgment. However, Orwell means what he says, and what he is saying is not essentially conservative. His main targets are not Stalinists or long-haired adolescents, but the leaders of English political and intellectual life, who he believes are guilty of large-scale perversion of language, and calculated acts of deception.

However, *1984* is Orwell's major work on language. The fact that this work is a novel and not an essay or treatise raises special difficulties of interpretation. A novel's content is refracted through its form. It is an elementary kind of misreading to regard every opinion in a novel as the author's, yet the majority of commentators on *1984* have done just that. The result has been to make him seem more definite and more simple-minded than he was. But the ideas in *1984* always have a source in the novel itself, which is clearly distinguished from the author's consciousness. The world of the novel is seen mostly through the eyes of Winston Smith, whose experience is totally contaminated by the manipulative techniques of Ingsoc. Into the narrative is inserted a treatise by Goldstein, arch-heretic against Big Brother, or probably another fiction from high up in Minitrue, the Ministry of Propaganda. Attached to the work is an Appendix on 'Newspeak', the language programme of Oceania. Whose voice speaks in the Appendix – Orwell's? Hardly. These are the opinions of an orthodox worker from the middle levels of Minitrue, someone like Syme but less critical. Orwell himself is everywhere but nowhere. The novel presents deliberately limited ideas, along with some of the means for understanding and criticizing these limitations, tracing them to sources in a particular social and political order. How far Orwell consciously worked through this critique we can never know, and this novelistic method of presenting ideas encourages such uncertainty. When does Orwell's understanding end, and his readers' own speculation begin? It is often impossible to say. In this situation the critic can only try to avoid two extremes. One is to claim Orwell's critical activity as his own, the other is in effect to rewrite Orwell's novel so that it confirms a new orthodoxy. Both perversions would find a happy home somewhere in Minitrue – another illustration of how relevant Orwell's satire is to the conditions of intellectual production in our society. But Orwell leaves us no single choice. By writing in this form, he has produced something that is tailor-made to be appropriated by contrary interests. Qualities that are admired in works of art, like irony, ambiguity, and multiple levels of meaning, are kinds of doublethink.

The action of *1984* takes place in London, chief city of 'Airstrip I', a province of Oceania. The world seems to be dominated by three large blocs, Oceania, Eastasia and Eurasia, in a permanent state of war, always two in alliance against the third in a war that may not exist, whose function according to Goldstein is largely economic and political, ensuring full employment, and justifying an austere and repressive regime. Oceania itself is said to consist of three groups, Inner Party (2 per cent), Outer Party (13 per cent), and Proles (85 per cent), or high, middle and low to use Goldstein's categories. The Inner Party are a ruling caste. The Outer Party see themselves as part of the governing class, but have no real power.

This unreliable account of the basic structure of Oceanic society is none the less the key to understanding the structure and function of the languages of Oceania. The Appendix refers to two languages, Oldspeak and Newspeak, with Newspeak destined to replace Oldspeak entirely by 2050, after which time Oceania will once again be a single linguistic community. However, what we are shown has a different structure and significance. The Proles speak a form of Oldspeak, and clearly will continue to do so. Newspeak is an artificial language, spoken by no one as a first language, probably understood only by Party members. However, Party members habitually use Oldspeak amongst themselves, and Goldstein writes in Oldspeak. This form of Oldspeak is very different from Proles' Oldspeak. The difference can be clarified through two terms associated with the modern sociolinguist, Basil Bernstein, 'elaborated code' and 'restricted code'.[4] For Bernstein, a restricted code, or use of language, is characterized by simple sentence-structures, limited reference and lack of abstract concepts and self-reflective operations. Elaborated code has the opposite qualities. Bernstein argues a correlation between restricted-code use and working-class speech in England, leading to working-class disadvantage in the educational system. He claims that the professional middle class have mastery of the two kinds of language, both restricted and elaborated codes. The middle-class speakers, in this view, have all the advantages of a restricted code, and also have access to a more powerful mode of language and thought.

Orwell's *1984* suggests an interesting variation on this scheme. Newspeak has many features of a restricted code: complexity is severely reduced, abstracts are limited, evaluation and criticism almost eliminated. So Newspeak turns out to be a particular kind of restricted code, one specifically designed for the ruling class. Proles seem unable to transcend their restricted code in *1984*, but party members are similarly limited by their own highly prestigious restricted code. Orwell here seems to have anticipated Bernstein's categories and Bernstein's emphasis on language and class, and language as an instrument of control, and he has added a devastating judgment on middle-class language and on the flexible options Bernstein saw as open to the middle-class speaker. The prestige language developed by the middle classes may be just another restricted code.

Orwell's account of language was based firmly on his understanding of forms of consciousness which he saw as growing directly out of prevailing modes of social and political organization. For Orwell, the rulers in a stratified society like post-Empire Britain or Stalinist Russia needed systematically to deceive the populace about their society's relationship to material reality. But plausible and systematic lying requires *self*-deception too, a willingness to entertain conviction about what one knows to be untrue. Since this self-delusion is voluntarily induced, it is doubly duplicitous. It is a kind of willed schizophrenia, to which Orwell in *1984* gave the definitive name 'doublethink'.

In the earlier essay 'Politics and the English Language', Orwell described the typical forms of the language of doublethink he found in contemporary discourse, in terms that are still applicable today.

In our time, political speech and writing are largely the defence of the indefensible . . . Thus political language has to consist largely of euphemism, question-begging and sheer cloudy vagueness. Defenceless villages are bombarded from the air, the inhabitants driven out into the countryside, the cattle machine-gunned, the huts set on fire with incendiary bullets: this is called pacification. Millions of peasants are robbed of their farms and sent trudging along the roads with no more than they can carry: this is called transfer of population or rectification of frontiers. People are imprisoned for years without trial, or shot in the back of the neck or sent to die of scurvy in Arctic lumber camps: this is called elimination of unreliable elements. Such phraseology is needed if one wants to name things without calling up mental pictures of them ('Politics and the English Language', ed. cit., p. 166).

In the essay the political function of this kind of language is clear, but Orwell makes no attempt to understand the subtleties of the associated state of mind. This is the advance to be found in *1984*. Here is the memorable evocation of Winston Smith's experience of doublethink in the novel:

His mind slid away into the labyrinthine world of doublethink. To know and not to know, to be conscious of complete truthfulness while telling carefully constructed lies, to hold simultaneously two opinions which cancelled out, knowing them to be contradictory and believing in both of them; to use logic against logic, to repudiate morality while laying claim to it, to believe that democracy was impossible and that the Party was the guardian of democracy; to forget whatever it was necessary to forget, then to draw it back into memory again at the moment when it was needed, and then promptly forget it again: and above all, to apply the same process to the process itself. That was the ultimate subtlety: consciously to induce unconsciousness, and then, once again, to become unconscious of the act of hypnosis you had just performed. Even to understand the word 'doublethink' involved the use of doublethink (*1984*, ed. cit., pp. 31–2).

Orwell in *1984* was fascinated with doublethink and the role of language in the processes of reality-control, but he did not lose his strongly commonsense and materialist convictions. Minitrue uses massive censorship and lies as well as language reform, and Minitrue is complemented by Miniluv and the Thought Police, who use physical torture on dissidents like Winston. It is against this background that the seemingly quaint devices of Newspeak gain a sinister power and significance. In the Appendix we are shown Newspeak as an ingenious experiment in the mutilation of language. In the novel we see Newspeak in action. The action is the curious kind of censorship that is Winston's job: rewriting past issues of *The Times* to falsify the records on which history is based. So the forms of Newspeak are intimately involved in the processes of censorship, or more generally the processes of 'reality control', as it is called in the novel.

The example Orwell explores at length in the novel is not in fact pure Newspeak, but a form of telegraphese, which is revealed as the target of the satire at this point. This is the instruction sent to Winston from some anonymous source:

times 3.12.83 reporting bb dayorder doubleplusungood refs unpersons rewrite fullwise upsub antefiling

He gives a translation of this into Oldspeak:

The reporting of Big Brother's Order for the Day in the Times of December 3rd 1983 is extremely unsatisfactory and makes reference to non-existent persons. Rewrite it in full and submit your draft to higher authority before filing.

In the expanded form the message seems clear enough. It's an instruction to Winston to perform the immoral act of falsifying records again. Though it is Winston's job to perform this act every day, day after day, he is still troubled by it when he is at home or alone and able to reflect. But at the moment of performing it, he is filled with excitement. He especially enjoys difficult problems,

> jobs so difficult and intricate that you could lose yourself in them as in the depths of a mathematical problem – delicate pieces of forgery in which you had nothing to guide you except your knowledge of the principles of Ingsoc and your estimate of what the Party wanted you to say (ibid., p. 38).

This gives us a clue about the function of the form itself. It is an instruction to rewrite which itself has to be rewritten to be understood. It is a curious kind of censorship, one that is designed to be seen through, or decoded. The problem of decoding is probably not difficult for Winston, but even a small problem helps. The new language is related systematically to the standard English form by a series of transformations, mostly deletions. The first sentence will serve to illustrate:

(The) reporting (of) B(ig) B(rother's) Order (for the) Day (in The) Times (of) December 3(rd) (19)83 (is) *extremely unsatisfactory* (and) (makes) ref(erence)s (to) *non-existent* persons (.)

Bracketed words or parts of words have been deleted and italicized elements have been substituted. There is some minor re-ordering. We can summarize the operations under three categories:

1 Deletions:
    articles (the)
    prepositions (of, for, in)
    conjunctions (and)
    modality and tense (is/was)
    punctuation
2 Substitutions:
    Oldspeak value-judgments by Newspeak value-judgments ('extremely unsatisfactory' by 'doubleplusungood'), words by numbers.
3 Reordering (shift of indications of place and time to early position)

The transformations seem to have two main functions. Indications of relationships between words or parts of a sentence are suppressed. Word-order takes over some of this function, but not all. Second, indications of the truth-value of the utterance are no longer possible. For instance, we can't say whether the reporting is now unsatisfactory or whether it always was. It isn't clear what is a noun and what is a verb; 'refs' could be either. If it is a verb it might be past or present, if a noun it has no tense. The result is a drastically limited language in which to represent complex relationships, but a useful language in which to be vague about when things happened, and whether they are certain, probable or only hypothetical. Value-judgments seem prominent, unambiguous, but uncomplex. These are the aims of Newspeak, according to the Appendix, but here we are shown them achieved by different linguistic means, not the childish grammar of Newspeak but something much more recognizable and adult, the language of memos, the language of administration.

Orwell seems to have regarded standard English as a neutral form of communication. However, even the language of the full version he gives is full of suppressions, using devices from the grammar of standard English to achieve the aims of Newspeak. Let us take the first phrase 'The reporting of Big Brother's Order for the Day'. Underlying the first three words is a sentence with the form '(X) reported'. We don't know who X is. He was some anonymous predecessor of Winston's, who has been made a linguistic unperson in this sentence. This form is so common and regular that it seems entirely innocent, to be explained purely on the grounds of economy. Maybe. But in this case it is emotionally convenient for Winston for there to be no mention of his superseded predecessor. This has the effect of dehumanizing the original 'error'. A further convenience can be seen later in the sentence, when we come to 'references'. This similarly comes from an underlying form '(X) refers to'. Again we ask who X is. The answer is interestingly uncertain: either the first X, or another unstated person Y, or Big Brother himself. It may seem probable that Big Brother was the person who made the erroneous reference, but both the others are possibilities, so that if the thought of Big Brother making an error seems unthinkable, the reader is given something else to think.

The syntactic form allows the blame to be shifted on to unperson X, who misreported the original speech, but this process of blaming him, which would perhaps trouble Winston since he knows better, is left implicit and unconscious. The blame, then, lands on both, and neither: a fine example of doublethink.

The surface form typical of this kind of language is achieved mainly by two related transformations. One is nominalization, turning verbs into nouns, e.g. 'report' to 'reporting', 'refer' to 'references'. Orwell describes the interchangeability of nouns and verbs as characteristic of Newspeak. The rule in the present case seems to be: nominalize all verbs, except imperatives. The effect of this rule is to remove tense and modality, i.e. indications of time or truth-value. The second rule is: delete all agents, except Big Brother. The effect of these two rules together is that the only kind of action which is coded as an action (i.e. through use of a verb) is the exercise of authority by whoever is doing the ordering: and the only active agent is Big Brother.

The effect of these transformations, which are very common in standard English, is similar to that of telegraphese, which only carries the process a stage further. Both kinds work by suppressions. Both involve a degree of censorship, but in neither is the censorship impenetrable. Through the compressed surface the underlying meaning is discernible, with effort. Or more precisely, meanings, because what is allowed is a multiplicity of meanings which are hard to criticize because they are only partially glimpsed and guessed at. So though a kind of censorship is involved, a more prominent function seems to be mystification, or doublethink. If we regard the expanded, standard English form as a kind of elaborated code, we reach a surprising conclusion. Oldspeak and Newspeak, far from being opposed as Orwell seemed to think, have essentially the same function. Newspeak merely carries the process one stage further.

Winston Smith's task is to rewrite the 'erroneous' article. The Order for the Day had praised an organization called the FFCC, singling out Comrade Withers for special mention. FFCC was now dissolved, and Comrade Withers and his associates had become unpersons. Winston is shown reflecting on what he will do, running through various alternatives before deciding on his solution. The solution was to replace Comrade Withers and the whole story by a piece of fiction about Comrade Ogilvy, an exemplary citizen of Oceania whose heroic death Big Brother will eulogize.

Orwell's satiric target here is not fictionality as such. Total fabrication of this kind was probably rare even in the media of wartime Britain. Orwell's real concern is with a perverse relationship between language and reality, shown by the kind of reasoning Winston uses. He is not turning experience and thoughts about experience into words. The input is a piece of language, plus an unspecific instruction to change it. Winston first analyses it structurally, and deduces what is wrong with it. He toys with possible drastic changes but decides on what is structurally a simple change. The original was, in outline, 'Big Brother praises FFCC and Comrade

Withers'. His version is 'Big Brother praises Comrade Ogilvy'.

So all he has done is to delete the forbidden organization, and replace 'Withers' by 'Ogilvy'. At a more abstract level, he has in fact preserved the original structure. Since Big Brother only praises what is plusgood, the original sentence had an underlying abstract form: 'Big Brother praises X (who is plusgood and male)'. Withers formerly had fitted this specification. Now that he is out of favour, he no longer qualifies for his place in the original sentence. The person and the name of Withers was less important than his specifications. So the substitution of the fictitious Ogilvy serves to restore the equilibrium.

Orwell is showing here a kind of communication in which the individual does not start from meanings he wishes to communicate, about experience which is important to him. In 'Politics and the English Language' Orwell had condemned the situation where 'The writer either has a meaning and cannot express it, or he inadvertently says something else, or he is almost indifferent as to whether his words mean anything or not'.[5] Here in *1984* Orwell shows this fault taken to an extreme. The complete article Winston produces comes from something as impersonal as a machine into which language is fed at one end, out of which comes fully formed apparently rational discourse. Winston describes the end product as 'a piece of pure fantasy' (*1984*, ed. cit., p. 40) but it is far from pure. Even the details that Winston invents, such as Ogilvy's precocious refusal of all toys except a drum, a submachine gun and a model helicopter at the age of three, are not a personal fantasy, they are the kind of detail which is prescribed by the Ingsoc ethic. The submachine gun might have been replaced by a rubber truncheon, as 'Ogilvy' could replace 'Withers', but a doll or a book would have been not permissible.

In this kind of communication, the material is always pre-packaged. It is the experience (real or imaginary) of others, already processed and coded in language. The basic meanings are prescribed, in the form of an underlying structure determining the required features and their permissible relationships. The individual has only the freedom to substitute particular details which conform to the underlying specifications. This makes the real meaning of these utterances their underlying structure. The actual surface forms are only stylistic variants. The real meaning of both *Times* articles, the Withers and the Ogilvy versions, is the same: Big Brother praises what is plusgood. This itself is a tautology because the only possible definition of 'plusgood', when everything else can be rewritten, is that which Big Brother praises. So the whole article is simply an expansion of 'plusgood' in the language-system, directly reflecting the ideology of Ingsoc. But though this is what Winston does, it is not what he supposes he is doing. He feels personal pride at having accurately produced a new meaning, in the very tones and syntactic forms of Big Brother. He even half-believes in the reality of the fiction he thinks he has created.

Orwell, himself a journalist, probably had in mind the conditions of journalistic production. Studies have shown how journalists rapidly learn the ethos of the particular paper they work for, and its standard treatment of staple topics. They find out which copy is accepted substantially unchanged, and which is rejected or altered beyond recognition. Professional pride such as motivates Winston leads them to try to predict what will be accepted. The rules at issue are never spelled out but are understood and internalized, and the system becomes self-regulating through anticipatory self-censorship.[6] Whatever comes in to the press office will be processed and reprocessed by a succession of people on the editorial staff till it conforms to these underlying stereotypes. The person responsible for the final form will, like Winston, have no first-hand knowledge of the truth or falsity of the story. He will be working on material already worked over by others, and his concern will be to make sure it is a 'good story' (by the standards of that paper), not a true one.

Winston carries out the whole process of rewriting with a minimum of guidance. He has to decode his instruction, and then interpret its real significance and try to obey it, using his intuitive sense of the unstated rules. This is a general feature of Oceanic society:

the individual has no freedom of choice in any direction whatever. On the other hand his actions are not regulated by law or by any clearly formulated code of behaviour. In Oceania there is no law. Thoughts and actions which, when detected, mean certain death, are not formally forbidden (*1984*, ed. cit., p. 169).

At first this seems a strange paradox. Oceania is the image of a totally regulated society yet has no regulations. The solution of this paradox lies in the mode of existence of the network of rules and regulations which control the actions of all members of the society, especially party members. The rules and regulations exist, but they have been totally deleted, so that they are disembodied, invisible, and hence unassailable. Without sanctions, of course, laws in this form would have no force. If there are effective sanctions, however, Orwell's paradox contains an important insight. When the language of control is backed up by the reality of power, the more massive the deletion, especially of the fact of power and coercion, the more powerful, mystified and irrational is the control. Anyone who can give orders without even acknowledging this in the surface of his utterance has access to an insidiously powerful form of command. For instance, someone who can say 'the door is open' and be interpreted as saying 'close the door' has issued an imperative which has been totally deleted yet is fully effective. The person who obeys accepts the reality of a power that has not been claimed, which has been completely mystified into the form of an apparently neutral, factual observation.

At the other extreme from an over-ingenious reinterpretation of utterances is the phenomenon Orwell calls 'Duckspeak' in the novel. This is the language used by party hacks. The writer of the Appendix refers to it as

a gabbling style of speech, at once staccato and monotonous. And this was exactly what was aimed at. The intention was to make speech, and especially speech on any subject not ideologically neutral, as nearly as possible independent of consciousness (*1984*, ed. cit., p. 248).

In the novel we are given an example of 'Duckspeak' in use. Winston is sitting in the cafeteria with Syme, a fellow worker in Minitrue, who is an expert on Newspeak. Syme gives an orthodox definition of Duckspeak. Winston observes what is happening at another table in the cafeteria, where a man is talking to a girl who Winston assumes is his secretary.

From time to time Winston caught some such remark as 'I think you're *so* right, I do *so* agree with you', uttered in a youthful rather silly feminine voice. But the other voice never stopped for an instant, even when the girl was speaking. The man's head was thrown back a little, and because of the angle at which he was sitting, his spectacles caught the light and presented to Winston two blank discs instead of eyes. What was slightly horrible, was that from the stream of sound that poured out of his mouth it was almost impossible to distinguish a single word. Just once Winston caught a phrase – 'complete and final elimination of Goldsteinism' – jerked out very rapidly and, as it seemed, all in one piece, like a line of type cast solid. For the rest it was just a noise, a quack-quackquacking (ibid.).

This dramatization allows us to generalize the phenomenon and apply it more widely to a more familiar world of discourse. The conversation is clearly not an exchange, but a kind of ritual in which the power of the male boss over his secretary is asserted and acknowledged as the sole content of communication. The message the boss is transmitting is not in fact about Goldsteinism but about his own orthodoxy and the power that accrues from this. The secretary similarly signals only her complete acceptance of the subordinate role. What the man says is almost incomprehensible. The surface form of his speech has almost no structure. The components have fused together like solid cast type. The lack of a surface structure deprives his speech of any deep structure, any deeper level of interpretation at which his speech makes sense. What he says would presumably make sense, or seem to make sense, if he slowed down his rate of delivery. It then would be jargonistic Oldspeak (not Newspeak, as the writer of the Appendix implies). Even more than with Winston's article, its content would be prescribed. The major difference would be in the way in which the prescription worked. With the article, a deep structure meaning determined the interpretation of the surface forms. In Duckspeak, the surface forms are independently produced in large chunks. Presumably the deep structure interpretation of the speech as a whole would reveal chaos and incoherence, but the words are said too quickly for this deep structure incoherence to be perceived.

Duckspeak itself is incompatible with doublethink, since it doesn't even allow singlethink. However, Duckspeak has a role to play in the operation of doublethink. We can see this in the discussion of words like Comintern in the Appendix. This word comes from 'Communist International' by an irregular transformational process, where 'munist' and 'ational' are deleted, and the two remaining parts fused together into a single three-syllable word. The parts taken out and the parts left are in both cases not meaningful units and this irrationality is part of the point. The result is 'a word that can be uttered almost without taking thought, whereas "Communist International" is a phrase over which one is obliged to linger at least momentarily' (*1984*, ed. cit., p. 248). Clearly Orwell sees it as a contemporary form of Duckspeak, but 'almost' is the giveaway. The difference between 'Communist International' and 'Comintern' is a difference of degree, not kind. Both are Duckspeak. Both allow doublethink, which in this case is a contradiction between a definite deep structure, and a re-appropriated surface structure. The difference between doublethink and Duckspeak is to be found not in the form of words themselves, but in how these are understood by whoever says or hears them. The higher up in the party, the more intense is the exercise of doublethink, according to Goldstein (ibid., p. 171). Someone in the Inner Party like O'Brien might know the history of the word 'Comintern', which parallels the history of Socialism, so in using the shortened, irrationalized form he might both know and not know that history. The result for him would be doublethink. Someone like the man in the cafe overheard by Winston could have used the fuller form, 'Communist International', without comprehension of that history or the component meanings of the word. For him the result is Duckspeak. So the fundamental antagonism between social classes in Oceania is expressed not only in different languages – Prolespeak and kinds of Newspeak – it is expressed in contrary ways of producing and interpreting the same language. The principle of contradiction becomes the condition of consciousness of the individual, even an individual as comparatively lowly in status as Winston. And even Inner Party members at times have recourse to Duckspeak. Doublethink and Duckspeak are alternative ways of coping with irrationality and contradiction. Duckspeak, which involves less thought and less effort, would be a necessary relief.

As we have seen, the account of language in the Appendix is usually inadequate for the world of *1984* as it is presented in the novel. Clearly we need to look again and more critically at the whole programme offered in the Appendix. If it is not a description of the language situation to be found in Oceania, what is it? The obvious answer is that this is a satire on language-planners and experts on language, not a prediction about developments in the English language. These are the theories about language which are encouraged by the rulers of Oceania. The ministry experts confidently predict that the Eleventh edition of the dictionary which is about to be produced will be definitive, and that 2050 will be the year for the final change-over to Newspeak. These predictions should be treated with the same scepticism as the periodic announcements that a final victory over Eastasia/Eurasia is at hand. The theories on which these predictions are based are offered for critical inspection by a sociologist of linguistics. The relation of this critique to Orwell's own views is intriguing, since the Newspeak theorists are trying to carry out a reform similar to the Basic English programme of Ogden, Chase and others, which Orwell in the 1930s saw as a positive weapon against the degeneration of English.

The basic premise of the Newspeak programme is a very crude

form of linguistic determinism, that is, the belief that language completely determines thought. In linguistics, thinkers like Whorf[7] have developed subtle forms of this theory, but the view in the Appendix is not subtle.

The purpose of Newspeak was not only to provide a medium of expression for the world-view and mental habits proper to the devotees of Ingsoc, but to make all other modes of thought impossible. It was intended that when Newspeak had been adopted once and for all and Oldspeak forgotten, a heretical thought – that is, a thought diverging from the principles of Ingsoc – should be literally unthinkable, at least so far as thought is dependent on words (*1984*, ed. cit., p. 241).

The method for achieving this control involves a simple but laborious method, based on a simple-minded understanding of language. Language is seen essentially as a set of words whose meaning is fixed and determined by dictionary entries. The lunatic logic of the Newspeak programme works by rewriting the dictionary, cancelling unwanted words and meanings. Quite apart from its implausible premise (in fact most people learn most words through use, not from a dictionary) this programme involves a number of contradictions. The aim of the dictionary-makers with their new words was 'to make sure what they meant: to make sure, that is to say, what ranges of words they cancelled by their existence' (ibid., p. 246). But this elimination also meant an *inclusion* of the meanings of the old words in certain new ones, which 'had their meanings extended until they contained within themselves whole batteries of words' (ibid., p. 245). So a single word in Newspeak might be immensely more meaningful than any Oldspeak word could be. The compression achieved by Newspeak (and the same could be said of Bernstein's restricted code) could correspond to impoverishment of thought, or to richness of significance. These are opposites, so the whole programme of Newspeak is built on a contradiction.

There is another contradiction to the programme. If the rulers of Oceania really believed that words totally controlled thought, they would not need to manufacture news, nor would they need the Thought Police and the brutal methods of the 'Ministry of Love'. Conversely, with total control over the repressive apparatus of the state and the media, why should they bother with the dictionary exercise?

The short answer to this is 'doublethink'. It seems essential for the rulers of this state both to believe totally in the power of language and mind over reality, and also to know that the party's rule is really based on its control over material instruments of oppression. There is also an economic function. Syme was 'one of the enormous team of experts now engaged in compiling the 11th Edition of the Newspeak Dictionary' (ibid., p. 42). Work on the dictionary corresponds to the use of war as an economic strategy. The 'war' guarantees full employment to the Proles, by generating endless useless tasks, such as the building of successive floating fortresses, each one scrapped as obsolete before it is used (ibid., p. 155). Outer Party members are similarly engaged in totally futile enterprises. Winston Smith's own job is a case in point. He rewrites past copies of *The Times*. With each item he assumes that up to a dozen others may be working on their own version, only one of which would be accepted. In the labyrinthine depths of the Records Department a whole army of workers was involved in this business of forgery. But for whom? The Proles do not seem to read back numbers of *The Times*. This is not a plot directed against the workers (other departments handle that), it is a plot against the academic historians of Oceania. These historians can rewrite the fallacious history books with less feeling of bad faith, though at some level they must know the worthlessness of their evidence. For these intellectual slaves we can see the function of the premise that language determines thought. In their impotence they are allowed to deal only with words, not thoughts or material and social existence. But the programme gives them the illusion that their impotence is power. Their ideology is clearly the direct product of the material conditions of their existence: how they are employed, and who their masters are.[8]

Orwell himself was not a linguist or an academic. 'Orwellian Linguistics' as in the title of this essay does not exist. If it did it might have one of two contrary meanings: either a narrow, bizarrely pedantic form of academic enquiry which ultimately serves the interests of the status quo, or a systematic demystifying study of language and power in a class society. Or, of course, both simultaneously, for a victim/expert in doublethink. Orwell's own relation to even the most radical and critical form of Orwellian linguistics would still be equivocal. He makes the crucial connections and raises urgent questions, but the connections remain problematic and the answers he suggests are either not enough or too much. Who or what, for instance, is responsible for using language in such a manner that people are deceived, confused, kept ignorant, and frozen in existing socio-economic roles? In 'The English Language' (1944, *Collected*

Essays, vol. III, pp. 40–6) Orwell answers 'the class system'. In 'Politics and the English Language' (1946, *Collected Essays*, vol. IV, pp. 156–70) he explains that 'our civilization is decadent'. Are these answers different, or ultimately compatible? *1984* is less explicit. In the novel, Orwell allows himself to know only what Winston Smith could know, and Winston never meets a manipulator who is not manipulated, and never grasps the key to the whole process.

The kind of answer Orwell gives in the essays is usually general and structural, pointing to causes beyond the individual. That kind of emphasis can lead to a sense of fatalism, since no individual action can affect the totality. However, in 'Politics and the English Language' Orwell makes it abundantly clear that then he thought the abuses he discussed could be combatted, that individuals might think before they wrote and let the meaning choose the word. In *1984* he takes precisely this theme, the attempt of an individual to challenge the system and achieve self-clarity if nothing more. The novel is deeply pessimistic in its effect because Winston fails so totally and inevitably. The pessimism may have had a personal source. When he wrote the novel Orwell was ill, and he was to die within a year of its publication. But pessimism follows inevitably from the terms of the novel. Someone like Winston attempting to challenge the system in the way he did was bound to fail.

Orwell's pessimism in *1984* poses the challenge: can anything be done? His understanding of a form of false consciousness is totally convincing as far as it goes. In fact, it is too convincing, because it is unable to contemplate any alternative to its own impotence and despair. To see the relevance, but also the partiality, of Orwell's perspective in *1984*, we might take examples from language used in the Vietnam war. It is reported that the American B–52 pilots who flew bombing missions in Southeast Asia during the Vietnam war invariably described them as 'protective reactions' on their flight reports.[9] Whatever 'protective reaction' might mean, it is obviously an inappropriate description for the destruction of peasant settlements by dropping bombs on them from a height of five miles. The whole terminology of the war – 'pacification', 'defoliation', 'resources control program', 'strategic hamlet', etc. – was a shockingly exact fulfilment of Orwell's vision. Pilots who talked of 'protective reactions' were not necessarily conspiring consciously to falsify reality through the misuse of language. The phrase was routine. It is difficult to pinpoint sources for such terms or to identify linguistic conspirators. American pilots who wrote 'protective reaction' in reports in the course of their daily duties were not deceiving anyone who did not already know. The deception or displacement is thoroughly routinized and apparently under-motivated, and responsibility for the process is hard to locate.

All this is what Orwell leads us to expect and helps us to understand. But there was another aspect of the Vietnam struggle. A radical critique of the whole war, its aims, methods and results, was possible and it was effective. Many people felt an Orwellian indignation at obscene euphemisms used to 'defend the indefensible', as he put it. The anti-war movement grew strong because people were able to go behind official pronouncements to recover more reliable sources of information, and they gained a disturbing insight into the minds of the makers of the war. Both these strategies are thoroughly Orwellian, and they can be effective when they give focus for a mass movement, rather than just the private rebellion of a Winston Smith.

Orwell's value as thinker about language is as a stimulus and a challenge. He was not a systematic theorist, and there are inconsistencies, confusions and gaps in any theory that can be drawn from his various works. He had no method of analysis beyond the application of common sense, the common sense of an observant, intelligent but idiosyncratic individual. But his work, predominantly *1984*, is a monument to a number of definitive premises about language and society. He saw clearly that the social structure acts on every aspect of personal behaviour, affecting active and passive linguistic experience. He was concerned especially with one aspect of social structure, inequality in the distribution of power. Particular relations are all variant realizations of a single structural opposition, between those who possess authorized power and those who lack it. It is in the material interests of the first group to maintain their authority over the second (and to persuade them that it really is in their best interests not to challenge this authority). The central asymmetry – *society is organized upon a principle of unequal power* – is sustained through a vast repertoire of behavioural convictions which relate role to role, status to status, institution to individual. In linguistic behaviour, Orwell saw this principle realized through forms of public communication. Newspapers, governments, bureaucracies and intellectuals cannot risk telling the truth because doing so might give others access to their own power-base. The defence of the power-differential is also carried out by a multitude of interpersonal strategies. The second half of *1984* is dominated by the dialogue between Winston and O'Brien, a symbol of the importance of this mode of exercising control through language.

In all these beliefs Orwell seems to us to have been essentially correct. Such things need saying now as much as they did when he wrote. Whatever other advances it has made, academic linguistics has not taken any account of these Orwellian insights. But there is no reason in principle why linguistics should not make a systematic study of the relations Orwell was concerned with, social structure and linguistic form, function and processes, using linguistic analysis as a way of uncovering ideological processes and complex states of mind. Such a linguistics would be of direct value in a critical account of contemporary culture. Whether or not this linguistics could draw in detail on Orwell's writing, Orwell would have made a significant contribution to its impact by affecting the general consciousness about language. Not many books by linguists have been able to alter a whole society's understanding of the role of language in its basic political and social processes. For all its imperfections, *1984* is an achievement on that scale.

2 · Rules and regulations

ROGER FOWLER and GUNTHER KRESS

It is well known that the linguistic forms of speech and writing express the social circumstances in which language occurs. The relationship of style to situation is very precise and functional, so that an analysis of linguistic structures reveals the contexts of language with considerable accuracy. Sociolinguists generally treat linguistic variation as an 'index' of social structure: because it is a product of social circumstances, it can be referred to as a sign of social circumstances, e.g. the nature of groups and the structure of personal interactions.

The analyses in this book are partly indexical, but we go further in our argument about the relationship between language structure and social structure. The forms of language in use are a *part of*, as well as a *consequence of*, social process. As a part of social process, language use is an instrument by means of which people manage their own behaviour, and influence that of others; by means of which social groupings are organized and the meanings available to those groups are determined. In this chapter we examine an aspect of the use of language to control the behaviour of other people, by analysing two examples of printed regulatory texts. We will argue that these texts, though by their nature less direct interactions than the face-to-face interviews studied in chapters 4 and 5, are no less 'manipulative' in function; and that part of the process by which language is used to exercise control involves control of the semantics of the relevant social group. (This will be explained below; basically, the argument is that the structure of the social varieties concerned requires the individual to learn exclusive concepts peculiar to the group.)

In this chapter we discuss an uncontroversial example of control: rules and regulations, and the language in which they are expressed. Rules are instructions for behaving in ways which will bring about an intended or desired state. Hence they presuppose a knower of the appropriate behaviour, who needs to transmit that knowledge to someone who does not have the knowledge. Knowledge is one source of power, and consequently, if both participants agree on their role-relationship, the application of power is unidirectional; there is no hint of negotiation for control. The source of the rules is in a hierarchical relationship to the addressees, in which it is assumed that he has the right to manipulate their behaviour. Superiority of knowledge and status gives the rule-maker the authority to issue commands, and we will shortly examine the syntax of commanding as it is manifested in our first text. We will rapidly discover that a certain deviousness complicates expression of the power relationship, however. Though commanding presupposes inequality of power, it does not necessarily imply conflict of interests. The rules announced in the first text below were drawn up by a member of a group for the communal benefit of that group. The group in question is a swimming club for children and their parents, run by the parents. The children all go to the same local school, and so both parents and children know each other independently of their membership of the swimming club. They are a community of friends; and the informal relationship of friendship seems to be in conflict with the more formal requirements of club organization. We argue that, in this text, the need for solidarity undermines clear expression of authority. To avoid alienating his members, the author of the swimming club rules resorts to a miscellany of syntactic stratagems to sweeten the pill.

Swimming club rules

1 Parents must accompany and take responsibility for their children at all times, unless the child is in the water in an instructed class. *Note –* In most cases this will mean one adult enrolling with one child, or, if they so wish, one adult with more than one child provided it is understood they are responsible for them.
2 Being absent for more than three consecutive sessions without explanation to the membership secretary means automatic expulsion.
3 No outside shoes will be worn when in the pool area.
4 Please respect the facilities and equipment, and take particular care with untrained children.
5 The age limits of the club are six months to eight years. For the six to eight years old instruction will be provided. Children may remain members for the completed term in which their eighth birthday falls.
6 There must be no more than twenty-four bodies in the pool at any one time.
7 Membership cards must always be carried and shown on request.

Here the author needs and seeks to direct the specific behaviour of his members. The speech act appropriate to this situation comes under the general category of *command*, and there are a large number of these in this text, with a variety of syntactic forms of expression. The most overt examples of command are 1 'Parents must accompany . . .' 4 'Please respect the facilities . . . and take particular care . . .' 6 'There must be no more than twenty-four bodies in the pool . . .' 7 'Membership cards must always be carried and shown'. Syntactically, 1, 6 and 7 are declarative sentences, while the two clauses in 4 are imperatives. Declaratives and imperatives express the relation between speaker and addressee in differing ways: the speech roles assigned in one case are 'giver of information' and 'recipient of information'; in the other 'commander' and 'commanded'. It is clear that the two forms are appropriate for two quite distinct kinds of power-relation: the imperative for one involving a considerable power differential, one where control may be exercised through the direct assertion of the roles of commander–commanded. The declarative, on the other hand, seemingly makes no specific claims about power-relations; the giving of information seems a neutral act. (This is in fact not the case: the giver of information also has the role of *speaker*, and there are conventions about who may and who may not be a speaker in any given situation – e.g. children should be seen and not heard; and everyone realizes when someone has 'spoken out of turn'. Also, a giver of information is a *knower* of information, and knowledge is a basis of power.) The 'command' in declaratives is not carried through speech-role directly, but modally, through the use of the modal verb *must*. In the imperative the source of the command is quite plain: *I*, the speaker/writer, command *you*, the addressee; but in the declarative with the modal 'must', the source of the authority is vague: it might be the speaker, equally it might not. The answer to the outraged question 'who says so?' is 'I' in the imperative, but in the declarative might be 'the committee', 'the people who own the pool', 'the caretaker', or 'I', or any number of other entities, 'common sense' included.

At this stage the unanswered questions are: where is the source of the vagueness, the need for obfuscation; second, why is there a switch, in just one case (4), from the modalized declarative form to the direct imperative form? We leave aside the first question for the moment, except to point out that it resides in the social relations between writer of rules and 'recipients' of the rules. The second question is illuminated by the conjunction of 'untrained children' and the age limit of six months at the lower end. 'Untrained' (explained as 'not toilet trained' in a later revision of these rules) hints that the dangers legislated against in rule 4 are critical and delicate. Non-toilet-trained babies could foul the pool; non-swimming-trained babies might drown. The seriousness of both eventualities increases the authority, hence the distance, of the writer, so that he can call upon the weight of the direct imperative.

Note, however, that the authority structure indicated by rule 4 is still not straightforward. 'Please' shows that this writer even at his most commanding is still negotiating for power – perhaps here also despairing, since what he requests, the close physical control of infants, is not really within the capability of parents.

As a general principle, we propose that the greater the power differential between the parties to a speech act of command, the more 'direct' the syntactic form (e.g. imperative) which may be chosen. Someone who enjoys absolute power can afford to be abrupt. The smaller the power distance the greater the amount of linguistic effort, of circumlocution (declaratives, particularly passives, e.g. rules 3 and 7). The swimming club rule-writer is in an ambivalent position of artificial authority, and needs to avoid curtness. He plays down even the very little power he does possess. The effect here is hesitancy. Let us now look at the varying syntactic realization of his acts of command. A command is a kind of speech-act which can be performed under appropriate conditions; it may be expressed through a variety of linguistic structures of which 'imperative' is just one.[1] We have started to give some reasons for choice among these variable expressions. We will now look more closely at three structures, how they are derived and what their motivations might be.

All commands require the following elements of meaning to be present in the underlying structure of the utterances which express them:

(a) *Commander* who is also *Speaker* (Cr/Sp)
(b) *Commanded* who is also *Addressee* (Cd/Ad)
(c) Verb of *commanding* (C)
(d) *Agent* of the action to be performed, who is the same person as Cd/Ad (Ag)
(e) *Proposition* referring to action to be performed (P)
(f) Displacement of time of action to *a point later than* time of utterance (W)

Thus the imperative 'take particular care with untrained children' is one way of expressing the following speech-act:

Cr/Sp	C	Cd/Ad	Ag	W	P
I	order	you	that	you	will	take particular care with untrained children

This, the least courteous of command structures, is derived by massive application of deletion transformations: Cr/Sp, C, Cd/Ad, Ag and W all disappear. Despite the deletions, imperatives are perfectly comprehensible. The addressee supplies the deleted elements from his knowledge of the non-linguistic context in which the speech act occurs. This linguistic dependence on context makes the situation itself remarkably salient or palpable. In effect the commander forces the commanded to take direct cognizance of those aspects of social context which make the speech-act valid – specifically, the commander declines to state that he has authority over the commanded (statements breed counter-statements and thus facilitate insubordination) but forces the addressee to acknowledge the power for himself.

Declaratives used as commands have a form such as

Cr/Sp	C	Cd/Ad	Ag	W	P
I	order	you	that parents	must	accompany their children

where Cd/Ad = Ag. In this case, the transformation of second person 'you' to third person 'parents' tempers the directness of the command: the addressee is allowed to pretend that the speaker is commanding someone else. We have already commented on 'must': our notation shows that Cr/Sp is a possible underlying subject of 'must', but the deletion of Cr/Sp in surface structure draws attention away from this possibility, suggesting that this is a need of the parents, not an imposed obligation.

Finally, a passive declarative such as 3 'No outside shoes will be worn when in the pool area', or 7 'Membership cards must always be carried and shown on request' has approximately the following underlying structure:

Cr/Sp	C	Cd/Ad	Ag	W	P
I	order	you	that you	will not	wear outside shoes

Passive, like imperative, but unlike declarative, involves deletion of agent. The effect is very different, however; the deleted agent of imperatives is instantly identifiable as addressee, whereas the person who does not wear outside shoes is not obviously 'you' but rather, coyly, 'someone' or 'everyone'. The effect is very like that of the third person transformation yielding 'parents' in rule 1. Similar interpersonal strategies are averting the eyes, turning one's back, sending personal greetings via a newspaper advertisement, speaking through the chairman, etc.

'Will' in rules 1, 3 and 5 signifies not only displacement of time but also a transformation from a statement of authority (cf. 'must') to an assertion about an impending state. The writer pretends confidence about a state which is to be the case. This use of 'will' is popular in proverbial or generalizing utterances of the kind 'boys will be boys' or 'cats will eat fish'. In the face of such a confident prediction as rule 3, the question 'who says so?' seems pathetically inappropriate.

There are two more important consequences of the passive. First, the naturally prominent first phrase in the sentence, which in actives is occupied by the agent of a process, is in passives occupied by the object. The object thus becomes focal: from an interest in 'parents carrying membership cards', attention is refocused on 'membership cards which must be carried'. Not only is the object given thematic prominence, but the agent is deleted as well. The persons become entirely uninteresting compared with the cards they must carry.

Second, the passive construction has a powerful neutralizing effect on the action or process being communicated. The auxiliary 'be' is introduced, so that 'carried' begins to look like an adjectival attribute of 'membership cards'. In the form 'will be carried' an attentive reader will see the passive form, and speculate about the deleted agent. The next stage from here would be 'membership cards *are* carried', in which the transformation from a *process* to a *state* is total. The point is that processes, being under the control of agents, imply the possibility of modification, decision; whereas states are perceived as unalterable and thus to be put up with. All 'be' forms classifying process as state are open to suspicion and should be inspected: cf. 'is understood', 'are responsible' in 1.

The deletion of agents in the truncated passive occurs not only in the main syntactic structure of rules such as 3 and 7, but also in phrases within sentences: 'instructed class' (1), 'untrained children' (4), 'instruction will be provided' (5) and 'completed term' (5). Presumably the deleted agents in the first three would have referred to officials of the club, in the fourth, to children, but deletions of this kind inevitably lead to indeterminacy. An underlying form of 1 might be 'someone instructs a class' leading, via 'the class is instructed by someone', 'the class is instructed', to the 'instructed class'. Here presumably the instructor is just that, a swimming instructor. In 5, however, the underlying form might be 'someone provides instruction', and this someone might be the instructor, it might be a member of the committee responsible for arranging the teaching, or it might be the whole committee itself. In 4 ('untrained children'), depending on what kind of training is being talked about, the trainer is either the parents or the swimming instructor. The point at issue is that the uncertainty about agency spreads a general vagueness through the rules, and a vagueness precisely in the area of *who does what*. The readers of the rules are left in a situation of helpless ignorance: apparently the knowers know, but seem to keep the ignorant from knowing. A dissatisfied member can be left very frustrated by not knowing where to turn for specific action. Here the process merely confers the power derived from relatively trivial knowledge on those who have it, and creates a class of those who do not have such power/knowledge. In more important contexts it works as a powerful means of control. Anyone who has ever come up against 'faceless bureaucracy' will know what this is about.

Those passives which have deleted though known agents (e.g. the members who must carry their cards) help to reinforce the general effect: because members can recover some of the agents, they may as casual readers be more willing to accept the blur, trusting that the other agents are equally readily recoverable.

A common counter-argument which is offered against such an analysis of deletion as the present is that what is involved here is a matter of 'simple economy'. The economy achieved here is never simple; and a very high price indeed is exacted for it.

Agent deletion is pervasive throughout this text, and the syntactic reduction which accompanies it results in a number of new noun-like compounds: 1 'instructed class', 4 'untrained children', 5 'completed term' have already been commented on in the context of agent-deletion. These reduced passives (and other sentence structures, as we shall see) are compressed into noun phrases – 'nominalized' – so that they can occur in positions in syntactic structure which might equally well be occupied by simple lexical items like 'child', 'parent', 'pool'. They become potentially equivalent to ordinary dictionary words, in that their meanings can be regarded as unitary, unanalysed. 'Untrained children', having been coded in a compact linguistic form, serves to crystallize a new concept, and to make it memorizable. This process of coding experience in new ways by inventing lexical items is known as *relexicalization*.[2] It is extensively used in the creation of specialized jargons, and significantly such jargons often involve *systems* of related terms, i.e. systematic classifications of concepts. Members of the club are required to accept a new classificatory principle for their children, one that is relevant and necessary in the system of concepts habitually employed by the club to categorize its members and their behaviour. Once this relexicalization begins, it may extend into a system that includes, say, 'trained', 'over-trained', 'under-trained', 'uninstructed', 'part-instructed', etc. The member cannot be sure how far the club's specialized classification system extends.

There are relexicalizations which are based on syntactic structures other than nominalization through truncated passives. In 3 we have 'outside shoes', and no doubt its complement 'inside shoes'; there is the 'pool area', a word which exists in the language of the world outside this club; however, with a large range of new terms being created, the nervous member of the club will be wary of relying on any continuity between his normal language and the language of the club. The most complex new nominal created here is in 2: 'Being absent for more than three consecutive sessions without explanation to the membership secretary' – here is a concept to master! Notice that the rule-writer evidently regards this as a difficult lexical item which has to be defined for the innocent addressee: i.e. his use of the definitional verb 'means'. Now 'means' is often used to equate two mutually substitutable linguistic items: e.g. ' "amour" means "love" ', ' "avuncular" means "behaving like an uncle" '. In the club rules, however, 'means' equates actions in a consequential relation: 1 'this will mean one adult enrolling . . .'. The use of 'means' here suggests the inevitable unalterability of the consequence.

The effect of the relexicalization is control through the one-way flow of knowledge. This device is probably more powerful than the direct control exercised in the commands analysed above. Whereas an obstinate individual might offer resistance to direct interpersonal manipulation, he or she would find it difficult to evade the control exercised through the new terminology of this society. The only strategies available would seem to be withdrawal from this club, or the construction of an alternative vocabulary; which might in fact amount to the same thing. However, for any member of the club, these terms constitute the categories which describe possible entities of the conceptual system which defines the 'world' of the club: and in that sense they control the user of that language.

In the light of this realization it pays to investigate the whole range of vocabulary used in any particular text: here we will look at two other nominals used in the rules, from the point of view of the analysis of processes which they reveal. First, 'responsibility', in 1. It occurs as the object of 'take': a transitive verb, and a verb signifying a physical process. The sense we get from this syntactic function is that 'responsibility' is something concrete, existing, real: something that can be taken. It is, however, an abstract word, and one which signifies not a single entity, but a relation between at least two participants: 'Someone is responsible for someone else'. This is collapsed into a single noun: the effect of this nominalization is to present a complex relation as a simple lexical item, and to introduce the process verb 'take'. We are not suggesting that the writer of these rules went through this sequence of syntactic changes; 'responsibility' is after all a word which is listed in any dictionary of English. The point is that the writer has a choice of either selecting a word such as 'responsibility', or using the fuller syntactic form 'be responsible for', preserving the state adjective 'responsible'. It is interesting to see the effect of substituting the latter form in the sentence. It has to be rewritten in a revealing way: 'Parents must accompany their children, and must be responsible for them at all times'. Why does the writer of the rules prefer the 'take' form? Perhaps he feels that an action ('take') directly under the control of an agent, and directly affecting an entity, ('responsibility') is more congenial to a command than the attribution of a quality to an individual ('be responsible'). Hence parents have to 'take responsibility'.[3]

The second nominalization is from 2, 'automatic expulsion'. 'Expulsion' like 'responsibility', is a collapsed form: the full version is 'someone expels you'. Presumably, if this full form were used, the writer would have to mention who would actually be doing the expelling: 'Being absent . . . means that X will expel you'. This embarrassing detail can be suppressed by using the noun. No expeller need be expressed, and so none can be challenged. It is also not quite clear where 'automatic' would fit in this form: 'automatically means', or 'means automatically', 'X automatically will', 'X will automatically', 'expel you automatically'? All of these possibilities carry different implications, and which one the writer might have had in mind is impossible to determine. Rather than trying to retrieve the underlying structure, it is more important to note that, by qualifying the noun in this way, a new term is being created: 'an automatic expulsion': an important term in the world of the club. And the possibility of other expulsions is opened: 'gradual', 'permanent', 'partial', 'temporary', etc.

The clearest and most familiar example of rules is a recipe in a cookbook. It has an unambiguous relation between speaker/writer and listener/reader, with one having full knowledge, the other having none. Recipes, however, are syntactically much simpler than the swimming club rules: imperatives are the only form of command used (take a clove of garlic . . .). By comparison, the rules of the swimming club show remarkable variety: only one imperative, and it qualified by a 'Please'; most of the commands showing uncertainty about the power-relation; deletion of relevant agents; control through the creation of a set of newly lexicalized categories. Then again, the rules are not as modalized as they might be: no 'should', 'possibly'. The writer has a model of what rules are, or should be; yet seems reluctant to use the overt form of, say, the cooking recipe. From this one might deduce what happens to be known to the writers of this essay, namely that the relation between the writer of the rules and the recipients of the rules is ambivalent: they are members of two overlapping communities with totally differing status relations. One community comprises the parents of children in one school, frequently meeting in informal situations not involving the club; the other, a committee formally constituted, drawn from these same parents to run a swimming club for their children. Hence the normal anonymity of the rule-writer is not the case here, and the power relations are complicated by the status differential assigned to some parents by their being put on the committee. Authority conflicts with friendship, and so the expression of authority becomes problematic.

Another way of thinking about the shifts and awkwardnesses in encoding this power relationship is in terms of the functions of the rules. These rules have to do at least two things at once. First, they are *directive*. Certain specific practical actions of the members have to be controlled, for reasons of hygiene, safety, protection of the physical facilities: presumably it is dangerous for there to be more than twenty-four bodies in the pool at the same time, and there has to be a rule prohibiting action which would lead to this potential danger. Second, they are *constitutive*. A club must have rules for it to count as a club: they are the token of its formal existence. So rule 7, for example, the one about membership cards, concerns the behaviour of members as members and not, pragmatically, as swimmers, parents, instructors, learners, etc., individuals engaged in the activity of swimming. The rules help to constitute the club as a theoretical social entity. There has to be a generally appropriate style, an 'official' style, and this style is both alien to the writer and obfuscatory as far as the practical organization of the swimming is concerned. But 'constitution' involves more than the definition of a social group: as we have seen, the choice of a style entails commitment to a perspective on the way the group is organized. A society is being cognitively, as well as formally, constituted, in the sense that the special language encodes a system of special concepts, a way of seeing the club; to the extent that the members accept this language, their world-view will be modified, albeit in a minute area of their experience.

The space between 'directive' and 'constitutive' can be seen as a continuum. At the directive end are the instructions on self-service petrol pumps, launderette machines, and in cookbooks. Here there is no ambiguity about power-relationships. The petrol company has all the knowledge, the customer none, the customer must carry out the instructions to the letter or he will not get his petrol, or will lose his money, damage the equipment, set fire to himself and the petrol station, etc. At the constitutive extreme are rules which do not apply to the specifics of behaviour, but are designed to define a community by offering a distinctive analysis of, or ideology of, that community's behaviour. Our next extract is close to that extreme. The dilemma of the club rules is that it falls somewhere in the indeterminate in-between, needing to regulate without compromising constitution, to constitute without obscuring the essentials of practical instruction.

General Regulations for Students

Preamble
The University can function effectively only if all its members can work peaceably in conditions which permit freedom of study, thought and expression within a framework of respect for other persons. The General Regulations exist to maintain these conditions:
(1) by the protection of free speech and lawful assembly within the University.
(2) by the protection of the right of all members or officers or employees of the University to discharge their duties.
(3) by the protection of the safety and property of all members or

officers or employees of the University while engaged in their duties
or academic pursuits.

(4) by the protection of the property of the University.

All students matriculating in the University shall, so long as they remain
in attendance, be bound by the following Regulations and by such other
Regulations as the University may from time to time determine.

1 *Age of Admission*

Those who intend to follow courses for University degrees and diplomas
are not normally admitted if they are under the age of seventeen years
on 1 October of the year of admission.

2 *Matriculation*

Matriculation is the act of placing a student's name upon the *matricula*
or roll of members of the University. Before being allowed to matriculate a student must have fulfilled the examination requirements laid
down by the University in respect of general entrance requirements and
in respect of course requirements for the programme of study which the
student wishes to pursue.

All persons entering the University as students in residence shall sign a
Declaration of Obedience to the Authorities of the University, in the
following terms: 'I hereby promise to conform to the discipline of the
University, and to all Statutes, Regulations and rules in force for the
time being, in so far as they concern me' (University of East Anglia,
Norwich, *Calendar*, 1977–8, p. 128).

This immediately recognizable institutional style is both unspeakable and unreadable. Its unspeakability lies in its remoteness from
any speech act which could be performed by a real individual. We
can experience this only as receivers, relating as addressees to an
institutional source. Most people are never called upon to write or
speak in this style productively, or if they are, like the author of the
club rules, they find the effacement of their everyday personal roles
extremely difficult to manage. Now the author of the club rules can
never go the whole way, because he has a certain practical content to
preserve, a directive function to enforce. His rules must be attended
to, or children drown. The University authorities, however, are
subject to no such hazard. The unspeakable style is by itself an act,
whatever its content; and the text does not have to be read, since it
does not apply to the specifics of people's behaviour.

We are not saying that this text is not intended to be manipula-
tory. From the point of view of the institution that published it, the
function of the text is to serve as an instrument in controlling

behaviour. This control is to be achieved not by regulating specific actions, but by enforcing a set of attitudes. Three points need to be made about the power-relationship expressed through this text. First, by adopting a familiar bureaucratic style of 'impersonality' (ready-made and available generally for official institutions in our society, and certainly not invented by the officers of the University of East Anglia) those people who were responsible for publishing the text have obscured the fact that they intend to control the behaviour of the people to whom the text is addressed. Second, there is a degree of over-kill here. The writer of the document is absolutely unidentifiable, and the addressees are absolutely depersonalized. In these respects the language is so unlike any discourse which might be spoken by one person to another person that the critical reader may well find the text alienating, symbolic of an utter separation of the interests of the source and the addressees (while both parties are, after all, members of the same university community). Third, not only is the nature of the communicative relationship obscured or mystified by the way language is used, so also is the content which is being communicated. This is a result of the text's being towards the constitutive end of the directive-constitutive continuum. The community to whom the text is addressed is given very little specific guidance about what activities are approved and what proscribed, and yet the structure of the language expresses an implicit and demanding orthodoxy, a special system of attitudes required of members of the community.

The language of the text is impersonal in the way that rate demands, government circulars, official notices are, and this impersonality has the same linguistic origins, and the same causes in the needs of institutions to interact with individuals in a formal manner. But the subject-matter, and the act of speech, are in fact far from impersonal. The regulations have for their topic a set of relationships between institution and addressee – rights and obligations, permitted and proscribed behaviour – and, to compound the interpersonal force of the text, the regulations not only describe but also *enact* an interpersonal relationship:[4] the text is a behaviour-controlling imperative, directed by the powerful at the powerless, saying 'I order you to . . .' even though few specific directions are furnished. In these circumstances the impersonality of the language is exceedingly conspicuous. There is no 'you', and the only first person pronouns which occur are the 'I' and 'me' in the quoted 'Declaration of Obedience'. The 'you' who is addressed by this text is consistently transformed into third person: 'a student', 'students', 'persons', 'those', 'they', etc. (cf. 'parents' above). The effect of this is to turn the person who is being addressed into someone who is being talked about; children whose parents talk about them to other people in their own presence, ignoring them, know how infuriating this is. There is no 'I' in the text: only 'the Authorities of the University' and 'the University', with 'the General Regulations' serving as an intermediary between source and addressee. Notice how both the source and the addressee are frequently expressed in plural form: 'the Authorities', 'students'. Pluralization aggrandizes and obscures the source. As with the royal plural: you can't really pin him down, but he seems to be more powerful than you. Pluralization of the addressee, on the other hand, confirms the source's refusal to treat the individual addressee as an individual person (cf. the doctor's 'how are we today?'). Such naming conventions can hardly fail to lead to distance and alienation.

Impersonality also arises from the total avoidance of any explicit command structure: there are no questions or imperatives, despite the strongly manipulative character of the speech act being performed. However, a weighty burden of authority is carried by the modal verbs 'shall', 'must' and 'may'. 'Shall' suggests an inexorable obligation, usually imposed on the student but, occasionally, in later paragraphs, the obligation of the university: 'The days on which students register shall be announced annually by the University . . .'. 'Must' means an absolute condition. The most frequent[5] modal attached to 'the University' is 'may', which ascribes a right, not an obligation: the University may if it chooses dispense with some condition, or has the right, if it chooses, to punish the breach of a regulation. 'May' connotes licensed capriciousness, and feels very threatening.[6]

In most styles that people find 'formal' and 'impersonal' two syntactic constructions are almost invariably found to be prevalent: *nominalization* and *passivization*. Both abound in this passage. Passives include 'engaged in their duties', 'bound by the following Regulations', 'not normally admitted', 'allowed to matriculate', 'laid down by the University'. Nominalization is a transformation which reduces a whole clause to its nucleus, the verb, and turns that into a noun. The first sentences yield (to cite only the clear cases):

| freedom | *derived from* | someone is free |
| study | | someone studies something |

thought	someone thinks
expression	someone expresses something
respect	someone respects somebody else
Regulations	someone regulates somebody else
protection	someone protects somebody or some-thing
speech	someone speaks
assembly	some people assemble

and so on. Many derived nominals can be spotted by their ending in *-ion*, *-ition*, *-ation*, *-ience*, *-ness*, *-ment*, etc., and many are learned words of classical origin: 'expression', 'protection', 'regulation', 'matriculation', 'declaration'. The impression of formality derives partly from their dignified etymological pedigree, partly from the fact that large numbers of scientific and technical terms have this form. We have already seen that nominalization facilitates *relexicalization*, the coding of a new, specialized, set of concepts in a new set of lexical terms. It seems as if the student can only conform to the regulations by learning a new technical vocabulary which expresses the relationships of which the regulations speak. 'Matriculation' illustrates the essence of this process. This arcane term, meaning admission to the register of students when entering the University for the first time, or the ceremony associated therewith, refers to one sole experience in the life of a person who goes to college. The word is absolutely no use to him in any other context, and by its intense specialization of meaning becomes talismanic in the relationship of student and university. The regulation seems to require the student to acquire the meaning of this word as a precondition for a well-formed relationship between the parties. It is a mumbo-jumbo as patent in its ritual function, and as impenetrable conceptually, as 'being absent for more than three consecutive sessions without explanation to the membership secretary'. Interestingly, both terms are introduced in definitional sentences – 'being absent ... means ... ', 'matriculation ... is ... '.

Another example of relexicalization, which illustrates how the process generates *systems* of new terms, is the series 'examination requirements', 'course requirements', 'general entrance requirements'. (These are technical qualifications which have to be looked up elsewhere in the *Calendar*.) Since the series is so patently productive, the student may well feel some unease lest it spawns other terms, unexpressed here and perhaps to be unleashed elsewhere –

'residence requirements', 'political affiliation requirements', 'dietary requirements' are all too plausible potential offspring of the system.

Nominalization is a process of syntactic reduction, as well as potential relexicalization. The personal participants, the 'someones' whoever they may be, are deleted as the clause turns into a noun; so is modality (thus many potential 'mays' and 'shalls' disappear). The deletion of references to persons is entirely compatible with the University's strategy, noted earlier, of suppressing 'I' and 'you': the single word 'Regulation', and all other words like it ('requirement', 'obedience', etc.) is effectively a euphemism, the nominalization allowing the University to avoid telling the truth in its full syntactic form: 'I, the University, require you, the student, to do such-and-such'; 'you, the student, obey me, the University'. Similarly with passives: 'not normally admitted' really means 'the University does not normally admit' – the passive structure, allowing agent-deletion, permits a discreet silence about *who* if anyone might refuse to admit the applicant. Usually the agents and patients can be retrieved in an analytic reading, though of course the style discourages such analysis. Sometimes nominalization or passivization makes it extremely difficult to infer the roles associated with the underlying verb: 'matriculation' again is a case in point: it is not clear, even if you read the sentences concerned carefully, who does what to whom, in this ritual. 'The act of placing a student's name. . . .' suggests that matriculation is something done *to* the student, but the next sentence, 'Before being allowed to matriculate . . .', implies that matriculation is reflexive, something a student does for/to himself. As the whole text is about relative responsibilities and obligations of the two parties, this is a typical and central ambivalence.

This is style as censorship. Although, in using this self-evidently extreme institutional style, the University is quite frank about the authority it claims, the style itself allows the details of the exercise of the mechanisms of control to be obscured, mystified.

Syntax may do something even more treacherous. Rather than just clouding the relational responsibilities of the deep structure (who does what to whom) it may actually *reverse* the distribution of rights and duties. Thus someone who has something done to him by another can be made responsible for his own suffering (cf. chapter 6 below, pp. 98–9, on the newspaper headline RIOTING BLACKS SHOT DEAD). A very useful linguistic device for suggesting this reversal is *thematization* through passivization. Consider, for example, the sentence

All students matriculating in the University shall, so long as they remain in attendance, be bound by the following Regulations and by such other Regulations as the University may from time to time determine.

The deep structure is actually something like

The University (AGENT) binds (PROCESS) all students (OBJECT) by Regulations (INSTRUMENT).

But in the passive surface structure, the nominal designating the object ('all students') has been placed in the position of theme, i.e. the left-most noun phrase in the sentence, and this is a position normally associated with the role of agent. The syntax strongly encourages one to read the first part of this sentence with the expectation that it is going to describe some action carried out by 'all students'; this illusion is heightened by the presence of an active verb of a subordinate clause ('matriculating') immediately following 'all students'; and by the extreme distance between the subject 'all students' and the main verb 'be bound', a distance which forces the reader to cling on to a hypothesis about the way the sentence is going to turn out. The easiest hypothesis is that we are waiting for a main verb which will tell us what action 'all students' perform; but this hypothesis will prove incorrect, since it is actually the University which is doing something. The reader has, however, made strong use of the hypothesis that 'all students' are the agent of the sentence, and is likely to retain some sense that the sentence does mean that.

Notice that the next sentence, 'Those who intend . . .', exhibits the same counterfactual reversal of roles: the initiator of the process retreats out of the thematic position (and is deleted, of course), leaving the people affected by the process to occupy a syntactic position which makes them appear responsible for their own fate of (in this case) exclusion from the University. Such role-transposition is appropriate to the ideology of the text, as we shall briefly show.

Linguistic variety is 'constitutive' – as we have seen, an important function of rules is to systematize the special concepts of the society they regulate.[7] Now there is something very odd about the way this text's language analyses the community it refers to. The General Regulations apply to individuals living and working in a large, complex community which encourages and stages a great variety of academic, social and domestic work and interaction. A university, particularly a residential one, is a hive of activity. But this language is used to neutralize the activity, and gives no sense of transaction or productivity. Pervasive nominalization accounts for a large part of the effect. As we have seen, nominalization of verbs permits deletion of reference to the persons responsible for and affected by the processes described by the verbs; nominalization can depersonalize, depopulate. It can also drain the language of actional vitality – an effect recognized in style handbooks which teach aspiring writers to prefer verbs to nouns. The processes and work which go on within the university are presented as nouns (study, assembly, academic pursuits); thinking, talking, writing etc. become, grotesquely, static 'things' located in a peaceful, stable landscape. Nominalization transforms the processes of studying and working into objects possessed by the institution, capital items to be accumulated, counted, deployed. The alternative view, that intellectual progress springs from work, dialogue, even conflict, is tacitly discouraged by this style.

Still on this subject of the peculiar analysis of people's actions, we may note the treatment of the subjects of such finite (i.e. non-nominalized) verbs as do occur. The presentation of a community in which people do not act is consolidated by some restrictions on what nouns occur as the subjects of verbs.[8] The most 'active' kind of clause-structure would be a transitive verb with a human subject and an object which undergoes change through the process described by the verb:

John opened the door.
The farmers cultivated maize.

The text avoids this construction almost totally apart from a very small number of clauses which spell out the obligations of students, and even in those the *meaning* could hardly be called 'transitive': signing a Declaration is a formal gesture, not a productive process. Avoidance of the fully transitive pattern is achieved by a small number of different strategies, of which nominalization is the most important one. Others are the use of abstract nouns or derived nominals as subjects, e.g. 'The University', 'conditions', 'the General Regulations', 'Matriculation', often plural (having the same effect as abstract, or compounding it); and a predilection for intransitive verbs, e.g. 'function', 'work', 'matriculating', etc. All these features contribute to a conception of the university as a quiet, static world in which individuals are separated from any action, process, change or productivity. It is a tightly governed community, but the governors

43

efface themselves as the mechanisms of control submit to the ideology of tranquillity. The only actions allowed are basically reflexive gestures by students: admission of responsibilities genuine or spurious.

We did not go in search of the two texts analysed in this chapter; we came across them in the normal course of our family and professional lives, and they impressed us as clear examples of the processes we wanted to describe. In the light of the analyses, is it possible to say anything more formal about similarities and differences between two texts which came our way by accident?

One theoretical point concerns the concept of *genre*: whether texts segregate themselves into recognizably different 'kinds' answering with any precision to the different communicative functions they are mustered to perform. Does *textual* structure as well as *sentence* structure respond to the demands of practical function? Are 'Rules' and 'Regulations' generically distinct sociolinguistic types in the definitive way that 'Sonnets' and 'Villanelles' differ among literary forms? In general, sociolinguistic genres exist like literary genres: a radio news bulletin is describably different from a hire purchase agreement, from an informal conversation, and so on; in actual use each of these is recognizable as what it is – thus enhancing the efficacy of the speech act it mediates – but genre category is a *problematic* in sociolinguistic intercourse. The problem affirms the power of the concept: for example, actors in white coats and horn-rimmed glasses speak of a headache remedy as if they were research scientists – we know they have been hired to present the genre 'TV advertisement' in the disguise of 'research report', so we take evasive action, recognizing that the speech act is hypocritical.

In the case of the rules and regulations, we are more impressed by their similarity than by their divergence. In his embarrassed way, the writer of the club rules has in mind some such model as the UEA regulations in which an institutional, impersonal style disguises the authoritarianism of the speech act of command that is being articulated. The effectiveness of the club rules depends on its addressees' sensing that the text belongs to the type of incontrovertible verbal authority which is so strikingly represented by our second text. The amateur's rules draw upon the power of the genre of which the regulations are a paradigm.

However, there is one important respect in which the rules depart from the extreme model of the regulations. The regulations have been drawn up primarily to create the atmosphere of a community in which authority is absolute if covert, and in which individual action is discouraged, quiet and stasis enjoined. The rules, on the other hand, retain a crucial directive function: their author envisages, and wants the members to envisage, a club in which certain actions are regularly carried out. This difference of function produces two major structural differences. First, the rules retain a firm loyalty to the syntactic expression of actions and processes: there are plenty of active, transitive verbs, and in one case ('take responsibility for'), a strongly transitive verb has been preferred, somewhat artificially, to an adjective ('be responsible for'), as if to encourage activity. The rules are much more oriented to action than the regulations. They are also much closer to a literal act of speech. One can imagine someone speaking the first text, whereas the second has been transformed away from any resemblance to the tones of a real voice. As we said, it is unspeakable, remote from any posture which could be taken up by any person ordering another around. This is a kind of linguistic dehumanization. It has the effect that the text is unreadable too: no one could reconstruct this as a credible piece of language without some distress, so remote is it from the human voice. In the authority-structure of the University, this probably does not matter: students are doubtless 'deemed to have read' the regulations, which from the University's point of view is just as good.

3 · The social values of speech and writing

GUNTHER KRESS

It is a commonplace that speech is prior to writing. Historically it preceded writing; even now, in the twentieth century most of the world's languages exist in spoken form only. In the so-called developed countries of the world the level of literacy is high; in some, like Britain, it is assumed to be total. But over the last three or four years the public has been made aware, through the publicity of the adult literacy campaign, that a startlingly high proportion of Britons are to all intents illiterate. This has come as a shock to many, for the condition of illiteracy or semi-literacy, once diagnosed, causes the awkward embarrassment usually associated with socially unacceptable illnesses. Illiterates regard themselves as stigmatized and are at pains to conceal their inability to read and write.*

But even if we ignore the substantial illiteracy within Britain, if we look only at those people who can read and write with some ease, we find that as far as the two uses of language go, the spoken use far out-strips the written. If we put speaking-hearing on the one hand against writing-reading on the other, then even for the most 'literate' among us the former occupies perhaps nine-tenths of our time as against the latter. For the majority of the population the proportion occupied by the spoken form is even higher. Furthermore, we need to make a distinction between passive and active use of the two modes. For while it is the case that most of us speak as much as we hear, all of us read more than we write. It is inconceivable that even the most prolific authors write more than they read. So on all counts the written mode of language is the less significant in terms of use, to quite an overwhelming degree; and differences of social class and occupation have no significant impact on this picture.

Yet this is not the whole story. If we ask different speakers about their attitudes towards their own language and the language of others we get surprising results. Most speakers regard their own spoken language as defective, ungrammatical, deformed, improper, deficient

* I would like to thank Ken Lodge for comments on an earlier version of this chapter.

in some way. Yet some speakers do not have this attitude to their own language. It is a curious phenomenon. One conventionally accepted interpretation argues something along these lines: 'It is an unfortunate fact that most regional and social dialects are corruptions or imperfect versions of the standard and correct form of English. The grammar of these dialects is defective or perhaps rudimentary.' Linguists have long argued against such views. The linguistic work of the last century and a half has made it clear that the different regional dialects of English have their own independent lineage back to Anglo-Saxon times. More recent linguistic research has focused on the social dimensions of dialect, and shown that social groups evolve distinctive dialects. 'Standard English' is thus shown to be one specific conjunction of geographical and social dialects. It is the case that this one form of English has a particularly high status; fairly loosely and generally speaking it is the language of those who enjoy a high level of education, wealth, economic and political power, and live within the geographical (and social and cultural) ambit of London. Anyone wishing to be identified with that group, or aspects of it, orients their linguistic habits on those of that group. 'Speaking nicely' is encouraged as desirable by many teachers and parents.

It is nevertheless surprising that the negative value-judgments placed on non-standard forms of English are so readily accepted by the users of these dialects. (That is not to say that there are not many social groupings and geographical places where 'standard English' is anything but highly valued!) Trudgill points out that females are more aware of and responsive to this social valuation than males; mothers tend to be more concerned about their children's language than fathers, women teachers more than men, and girls tend to be more responsive to such pressures than boys. Indeed in a study which Trudgill carried out in Norwich,[1] he found that working-class forms of speech were regarded as more masculine than middle-class forms, and consequently males tended to adjust their language in that direction – 'downwards' rather than 'upwards'. Clearly such valuations are social rather than grammatical. Yet the judgments which speakers make about their own and other speakers' speech are expressed in grammatical rather than in sociological terms. Appeal is made to notions of grammatical correctness rather than to facts of social structure.

These are judgments made on *speech*, but the standards of the judgment are derived from conceptions about the *written* and not the spoken form of the language. In other words, there is a double mis-carriage of judgment. Firstly, social value-judgments are expressed, inappropriately, in grammatical terms. Second, one mode of lan-guage, speech, is judged, inappropriately, in terms of another mode of language, writing.

The criticism which is most often made of spoken language is that it is marred by incomplete sentences, hesitations, pauses, repetitions, false starts, and so on.[2] Interestingly, very few people are aware of these things when they hear spoken language, particularly when they are themselves engaged in conversation. We have to 'distance' our-selves from the conversation quite self-consciously before such features of language impinge on our awareness. Indeed, the occasion for this criticism usually arises in situations where a distancing arises accidentally or coincidentally: for instance, someone might be an uninvolved observer of speech, or might be maliciously finding fault with another speaker. Most frequently, the distancing arises when the language used is 'translated' from one medium to another, that is, when speech is 'transcribed' and presented in written form.

It is quite true that writing contains none of the features men-tioned above, nor a good many others found in speech. There are two related reasons for this. First, speech is instantaneous, writing is not; second, each employs a distinctively characteristic medium, aspects of which have influenced their very structure. To deal with the first point. The phrase 'thinking aloud' in its everyday use provides a very useful insight. Thought and language are intimately related; certain forms of thought are impossible without language. The words and structure of a language constitute the matter of those forms of thought. Speaking aloud in a spontaneous manner is thus the closest we can come to the core of thought and to the process of thinking. From this point of view thought exists in the forms and structures of language – conversely, the forms and structures of language represent thought. The process of articulation of language represents the process of thinking. Seen in this light, the features of speech mentioned above have a plausible explanation.[3] They record the process of thinking. Far from regarding such matters as defects, we can regard them as providing us with meaning of a most interest-ing and critical kind. Signs which indicate 'thinking in process' are hardly meaningless. They enable us to witness and understand the choices a speaker may have made, accepted, rejected, or further modified. This adds a richness of understanding and interpretation to the 'message' which hearers draw on and use in responses to and assessments of speakers and messages. They are meanings which we disregard at our peril. To classify these matters as defects is a grotesque failure to appreciate what is actually at stake.

There is another meaning expressed in these characteristics of speech. To the extent that spontaneous speech, with its abandoned forms, new starts, hesitations, permits us as hearers direct access to undisguised processes of thinking, the speaker is exposed and vulnerable to a considerable extent. Such language is therefore most likely where no threat is felt, where the speaker is secure. If the context is threatening, the only possible response for many speakers is silence. Thus spontaneous speech expresses meanings about the speaker's perception of the social context over and above the other meanings carried.

Writing, by contrast, is not spontaneous. Writing is the antithesis of spontaneity, and countless chewed pencil-ends bear witness to that fact. Hesitations, false starts, pauses, *are* there in writing: in crossed out phrases and lines, torn up first, second, third drafts, blank sheets of paper. They are, however, edited out. Interestingly, the more important and formal a written document, the less likely we are to leave behind any traces of our editorial work. In fact one could quite readily construct a hierarchy of formality by plotting the amount of editing which has been performed on a text. Our editing efforts may go much further than this. As writing has permanence, I can come back to a passage that I have written some time ago and attempt to re-write it for any number of reasons: to take into account new insights, new information, a reassessment of my relation to the audience, and so on. The finished product bears no immediate and visible signs of this. (We argue later in this book that some traces of editing may remain, though they are of a more covert, less accessible form.) Editing, care, circumspection are thus hallmarks of the written language.

So much for differences between speech and writing which arise from the instantaneous and spontaneous nature of one, and the non-spontaneous, planned and edited nature of the other. The differences in the media employed in speech and writing are apparent, in fact, so apparent and obvious that their consequences have hardly been explored. Both need to convey a range of similar meanings, and it is important to know how these meanings are realized in each medium. But beyond this, each expresses meanings which are proper to one medium alone, and which, if they occur in the other, have to be 'translated' in some way.

To take this second point first. Very brief reflection will show that speech occurs in many situations in which writing never occurs. Conversations are always carried on in spoken language. Therefore a whole range of meanings which have to do with the interpersonal nature of conversation occur in speech, but never in writing. For instance, so-called tag-questions ('You do take sugar, *don't you?*', 'You'll come, *won't you?*', 'He's twelve, *is he?*', 'You took it, *did you?*') never occur in writing (except of course in the reporting of speech). These questions are concerned with the mechanics of interpersonal relations, establishing rapport, seeking confirmation, eliciting support, and so on. There is a whole range of linguistic forms which express meanings of this kind, the 'you knows', 'sort ofs' of spoken language. In addition, there are the syntactic forms which are appropriate to interpersonal exchange: questions and commands. Seen in this light, writing is a limited code utilizing a narrower range of linguistic forms and devices than speech.

The two modes of language do, however, also express broadly similar meanings. Here it is interesting to analyse the effect which the medium itself has had on the manner in which specific meanings are expressed. Take as an example the means for conveying emphasis. In speech there is a range of devices to achieve emphasis, each of course with its own meaning. A speaker may make one item louder than the surrounding items, or longer, or pause before it, or say it with a pronounced pitch-movement, or several of these together. So in response to 'Did you say fifty?' a speaker might say 'No, fif-teeeeeen', or 'No, fif*teen*,' (with '*teen*' pronounced very loudly) or 'No, fif*teen*' (with a marked fall in pitch from high to low on 'teen'). All of these could be used together. In writing (which does not attempt to imitate speech) prominence would have to be achieved by different means. (Of course, the need for a response of the kind mentioned is unlikely in a context of writing.) Here the place of an item in the sequence of the linear structure is likely to have emphatic meaning. Obvious places are first and last position in a sentence. English has a range of syntactic devices which permit writers to place items in such positions; in the case of the example above it could be a form like 'Fifteen is what he said', or 'It was fifteen that he wanted'. Here syntax is used to create positions of special emphasis. One major explanation for the frequency of the passive in English is its function in making items focal: 'He wanted fifteen', 'Fifteen were wanted'.[4] (The situation is somewhat complicated by the fact that most readers silently 'speak' written language, so that the emphatic devices of speech tend to be present as well as those of the written form. For example, in 'It was fifteen that he wanted' a silent reading would probably place marked pitch-movement on '*fif*teen' with a fall from high to low.)

It seems, then, that English has certain syntactic forms which are predominantly used as devices for expressing meanings specifically through the written form of the language. The greater range and flexibility of expression of speech is 'translated' into a range of syntactic forms in writing. But not all meanings can be 'translated'. There are 'attitudinal' meanings, modalities of all kinds, which exist in speech and not in writing. When they do appear in writing it is very much as quotation forms: '"No, fifteen", she said feelingly (with annoyance, indignantly', etc.). Such modalities are automatically expressed in speech, and are understood by competent speakers without special pointing out: imagine the oddness of a speaker saying, 'No, fifteen, (I'm saying) indignantly'. All competent hearers hear indignation if it is 'there' or do not hear it if it is not there.

In many respects, therefore, speech is richer in linguistic forms and in expressive devices than writing. From this point of view one could easily arrive at a negative judgment about writing as compared with speech. It is in itself interesting and revealing that such judgments are never made.

But perhaps the major criticism levelled at speech is its alleged 'incompleteness', 'lack of structure', 'broken sentences'. The implicit and unstated assumption underlying criticisms of this nature is that the sentence is the basic unit of language, both speech and writing. It is the case that sentences are the basic constituents of written texts. The sentence is not, however, the basic unit of speech. The work of Michael Halliday suggests that the relevant and operative structural principle in speech is concerned with marking out appropriate units of information (as judged by the speaker).[5] Intonation (the significant pitch-movements of the human voice) is used to realize this structure. The relevant structural unit is the information unit; frequently this coincides with a clause, rarely with a sentence. As an example, here is a stretch of speech transcribed from a report by a foreign correspondent on the 9 p.m. news service of the BBC: 'Probably the most important and certainly the most difficult of Mr Carter's job is to break Americans of this habit of driving everywhere in huge cars which often get as little as ten miles to the gallon sometimes even less.' This is unlikely to be 'spontaneous' speech; more likely it was scripted in some way before it was spoken. Nevertheless, we can discern some of the features of speech; there are discernible divisions within the text, which are motivated by the speaker's wish to present chunks of information, and within those chunks to present some pieces of information as *new* to the speaker. We can mark off the units between //, underlining those words which have intonational prominence.

/ / Probably the most important // and certainly the most difficult part of Mr Carter's job // is to break Americans of this habit // of driving everywhere // in huge cars // which often get as little // as ten miles to the gallon // sometimes even less //. The units between the slashes are given unity by having one major pitch-movement within them, and an overall unifying pitch-contour. The pitch-prominence picks out the element which the speaker wishes to present as informationally focal (because *new*) relative to which the rest of the unit is presented as non-*new*. The prominent element may occur late in the unit / / Probably the most important //; or early: // sometimes even less //; or anywhere else. It is important to notice that these units may correspond to traditional units of syntax (clauses, phrases, for example), but need not. For instance // and certainly the most difficult part of Mr Carter's job // is neither a clause nor a phrase, it is less than one and more than the other.

Spontaneous speech is often characterized by greater complexity of structure, a great variety of information-units, and variety in the internal structure of information-units. Additionally, as I observed above, where speakers feel unthreatened and their speech is close to the neurological assembly of language, there may be a number of embedded information-units, incomplete information-units, and hesitations preceding the informationally prominent elements. Listeners characteristically do not note these either as particularly complex or as ill-formed or incomplete. Frequently one finds listeners constructing the text simultaneously with the speaker, so that they insert the correct items in the speaker's text; interestingly the items tend to be not only syntactically correct but also lexically correct. This may well point to principles of textual structuring of a semantic kind which we do not understand at the moment, but which operate in parallel to syntactic and informational structuring. The cohesion of spontaneous speech is as strong as that of writing; though it is not always possible to fit a grid of sentence-structure neatly onto the structure of speech.

Hence what is often interpreted as incompleteness, lack of structure, etc., points to a different type of structure, a different order of structuring, in speech. Despite protestations about the primacy of speech, modern linguistics has very little indeed to say about the grammatical organization of the spoken language. Without acknowledging that this is so, much of modern linguistic work is about an idealized version of language, remarkable mainly for its remoteness from actual language use, and, in particular, speech.

If we put together the realization about the actual uses of speech and writing with the valuations attached to either, we are forced to look for a new interpretation. In crude class (or socio-economic) terms, it is the case that all groups use speech much more than writing. Yet it is also the case that speakers from a lower class (or socio-economic group) disvalue their own speech when asked by others to make judgments. In terms of the *active* use of the written form – writing language rather than only reading it – it is probable that only members of higher socio-economic groups write with any appreciable frequency at all; and it is probably also true that these groups read appreciably more than the lower groups. At any rate it may well be the case that the group which makes most active use of the written form of the language begins to see it as the 'real' form: it is permanent; it is conservative in its effects – the language of yesterday is as accessible as the language of today; it can be modified without embarrassment, for I can edit a written message as heavily as I choose and leave no trace; it has a normative influence removed from the contingencies of time and place. When we put these characteristics together with the fact that (just as only some of the world's languages are written) only one of the many English socio-geographical dialects has a written representation (standard southern middle-class English), we begin to see that the command by one social group of the active use of the written medium, taken together with that medium's pervasiveness and constancy over time, can readily lead to the valuation of the written as higher than the spoken form. And this valuation is accepted to a large extent even by those whose main or only use of language is spoken. Many influences work for such valuations. The effect of the educational system – ostensibly based solely on the mastery of written language; the reinforcing and causally prior effects of the social system, where those in positions of power and control attempt to approximate in speaking to a language which takes the written version as the standard. Though the process operates largely invisibly, there are some exceptions: the attempts to get children to speak 'nicely'; the BBC's influence exercised through a pronunciation unit, and an editing policy which ruthlessly cuts pauses, gaps, hesitations and repetitions from spoken language; to the promotion of people with the right accent. On the whole the process is covert, though all-pervasive.

Yet sometimes one gets a peculiarly sharp insight into the imposition of the value-system, and the text below is one such case. The first extract is a speech therapist's transcription of a tape made by one of her patients, an 8-year-old boy. He was given a picture-book story to look at and was then asked to re-tell it. Here is the speech therapist's transcription:

(a) That's a bus and driving down the road and the drive round road and try and mend them is stop try stop running away try catch him and can't. He see engine him follow him Make funny funny funny er pictures and he run away and go in tunnel and his bus go away.

In the normal course of speech therapy practice a therapist would not make transcripts of tapes as that is a very time-consuming activity; this transcript was kindly made for me by a speech therapist as part of some material for a lecture. However, though actual written transcriptions are probably rarely made, in the course of treatment a therapist needs to make such transcripts 'silently', for they represent the basis on which he or she will recommend and initiate treatment. This text is thus unusual only in so far as it makes overt an activity which a therapist needs constantly to engage in anyway. Although the speech therapist will attempt to transcribe what he or she 'actually hears' on the tape, the transcript is in fact determined by a theory of language which the therapist holds, consciously or unconsciously. The transcript therefore is an interpretation guided by a more or less articulated theory of language norms and of language disorders.

I want to suggest that this is a sharply focused example of something which occurs constantly in our interactions with others. We construct silent transcripts of other people's speech, and these transcripts incorporate our theories of language (what we regard as appropriate, proper) and our assumptions about deficiencies in the speech of others. As an anecdotal example I offer the following. I had just taken up a new job in England, after working in Germany for a year. I wanted to ask one of my colleagues about the 'social life' in the new place but halfway through uttering my question I thought that 'social life' would sound too pompous, and changed it to 'parties'. Consequently my question came out as 'Have you got much (– social life –) parties here?' He interpreted this as the mistake of a German learner of English, and frequently afterwards constructed little jokes around this one 'lapse'. He had acted exactly like the speech therapist: constructing a transcription, and interpreting on the basis of a theory of the language problems of a German learner. Had an English speaker made this 'error' it is very likely that he would not have 'heard' it at all. In our everyday interactions, I suggest, we proceed very much in this way. Instead of the physiological or psychological pathologies that the speech therapist frequently deals with, we recognize social pathologies. However, speech therapy is beginning to handle the treatment of such social pathologies, so that the dividing line between the physiological/psychological and the social is perhaps much more conventionally drawn than we might assume.

The transcript represents the child as nearly without command of syntax; judgments about lack of sentence structure, confusions about tense and time, gender and number, etc., come easily as responses to such a transcript. School reports by teachers which I have seen make such judgments on children, and on children's intellectual capacities: 'lack of logical thinking', 'underdeveloped grasp of the concepts of time', 'limited or backward development', 'no concept of number', 'limited imaginative ability' are some examples. Though not presented as judgments about their language these 'assessments' of 'intellectual abilities' may stem from responses to the children's language. These judgments stay with the child, and may well influence the next teacher's perception of the child's abilities. In the case of the speech therapist the process is overt: while teachers' reports are mainly 'confidential' and the corrective actions that they take remain to that extent covert, a speech therapist has to recommend 'treatment', and attempt to implement it. I shall try to point out some of the 'problems' which the therapist might draw out of this transcript, and the assessment of the child that might result from it. (I ought to point out that I know very little about the kinds of treatment that speech therapists undertake.)

First, the transcript suggests that the child has no conception of *sentence*, which the written model assumes is the basic unit of language. On a conceptual level, the sentence is assumed to be the basic unit of thought, expressing one whole idea, etc. If the therapist wants to make psychological/intellectual judgments, then this would be the kind of judgment that he or she might make. Indeed it is difficult to conceive of speech therapy without speech psychology, and in most speech therapy training programmes psychology forms an important component. Second, there is no evidence of grammatically developed connections between the rudimentary sentences, so that logical order and sequence seem to be missing (from the language and hence from the child's intellectual make-up). Third, the child has a weak or undeveloped notion of causality, shown by the absence of grammatically expressed subject/actors. So instead of saying '*they* drive', '*It* has stopped', '*it* running away', '*They* try and catch him', etc. he makes no mention of the actor. Fourth, the child has no command of tense: 'is stop', 'He see engine', 'he run away', 'go in tunnel'. From this evidence the speech therapist can make deductions about the child's knowledge and perception of time. Fifth, one interpretation of the data would suggest that the child has no knowledge of syntactic agreement, that is, he says 'he see engine', 'him follow', instead of 'he see*s* (the) engine', 'he follow*s*'. It is not clear what lack of syntactic agreement suggests on the conceptual level, other than a disjunction between the subject (/actor) and the action carried out by him or her. Certainly, the effect would be to contribute further to the sense of fragmentation. Overall, the impression is of incoherent speech, pointing to an incoherent perceptual and intellectual state. I am, of course, not saying that the speech therapist would make these particular psychological assumptions fully or overtly. But I am saying that they are suggested by the syntactic deficiencies which the analysis encoded in this transcription assigns to the child's language. In constructing a programme of treatment which was more than a superficial tinkering, a speech therapist would be forced willy-nilly to speculate about such things.

If we look at the same extract as speech rather than as a deformation of the norms of the writing model a different picture begins to emerge. Below is my transcription of the tape; I submitted it to a group of speech therapists, including the one who had made the original transcript, and they agreed with my 'reading'. Again it is based on and incorporates a theory, as it necessarily must. I have marked off the information units by //, and underlined the word within each unit where the major pitch movement occurs. (Where it was difficult to hear what the child said, I have given the alternatives which seemed plausible.)

(b) // I saw a bus // a . . . driving down the <u>road</u> // and it drive s there (that) // round the (na) <u>road</u> // an and try and <u>mend</u> them // is s stop p // try // that were running <u>away</u> // and try to (a) <u>catch</u> him // and can't // He see an <u>engine</u> // it <u>follow</u> him // make funny funny a funny a

pictures // and he ran <u>away</u> // and he go in <u>tunnel</u> // and his bus go
<u>away</u> //

The context which we have to take into account when evaluating
this language[6] is that of an 8-year-old boy taken to an office in a place
described as a hospital, talking to a strange person. Most 'normal'
8-year-olds will become worried by this situation. The greatest
difficulty in listening to the tape was that the child talked very softly,
timidly; and that would be the case with most children in that
situation.

The first thing that emerges is that the passage consists of clearly
marked units, not sentences, but the intonationally defined units of
information that speech consists of. In most cases the information
unit consists of one clause; 'I saw a bus', 'driving down the road', 'it
drive s there'; in some cases they are not clauses: 'round the road',
and in some cases they are larger than one clause: (defining a clause
as that syntactic unit which contains a verb, finite or non-finite) 'and
try to catch him', 'and try and mend them'. So, on the one hand,
there are the appropriate units of speech, information units, clearly
marked, and, on the other hand, we see the complexity of the content of each information unit, sometimes a single clause, sometimes
less than one clause, sometimes more (// and try to catch him // :
(1) *and try* (2) *to catch him*). Far from a lack of order, and far from
simplicity, the child's language shows the appropriate units of
speech, in order, with quite considerable complexity of internal
structure. In reply to the criticism that the child has no conception
of the sentence, one would say that sentences are inappropriate
units here: the child does, however, have a clear conception of the
appropriate unit of speech, information units, which are signalled by
means of intonation. The child has, furthermore, a clear conception
of the syntactic unit of *clause* (at least one verb, finite or non-finite,
with a subject which may be present '*I* saw a bus' or understood '[*it*
was] driving down the road'). Once we apply this model of speech
other things become clearer. Some of the apparently incomplete
units are explained by the child's notion of 'syntactically understood'. For instance, 'and try and mend them': the two verbs *try* and
mend do not have subjects expressed. But as the child is retelling a
story, which was illustrated with a series of pictures, he may well
feel that the person he is telling the story to knows who the subjects
of the two verbs are.

As far as the second point, lack of connection between the units, is concerned, the placing of the intonation focus (the major pitch movement) shows that the child has a clear idea of the progression of a story: if we list the series of focal elements, we see that they constitute the bones of the story. 'Bus' (the story is about the adventures of a bus), 'road' (it sets off by itself down the road), 'drive' (the action concerns its driving in various places and situations), 'road' (explaining the 'there', but also the later episode where the bus leaves the road). The third point, about the child's weakly developed sense of causality, is partly answered by his notion of understood subjects, but in part, is a reflection of the kind of story that it is: 'normal' human causation is suspended by the very nature of the genre, as a bus drives off by itself, without a driver. This is of course a challenge, on the one hand, to the child's knowledge of the world, and on the other an attempt to engage his imagination. Where judgments of psychological adequacy are at stake this may be a peculiarly unfortunate story to choose. If the child responds to the imaginative challenge, he will be using an acausal syntax. And this could leave him open to a quite unjustified description and diagnosis.

The fourth point, that the child has no conception of tense, has a slightly more complex answer, and one which takes us back into consideration of the larger social interpretations. In the child's local dialect (a low socio-economic form of Norwich English, roughly speaking) verbs are not marked for third person, or for past and present tense. So a speaker might say: 'she wash and cook for him', instead of 'she wash*es* and cook*s* for him', or 'she washed and cooked for him'. The absence of third person marking can be explained in two ways: either speakers of this dialect cannot distinguish third from second and first person, or else they do without overt marking of the third person, just as standard English doesn't mark first and second person (though other languages do – e.g. German ich wasch*e*, du wäsch*st*, er wäsch*t*). The former is as implausible about Norwich English as it is about standard English. All the Norfolk people I have met can distinguish self from other. It just happens to be the case that Norfolk English does not regard this as an important distinction to mark grammatically. But Norfolk speakers also say 'she wash and cook for him for five years and look what he do to her now'. The same explanation as before is possible, though here complicated somewhat by the fact that the so-called past and present tenses in English have, among other things the function of making an utterance either 'remote', or 'current'.[7] If I say 'I thought you were going to come early' this doesn't necessarily mean that it is a statement about a thought I had in the past; I very much think it now, I just want to distance myself from this accusation somewhat. So it seems that Norfolk English has a different system of marking distance of this kind. However, speakers of standard English are unlikely to operate with a theory of language which permits such an assessment of different forms of English. Instead they are more likely to assume that their own language is correct or proper and that its classifications are the natural and correct ones; so by their standards the dialect is deficient. From this judgment it is a very short step to making judgments about the intellectual capacities of speakers of the language. Perhaps we would hesitate to make such judgments about 'normal' speakers of an English dialect (though I suspect that such things are said and thought). We might be much more ready to pass such judgments on someone whom we met in a speech therapist's office; and we might do so quite confidently about the speaker of another language. The fifth point, about syntactic agreement, is also taken care of by what I have said so far: namely that Norwich English has rules which differ from standard English.

So, working with a different model of language, it is possible to construct a totally different account of this child's linguistic abilities and disabilities from the one which is implicit in the speech therapist's transcription. The two accounts are just about incompatible: one shows a pretty well completely competent 8-year-old user of speech; the other presents us with the picture of a nearly asyntactic, illogical, incomprehensible language, and language-user. The psychological inferences drawn from either analysis are equally disparate. Now it is the case that the child was referred to a speech therapist, and other children in his class were not, so presumably he had some speech problem which the teacher recognized. I will briefly focus on three examples in this text, and attempt to explain them. The first is: 'round $\left. \begin{matrix} \text{the} \\ \text{na} \end{matrix} \right\}$ road'. There are a number of possible hearings for this; some would involve classifying the child as an incompetent speaker. If we look at the boundary of 'round' and 'the' ('round the') we find two consonants following each other. Both are 'dental', that is, produced with the tongue touching the teeth. *d* is a plosive, *th* is a fricative; both are voiced sounds. The two sounds *d* and *th* therefore share their voicedness, and more importantly, they are articulated with the speech organs in a very similar position. The most common strategy adopted by speakers in such a situation is to merge the two sounds. *d* in word-final position tends not to be pronounced in many English words, so that it has a tendency to become assimilated to the following *th*. When this has happened we have the *th* remaining. It is now 'next to' the *n* of 'roun(d)'. *n* is pronounced with the speech organs in a position very close to that of *th*; furthermore, it is, again, a voiced consonant, and like *th* it is a *continuant* (that is, a sound that continues on, unlike *d* which 'explodes' and is then finished). Assimilation can now occur again, with the *th* being assimilated to the *n*. Now the remaining sounds are *roun* and the neutral *a* sound of *the*, and we have *roun na* or *rouna*. The phonetic process followed by the child is totally typical of speech, whether of adults or children, educated or not. The important point to note, though, is that *syntactically* all the elements of the structure are present, and it is perfectly well formed and grammatical.[8] We can give a convincing and plausible account of this error. However, if we approach the same data with a different theory we can give an account in terms of speech disability and syntactical deficiency.

The next example centres on the child's command of tense: $\left.\begin{array}{c}\text{'is}\\\text{has}\end{array}\right\}$ s stop p'. On hearing the section of the tape it was quite clear that the child pronounced the *p* of sto*p* either particularly strongly, lengthened it, or doubled it. A normal final *p* is not exploded, that is, it does not have the release of air which occurs elsewhere with a plosive consonant (p, k, t). When it is followed by the *t* of the past tense (*-ed* is pronounced as *t* after voiceless *p*, again by assimilation), speakers may explode the *t*, or they may not (try saying *stopped* as clearly as you can, then with less care, to see the difference). It seems, then, that the child has heard that a complex double consonant occurs at the end of the word *stopped*, and he is attempting to reproduce this in some way. He may or he may not realize that the significance of the complex consonant has to do with tense. We cannot be certain about this unless we hear him saying *stop* in the present tense. $\left.\begin{array}{c}\text{'is}\\\text{has}\end{array}\right\}$ s stop' presents the same problem. The form which the child has heard, and is attempting to reproduce may be 'it is stopped', 'it's stopped', probably 'it has stopped'. What we seem to have is the *i* of *it*, the *s* of *has*, and an extra *s*.

There are other interpretations: for instance, the child may have started with the 'is' of the present tense, changed his mind and gone on to restart using the 'has' form. The phonological complexity of the utterance points to a syntactic complexity (and that, in turn, to conceptual complexity) which is very much in the direction of the normal language-learning strategies employed by all children. Moreover, the apparently defective phonological forms can be explained as a conjunction of normal phonological economies and the rules of his local dialect. Such an interpretation is a long remove from judgments about phonological, syntactic, logical, and conceptual deficiencies which a different theory of language (based on written language as a norm) might impose on the data and on the child.

To end the discussion of this text, I will give my interpretation of the tape-recording, based on the transcription I made, and the theoretical evaluation outlined above.

(c) I saw a bus, driving down the road; and it drives there, round the road, and try and mend them. It has stopped, try . . . (inaudible) running away, and try to catch him and can't. He see an engine, it follow him, make funny, funny, funny pictures. And he ran away and he go in tunnel, and his bus go away.

In this interpretation I have left the Norfolk forms, though as they differ systematically from standard English, it could be argued that they might be normalized to show the underlying competence of the child more clearly. However, it seems better to get away from the notion of one form of language as the norm in terms of which all others have to be described. Norfolk English is as regular and rule-governed as standard English, though its rules are, in part, different ones. The child does have some problems, but by no means as severe as we might be led to believe from the initial transcript. The speech therapist will need to recommend some form of treatment, and that depends on her diagnosis of the child's problems. That diagnosis is revealed, in its initial stage, in the transcription she made, and it forms the basic data for any further analysis and evaluation. It is not difficult to see how an inappropriate treatment could proceed from such initial analyses; and how disastrous they might turn out to be in some cases.

The child is powerless in this situation. An initial classification by a teacher has brought him to an expert. On the face of it the expert offers a service dealing with a specific pathology. The service appears neutral, non-ideological. But as I attempted to show, its diagnoses and treatments rest on a linguistic theory, and this linguistic theory is (as any theory) ideological. It contains assumptions about society and its structure, and is locked into a social theory. Hence the practice of speech therapy is an institution which is part of the larger ideological structure of a society. In this respect it behaves like other professions (see for instance the critique of psycho-analysis offered by critics on the left). Speech therapy has extended its scope to include matters of a social kind: questions of linguistic deprivation, social dialects, and their effects on the child and its performance in education. If it operates with a linguistic theory which is based (however implicitly) on the norms of the written language it will bring to bear all the valuations which attach to that mode of language in the treatments it offers, and impose them on those who may not be users of that mode.

The child's situation, and his relation to the institution of speech therapy, can serve as a convenient symbol of the relation between the users of the spoken and the users of the written mode of language. We can draw out some of the characteristic features of the relation.

Speech therapist	Child
professional	patient
middle-class	working-class
adult	child
(representative of) institution	individual
valuer/categorizer	evaluated/categorized
(user of) high language	(user of) low language
(oriented on) the written model	(oriented on) the spoken model

The effect of these characteristics is that the one is powerful, the other powerless. The relation symbolizes others of a similar type in a society: teacher–pupil, professional–client, manager–managed, etc. The underlying power-differentials are realized in countless situations and relation-types. In each of these situations there is a 'therapist' making a 'diagnosis', and a 'patient' who will be 'treated' on the basis of the diagnosis: whether it be a job-applicant, an aspirant for promotion, or simply a casual acquaintance. One of the most potent (because most covert) bases for such diagnoses, and one of the most powerful means of perpetuating the basic dichotomy, rests on the unacknowledged and misunderstood relation between the two distinct modes of language, speech and writing.

4 · Interviews

GUNTHER KRESS and ROGER FOWLER

All language is addressed to someone, and involves an addressee as well as an addresser; it is relational. We suggest that communicative relationships are generally asymmetrical, in the sense that one participant has more authority than the other(s); that differences of class or status are at issue in discourse; the relationship is more or less competitive, a negotiation for power. In conversation, any appearance of intimacy, solidarity and co-operation is generally illusory. Speakers act out their socially ascribed roles in contending for attention, for the right to initiate new segments of the conversation, to introduce new topics, to 'hold the floor'. The influence of these underlying social relationships can be seen in the structure of linguistic choices.

To show that these forces act upon the structure of informal conversation would require a very long and complex analysis beyond the scope of this book. In this chapter we examine a rather simple and clear genre of face-to-face discourse socially structured, the *interview*. In interviews, the participants are obviously differentiated by their individual purposes, their differences in status, their roles, so that this mode of conversation exhibits an inequality, a skew in the distribution of power. And the language reflects this inequality.

The basic fact is that the interviewer has power *qua* interviewer. He is in control of the mechanics of the interview: he starts it, he has the right to ask questions, and he has the privilege of terminating it. Through his choice of questions he selects the topics which may be introduced and, as we shall see, he even has the prerogative to ask questions so designed structurally that *no* new information can be introduced. The interviewee only has the right to ask questions in the very rare, and often merely token, situation of being given explicit permission to do so. The interviewer may, even then, refuse to answer a question, may without penalty plead lack of expertise or irrelevance; yet failing to answer the question, or deviating from the drift of the question, is the most damning sin the interviewee can commit. In the hands of an experienced practitioner, the devices for

63

control granted to the interviewer by the format and situation of the interview itself constitute a formidable armoury.

Typically – and certainly in the two interviews we are going to examine – the statuses of powerful and powerless ascribed by the format of the interview to Ir (Interviewer) and Ie (Interviewee) respectively coincide with a power differential which they occupy for reasons external to the interview itself: employer/unemployed, teacher/potential pupil, adult/youth, etc. But in passing it is worth pointing out that this correspondence is not always so neat. The junior reporter who is sent to interview the busy politician, or government minister passing through, may find it difficult to assert his power as interviewer, since the status differential that relates them generally is so obviously the inverse of the one produced by the interview situation. But that same government minister may find it difficult to assert his power in an interview just before a general election, even against a junior reporter.

If we regard the interview as a kind of conversation, it is a peculiar one, in that the formal rules of status relation, and the means for their expression in language, are exceptionally overt, strict, and legitimized by the interview genre. To what extent these devices are actually used by the participants, or adhered to, can be regarded as depending on factors brought into the interview from outside, factors relating to pre-existent social statuses of the participants.

Seeing interviews as peculiar conversations may lead us conversely to regard conversations as peculiar kinds of interviews. This is a hypothesis which we tentatively make: in the conversations which we and our students have more or less formally analysed, it has been the case that the speakers, even when they regard themselves as equals, friends, etc., have used some forms which recall the power-differential signals found in the interview. If this hypothesis is valid, it may be explained by the inherent asymmetry of all social communication.

The texts which we analyse here come from very familiar kinds of interview situation, and we believe that they are typical interview language. They were collected by students in the course of their undergraduate work in sociolinguistics, with the permission of the people involved. To the extent that the participants were aware of being recorded, self-consciousness may have introduced a slight distorting factor, though it is our experience that speakers are not usually put off by the presence of a tape-recorder, or at least, quickly come to ignore it and get down to the more engaging purpose of their conversation. The first interview was recorded in the offices of a commercial employment agency. The second was recorded at the University of East Anglia, and is one of the thousands of interviews of sixth-formers applying for admission to university conducted every year. Both interviews were, then, routine affairs.

Any complete analysis of face-to-face spoken interaction would ideally contain statements, as full as possible, about the situation in which it took place, the participants, their purposes, etc. We do not have this information in the case of the first interview, except one fact which may be informative, that the Ie Mary (the name, like all others in these texts, is fictitious) is West Indian.

Liz: Take a seat, Mary.
(*Pause as she reads the card*)
Do you mind what area it is, just sort of West End or City or . . . ?
Mary: No, just City probably.
Liz: Is local OK if it . . . if we've got local, you don't mind. The
5 money's a little bit less, it might be sort of twenty-eight if it's local. Or would you prefer to go up town and get more money?
Mary: I'd prefer to go up town.
Liz: Fine. So I'll put the salary down as thirty. I'll have a look through for you, see what we've. . . . Done an IBM 029 and 059 at
10 college?
Mary: 029 only.
Liz: You haven't done the 059?
Mary: No, IBM 029 only.
Liz: Not even at college?
15 *Mary:* No.
Liz: You've never done any temporary work using it, no?
Mary: Temporary work, no.
Liz: Here's one, no it's no good, it's for a minimum of two years' experience . . .
20 *Mary:* Yeah.
Liz: But if they say sort of trained, they'll train you in their own system 'cause they'd 'cause a lot of companies haven't got IBM any more, a lot of companies here got ICL, Univac and a new one out, apparently called CMC. I don't know, I haven't sort of seen it or
25 anything but we've got sort of several sort of companies that do this CMC now so . . . Univac, that's a different machine to an 029, see there's nothing . . . Univac is a sev . . . 1701 I think. You don't know . . . do you know how fast you are? I mean, how many key depressions?
30 *Mary:* No, Mrs Kelly tell me how much.
Liz: Oh, yeah, but I don't know where it's . . . you haven't got any

idea because Mrs Kelly is off sick and she's . . . she's got your
certificate.

Mary: I don't know how many.

35 *Liz:* If you . . . oh, there's one here for a punch operator with experience on an ICL. 'Do not send along applicants who have not got
ICL experience.' Obviously they've had a lot of people being offered
it, that are IBM. There's nothing at the moment but we can keep
your card on permanent and temporary and um you know if we get

40 anything come in 'cause we get the new jobs in every day; oh, I'll
just check the new jobs. No, they're all local, they're for IBM anyway. Um, as the new jobs come in each day I'll ring them up and ask
them if they will take you without you know even if it's um if they
train you on an ICL or something. I'll ask them each day when jobs

45 come in. But there seems to be a lot of experienced punch operators
around.

Mary: Really?

Liz: We've had quite . . . we've had two in this morning so you
know so they're usually scarce, quite scarce, punch operators, but at

50 the moment there seem to be a lot around, but I can drop you a line,
but if you can ring in regularly for temporary work and I'll get Mrs
Kelly to send your certificate off to you. OK?

Mary: Yeah, but . . .

Liz: All right?

55 *Mary:* Yeah, could you send it off in this thing, because I don't
want it to get spoiled, you know? That's why she told me to come
and collect it myself.

Liz: Oh, you want us to send it off in this.

Mary: Yeah.

60 *Liz:* OK.

Mary: That's why I brought it in. I've already paid for it.

Liz: All right, I'll send it back to you in that then, as soon as I can
find what she's done with it. OK. Thanks for coming in Mary. I'll
get in touch with you. All right?

65 *Mary:* Bye-bye.

Liz: Bye-bye.

Liz, the interviewer, begins the interview, as one would expect.
To do so, she uses a conventional invitation to sit down, a command
in imperative syntax. The conventionality of this opening might lull
us into treating it as 'just a phrase', without any meaning. We should
ask, however, what other 'conventional' forms would have been
available to Liz: a phrase is significant if it is taken from a range of
alternative options. She might have said 'Won't you take a seat?', or
'Let me get you a chair', she might have silently gestured to a chair,

or whatever. It is instructive to ask whether any of these alternative forms would have been appropriate, or, taking it one stage further, which would be inappropriate, and in what circumstances. Could Liz invite the branch manager to 'Pull up a chair, Charles!', and if so, what would be inferred about the relationship between the two? Just because a linguistic form is conventional, we must not assume that it is meaningless; we must be alert to the significances of the conventional. In this case, out of the possible opening moves, Liz chooses one cast in the most direct form of command, an imperative; and Mary acquiesces. Moreover, she obeys the command, and then remains silent while Liz reads the card. This illustrates very clearly the power of speech-roles: in a command the two roles are those of 'commander' and 'commanded', and for the latter the obligations of the role are discharged with the carrying out of the command. Occupying the powerless role of Ie, Mary cannot begin the next 'turn' in the interview, so she remains silent.

The way in which Liz addresses Mary is also significant: she feels perfectly free to use her first name, whereas Mary does not once use Liz's name. In fact, Mary does not address Liz by any name. The use of terms of address is strictly regulated in any society. English has rules which seem somewhat less formal than those of continental Europe; they are none the less quite strict, and clearly understood by members of our society.[1] Mary is not entitled to use the first name (and if she does not know what Liz's name is, she has no power to request to know it): address by first name signals either intimacy or condescension, and neither of these postures is allowed Mary in this situation, though Liz is permitted the latter.

Liz now moves into the interview proper, and asks her first question: 'Do you mind . . .'. This is a yes/no question, so called because its structure permits only the answer 'yes' or the answer 'no'. Mary is in effect asked to give up her right of decision here, and she obliges with the answer 'No'. However, the question is in fact trickier than this analysis indicates. Inside the yes/no question there is another question of a different structural type, a 'wh- question' (see below): although this is not absolutely transparent on the surface, Liz is not only asking Mary whether she minds what area it is, but also what area she wants, West End or City or. . . . Mary responds negatively to 'Do you mind?', but affirmatively to the wh-question with 'City', so that there is a contradiction in her answers: no, I don't mind what area; yes, I want City. She shows herself compliant in terms of the first question, which was seemingly not a real question. The lack of genuine alternatives in the first question can be brought out by answering differently from Mary: 'Do you mind what area it is?', 'Yes, I do mind'. This could probably not be said without emphasis on 'do': 'Yes, I *do* mind', and such a response could be interpreted as a direct challenge. One only asks whether someone minds something if one is confident that the person cannot object to the something. If the person questioned is powerful one presumably assumes that they do mind, and so one does not ask.

Thus Mary's answer to the second question is also a challenge to Liz, for while asserting that she does not mind, Mary implies that she *does* mind, thereby rejecting Liz's assessment of her as the sort of person who hasn't got the right to mind. It is this implicit challenge which makes it necessary for Mary to hedge her answer about with 'softeners' or *modalities*:[2] 'just', and 'probably'. It is not that she is uncertain and so uses 'probably', or that she is undemanding and uses 'just'. There is an embarrassment to cover over, the embarrassment of the powerless challenging the powerful. Note also that Mary repeats one of Liz's own words, 'just': Ie signals submissiveness by adopting Ir's terms – this happens a lot: cf. lines 6–7 and 16–17. But why does *Liz* need to use the modalities 'just' and 'sort of'? The motive cannot be humility or submissiveness, since the whole context authorizes Liz's role of dominance; it is, we suggest, a half-apologetic gesture, a cover for the naked exercise of power. Confirmation for this reading comes in the next line: '. . . if we've got local, you don't mind'. Characteristically it is preceded by another yes/no question: 'Is local OK if it . . .'. Liz has ignored Mary's response to the specific question (what area do you want?), and has taken note only of Mary's expected blanket agreement to the initial, coercive 'Do you mind?'

If interviews are for eliciting information from those who have it by those who do not, then Liz is going about it in a strange way. Yes/no questions cannot be used to extend the scope of a conversation, because the questioner, in using them, restricts the information which is introduced. In wh- questions, on the other hand (questions which begin with the words 'which', 'where', 'who', 'when', 'why', etc., including 'how') the addressee is asked to introduce new factual material. Rewriting the questions so far considered, they might have taken forms like 'Where would you like to work?', 'Why don't you want local?' which would have given Mary the opportunity to elaborate her wishes and motives. The answers to such potential questions all come from Liz: she assumes that she knows fully what is in Mary's mind and can answer the questions for her, so she does not ask the questions, but simply provides the answers: 'If we've got local, you don't mind' (4), 'You don't know . . .' (27). This technique is infuriatingly familiar to children, pupils, patients, examinees, people in very powerless roles. The problem arises why Liz asks any questions at all – that is, even the yes/no questions. The explanation might be that they are to establish Mary's agreement or disagreement with Liz's assumptions about her wishes, but this is implausible given the total disregard by Liz of Mary's wishes (line 4). Liz is not asking for information, either of a general factual kind, or about Mary's wishes. The answer must be that she is simply interested in putting Mary through the hoops. This sounds cynical, but there is no other conclusion to be drawn. The benefit to Liz, or her organization, or to any interviewer of this kind (doctor, teacher, parent, examiner) is that the performance of an interview was carried through: the interviewee was questioned, acquiesced in the performance, and has no formal grounds for complaint afterwards. This is a frequent occurrence in everyday life: 'but I asked you . . .', 'but you agreed . . .', 'but you had every opportunity to say . . .'. More than that, the interviewee has been forced to perform something not in itself worthwhile or productive, but in the performance a reaffirmation of the social relations between the participants. The function of such performances could be seen as very similar to the ritual affirmations of subjection, allegiance and domination known from so many societies. The function of the performance is a re-enactment, and thereby re-creation, of the relationship of control and subjection.

Nevertheless, Mary did respond inappropriately to Liz's first question, stating a preference when she should have left a decision to Liz. Such a transgression should have unpleasant consequences. In line 4 Liz responds to Mary's expression of preference, but she does so through a question, as though she had not in fact heard Mary's preference: 'Or would you prefer to go up town and get more money?' This is actually what Mary had asked for with 'City'. But this strictly redundant question of Liz's fits in with the principle of the ritual interview that all information must come from Ir, Ie having the function simply of filling the required complementary role of Ie. Mary is now entitled to entertain this proposition, as it has come from the authorized source. She responds affirmatively, by a perfect copy of the substance of Liz's question, except that she omits the embarrassing motive 'I want more money'. Throughout the interview Mary tends to take over words, phrases and clauses directly from Liz's language. The yes/no questions ensure that Mary cannot introduce new material; and her willingness to let Ir control the content extends to the detail of adhering to the actual language used by Ir. The process can be understood by referring it to a common and well-understood rule in everyday language: inferiors do not normally substitute alternatives for words previously used by their superiors. To do so would be regarded as an impertinent attempt at 'correction', even if the substituted word might be much more accurate and appropriate.

In line 9 Liz asks 'Done an IBM 029 and 059 at college?' – another yes/no question, and another tricky one, since the range of acceptable answers is smaller than the range of possibilities offered by the question (compare the difficulty of giving a simple, polite answer to 'Milk and sugar?' for a guest who doesn't use sugar). Although Mary has indeed used an 029, she has to answer the question as a whole negatively: 'only' meaning 'not the whole X'. Liz has established all the information she needs, but she asks this question three more times (lines 12–16), and each time Mary is forced to answer negatively. The purpose of this questioning cannot be to get information from Mary; its function is to humiliate Mary, to punish her for her initial transgression.

In lines 21–29 Liz speaks to Mary while going through her files of jobs. Basically, her comments continue the humiliation of Mary, showing the riches in the files but inaccessible to an unskilled girl, but there are two new points worth noting. First, the alternation in the pronouns which Liz uses. She sometimes refers to herself as 'I', and at other times as 'we': when she is referring to specific actions she is carrying out, she tends to use 'I'; when she is referring to herself as part of the company, she uses 'we'. '. . . *I* haven't sort of seen it or anything but *we*'ve got sort of several companies . . .': here the distinction between individual and organization seems clear. However, in other instances it is less so: line 38 '. . . *we* can keep your card . . .' and line 42 '. . . *I*'ll ring them up . . .'. In such examples the use of 'I' and 'we' could have been reversed without any challenge to the classification of herself as either individual or as representative of the agency. As far as the interviewee is concerned, this apparently unmotivated switching of pronouns tends to mystify the roles of the interviewer. Mary cannot be sure who addresses her and whom she is addressing. She may feel hostile to Liz only to discover that it is the company which is to blame, or feel that she is with

an efficient agency only to find that she owes any help she may be
getting to the action of an individual. In this situation the interviewer
enjoys all the privileges of power without any of the responsibilities.

The second point concerns the revealing slip of the tongue in line
28: 'You don't know . . . do you know how fast you are?' Liz starts
to put a question concerning information she has, or thinks she has,
about Mary in the syntactic form of a declarative. She has already
done this twice: 'if we've got local you don't mind' (4) 'You've never
done any temporary work using it, no?' (16). This sort of question,
totally anticipating the addressee's response, is manifestly an expression of the power of the very powerful, and it is not surprising that it
is found in this extremely asymmetrical interview. Liz's rephrasing
as a 'real' question is a concession, a modulation of the blatant
expression of Liz's total authority (cf. the modalities noted in line 3).

Up to line 52, Mary's contributions to this conversation have been
confined to 'yes' and 'no', sometimes in the simple form 'yeah', 'no',
sometimes in the extended form of repetition or negated repetition of
parts of the question to which she is responding: 'how many key
depressions?' 'I don't know how many'. She has not once taken the
initiative, or sought to extend the content of the interview in any
way, however slight. The one exception occurs in line 53. Liz has
wound up the interview in lines 51–2: 'I'll get Mrs Kelly to send
your certificate off to you. OK?' 'OK?' is, as far as Liz is concerned,
the final yes/no question, seeking the confidently expected assent.
Mary, in keeping with her role as powerless Ie, answers 'yeah'; she
follows this with a 'but', however. 'But', like 'only', is a 'partial
negation', conveying partial agreement with what has gone before,
and also reservation. If Mary had felt more powerful, she could
have answered 'no' to the 'OK?' As it is, she has to make this tentative intervention. Liz ignores it, or rather acts as though it had not
occurred. Her 'all right?' is a response to Mary's continued presence,
when she should presumably now be halfway to the door, and also
to the fact of Mary's having spoken. It is not, significantly, a
response to the meaning (reservation) of Mary's 'but'. An appropriate response, in a flexible conversation, would have been an enquir-
ing 'yes?', or even 'Is there something I can do?'. But Liz's 'all
right?' is just another overt question seeking agreement that everything has been settled, and again a covert statement that the interview is finished. Mary's response is again two-fold: agreement to the
request, and then the statement of her wish: 'Yeah, could you send
it off in this thing . . .?' This is in fact a command, but a highly

transformed one. If we imagine the situation in which Liz might ask Mary to post something back to her, she would probably use a form such as 'Look, send it back to us in this thing' – that is, she would very likely use an imperative. Mary uses a tentative form, a question, and modalizes it even further by using the past tense 'could' rather than the more direct present 'can'.[3] Thus the only part of the conversation in which Mary attempts to direct Liz's behaviour is done in provisional, uncoercive language which is entirely in keeping with the submissive position in which the interview mode, and the economic circumstances which authorize that mode, place Mary.

The asymmetry in the distribution of power, and the clarity of the formal rules that give this inequality linguistic expression, suggest that this particular interview might be a paradigm example of one end of the interview spectrum, namely that furthest removed from egalitarian 'ordinary' conversation. The next text, in which the class and power differential is not so great, and in which the interviewer actually possesses something he wants to be able to give the interviewee (a place at university) and which the interviewee may actually want to take, might *prima facie* promise to be more democratic, more co-operative. Nevertheless, since this is still in the formal mode of the interview, we would expect the linguistic mechanisms to be similar, changed in only minor ways to reflect differences in the social relations in this interview compared with those in the first.

Dr Jones: The first thing I want to say, if you have any objection to this machine going on, if (*inaudible*) then kick it.
Brian Gentle: No, it won't put me off.
Jones: Good, fine, I'll try not to let it put *me* off. The things we go
5 through for the sake of linguistics! Good. Let's sort you out, then. You are indeed Mr Brian Gentle, of (*candidate's address*). I thought I'd make quite certain (*laughter from Ie*) I've got the right person. (*Pause*) Er. yes . . . I don't know ———— School . . . and you're 18.8, which means you're really sort of the average age. (*Assenting*
10 *noises*) Good, fine . . . fine, then, have you been able to spend the whole day with us? Were you here for the Dean's talk?
Brian: Yes, I was. Yes, I was. And then I was sort of, er, had a look round, got here about half past eleven, er, then straight into the talk, and then sort of looked around the Library, and, er, the bookshops.
15 *Jones:* So, you've had the full treatment?
Brian: Yeah.
Jones: Lunch?
Brian: Er, yes, I had something to eat.
Jones: Which one? Down in the . . .

20 *Brian:* Er, yeah, down by the coffee bar.
  Jones: Yeah, which one, the one at the end ...
  Brian: Yes.
  Jones: ... or fairly near the centre of the University?
  Brian: Yes, the one sort of at the centre of the ...
25 *Jones:* Ah, yes, a great place for chips and hot pies, isn't it?
  Brian: Er, yes, that's right.
  Jones: Good, then. Er ... well, now that you've had, you've had a
  chance to read the Prospectus at some stage and then you've had the
  Dean's talk, do you find the system, er, makes sense?
30 *Brian:* Yes, I think I'm, er, beginning to understand it better now,
  and I must say, I'm quite sort of impressed ... I quite like the idea
  of, er, sort of, er, sort of flexibility, I think is the key word, isn't it?
  ... in the sort of Prospectus.
  Jones: So they tell us!
35 *Brian:* And yeah (*laughter*), and it seems to me as well, that the, er,
  the exam system is, er, (*sounds of agreement from Ir*) a much better
  idea, if you sort of, er, take it, the whole, the whole um, six terms,
  and um, you know, work it out on assessment like that, rather than
  sort of three hours, pass or fail, sort of.
40 *Jones:* How are you getting on with your *Don Juan*?
  Brian: Er, um, I quite like it really, it's er, part of it I find, er sort
  of, er, a bit contrived, but I suppose that's er, that's sort of Byron's
  style that er, um ...
45 *Jones:* (*interrupting*) What is Byron's style?
  Brian: One, I think generally, he's er, it's um somewhat satirical
  style in that ...
  Jones: Uh huh (*general encouraging noises*).
  Brian: ... Uh, he's particularly in *Don Juan*, he's sort of bringing
50 out the, er, bitterness of his sort of family life I mean, his wife, er
  left him on er ...

Some contrasts and comparisons between the two interviews can be
predicted from the analysis of the first text, so we will mention them
only briefly. As before, the main linguistic device which Ir uses to
control Ie's contributions to the conversation is questioning. In this
short text Ir asks no fewer than ten questions, whereas Ie asks only
one (line 32), and that one is merely a 'tag question', a request for
support, and doesn't demand an answer. The sequence of questions
allows Dr Jones to keep Brian Gentle moving along, and allows him
to determine what Brian talks about. A striking difference from the
first interview is the use of wh- questions (lines 19, 21, 40, 45) which
encourage Ie to introduce new material. The two wh- questions in

the latter part of the interview are very open and general indeed and are used to prod the candidate into saying whatever he can say about the topics queried: having asked 'What . . .?' Ir has let Ie loose on his own. Interestingly, Brian, quite unlike Mary in the previous text, interprets some of the yes/no questions as invitations to comment generally rather than just answer 'yes' or 'no': see his response to the questions in lines 10–11, and 29. In this connection, compare an awkward fragment of exchange between Ir and Ie in another admissions interview, conducted and recorded by Roger Fowler:

RF: Have you heard from any of the other universities you applied to?
Ie: Yes. (*Pause*) Do you want me to tell you the, er . . .?
RF: Yes please.

Whereas the yes/no questions in the job interview were used to effect control with *closure* of Ie's language, in the admissions interviews the convention requires candidates to be expansive; Brian will be penalized if he does not treat the questions as opportunities to reveal his intellectual independence, whereas for Mary to do so would be tantamount to unco-operativeness or even rebelliousness. Yet for Brian, as for Mary, the questioning is still a mechanism of control, Ir is still vested with an unchallengeable authority. Thus Brian treads a tightrope; and we would expect his ambivalent status to be reflected in the structure of his utterances. We would also expect this insecurity to have its effect on the interviewer's language, since, as we have seen, language usage is essentially relational, each speaker's utterances being influenced by his awareness of the status of the addressee. In a sense, Dr. Jones, though formally in control, is almost as much on the spot as Brian. The complexity of their relationship produces an embarrassed self-consciousness about roles which is mirrored in the language.

Uncertainty about roles is evidenced from the beginning of the interview. The interviewer tries to put the interviewee at his ease with the invitation to kick the tape-recorder. The inaudible segment in line 2 was probably something like 'if *it puts you off* then kick it'. Of course, Ie is hardly in any position to request that the machine be turned off, but his response, 'No', suggests that he has interpreted Dr Jones's first utterance as a question, though on the surface it was an 'if . . . then' hypothetical with an embedded imperative ('kick it'). Whereas Liz ignored Mary's response to her first question, Dr Jones takes up Brian's answer: 'Good, fine, I'll try not to let it put *me* off'. On the tape recording, 'me' is emphatic, through having a prominent pitch movement placed on it. The interpretation which this leads to is a contrastive one; a paraphrase might be: this sort of thing would put anyone (including *you*) off, I have to try not to let it put *me* off. In other words, Dr Jones interprets Brian's assurance as being conventionally required, and hence not real; he takes it on himself to acknowledge on Brian's behalf the real difficulty introduced into this situation. Both Dr Jones and Liz take for granted Ie's obligation to agree with their first request, but only Dr Jones overtly acknowledges the concurrence, and even goes further, putting himself into Brian's place. Dr Jones has no reason to be put off by the machine, since he places nothing at stake by participating in the interview; but his consciousness of the roles being called upon in this performance causes him in effect to empathize with Brian.

Predictably, consciousness of role makes a greater impact on the language of Ie than of Ir. Brian Gentle's status here is extremely ambiguous. In his role of Ie, he occupies an inferior status in relation to Ir, and this distance is reinforced by the external (though not unrelated) facts that he is younger than Dr Jones, that Dr Jones is highly educated, a salary-earner, and a member of an institution in relation to which Brian is still merely a supplicant. But notwithstanding the social distance between the two participants, Brian's position is, unlike Mary's, not one of complete subordination. His situation requires him to be polite, unrebellious, modest, but at the same time he has to prove himself a worthy potential member of Dr Jones's intellectual community, and this demands adequate confidence and independence of opinion. This conflict shows itself linguistically in two aspects of his language: an exaggerated use of markers of diffidence, and a tendency to give himself non-agentive semantic roles in his sentences, yet placing references to himself in the subject position in syntax.

On the first point, markers of diffidence, take, for instance, the 'er's' and 'um's' and 'sort of's'. These are endemic in Brian's discourse, almost absent from Dr Jones's. Several explanations might be entertained. One which would be partly true but much too simple would be that Brian is (as an individual) inarticulate and unconfident. It is much more likely that these signs of diffidence typify him as a member of an underprivileged class (young, etc.) and are intensified by his current extremely disadvantaged position as an applicant being interviewed: that is, his behaviour here as an individual is the conditioned behaviour of a class intensified by being in a typical conditioning situation to which members of that class are habitually exposed – enforced encounters with authorized representatives of the dominant class of elders, employers, etc. As far as Brian's speech as a whole is concerned, they are also a device for diffidence in that they 'soften' his utterance, allow him to avoid seeming over-confident or arrogant in his judgments. In this connection, the positioning of some of his modalities is significant: most of the key content words, the most informative words, are heavily modalized: 'er, sort of, er, sort of flexibility' (32), 'er, sort of, er, a bit contrived' (41-2), 'um somewhat satirical' (46). If he is wrong with these judgments, his offence is mitigated by the fact that he has qualified them. And this positioning of modalities before key lexical items does, in fact, fall in with a common pattern in people's elaborated, discursive speech: placing pauses, hesitation fillers ('er') and qualifiers ('somewhat') before major lexical foci, a habit which is said to go with the conscious planning of careful speech.[4] So some of this interviewee's qualifiers stem from a coincidence of two quite opposed sociolinguistic forces, the diffidence and embarrassment of the underprivileged and the cautiousness of one who claims to be intellectually precise. This convergence is a nice symbol of the precarious ambiguity of the candidate who is powerless yet bidding for a place in an institution which will bestow power upon him.

The difficulty of this double position is reflected in another range of structural facts, this time not so obvious on the surface: the avoidance, referred to above, of agentive roles for himself while still putting himself in subject position in the syntax. Consider, for instance, the exchange in lines 27 on:

Jones: . . . now that you've had, you've had a chance to read the Prospectus . . . do you find the system, er, makes sense?
Brian: Yes, I think I'm, er, beginning to understand it better now . . .

The interviewer's question might be taken in at least two ways, either about the inherent sensibleness of the system (or its stupidity), or about its complexity, which presents problems to an outsider. Brian's answer is a response to the second meaning, as one would expect: to respond to the first ('is the system sensible?') would mean either handing out gratuitous insults or setting oneself up as a competent judge. In the second meaning ('can you make sense of the system?'), the wisdom of the system is not in question; its complexity is presupposed, mastery of this complexity would reflect favourably on the candidate, so the beginning of mastery will, too.

Looking at the structure of Brian's responses more closely reveals some interesting facts about syntax and meaning. In 'I'm beginning to understand it better now', 'I' is syntactic subject but not the semantic *agent* of the verb. The verb 'understand' is one of mental process, the stimulus of the process being 'it' (the system). 'I' acts as the experiencer of the mental process, or to put it another way, 'I' is affected by a mental process which is caused by 'it'. Of the two roles present in this clause, agent and affected participant, the speaker has chosen the latter – the more 'passive' of the two. If we assign the two roles on the scale of power, it is clear that the role of affected will be closer to the 'minus' end of that scale than that of agent. However, Brian still gives himself the syntactic position of subject, despite the non-active meaning of his participation: he doesn't say 'the Prospectus helps *me* understand it'; cf. below.

Compare lines 40 on: 'How are you getting on with your *Don Juan*?' 'Er, um, I quite like it really'. The structure of the question allows the addressee to cast himself in an agentive role; he could have said something like 'I've read the whole poem', but he eschews that option, answering 'I quite like it'. He assigns to himself the role of affected participant, for 'liking', like 'understanding', is a mental process, not an action, and someone who 'likes' is not an agent. 'Liking' is treated in our society as being outside our control: it is regarded as unreasonable and nonsensical to *order* someone to like Schoenberg or anchovies, since those are things that one can't *decide* to do – one either does, or not. (Again, he chooses the syntactic position of subject, however.) Similarly with 'I find the plot a bit contrived': 'I' is affected participant but subject. Contrast almost any other answer he might have given – 'I've read the first four cantos, and now I'm working on the plot', both clauses in which he is both subject and agent. One begins to suspect that there is a systematic, and skewed, presentation of self going on here. Brian tends to interpret questions not agentively ('What are you doing with/to *Don Juan*?') but very closely akin to passively ('What is *Don Juan* doing to you?'). There are other examples throughout the interview. He seems to have adopted (probably unconsciously) a linguistic process designed to indicate an inferior, but not totally inferior, role in the interview. It involves a transformation of the set of the interviewee's perceptions and experiences into another set judged appropriate for this occasion.

But, as we have hinted, this transformation is not absolutely carried through; in fact, it is curbed somewhere near the point of balance between powerlessness and power, the point of ambivalence

77

that we noted earlier. Notice that Brian's language preserves plenty of 'I's'. In most cases in this text, this surface structure form stands for the semantic role 'affected participant', but the interesting fact is that the surface syntax is of the form which we normally associate with the agent role – he presents himself as a pseudo-agent. He avoids putting himself in overtly passive or objective roles. He would not say 'It bores/impresses me' but 'I find it boring/impressive'. In this way, the *content* of what he says remains relatively humble in its self-characterization, but the *syntax* rescues him from appearing an utter mouse. Once again, an instance of self-correction turns out to be very revealing. This is lines 12–13: 'And then I was sort of, er, had a look round . . .' He launches out on a passive structure, which if he had completed it would have continued as something like 'And then I was sort of *shown round* . . .' – an analysis which would have reflected the reality of the morning's events, since candidates are in fact given a guided tour of the campus by undergraduates. Brian cannot say this because his transformation of events requires him to suppress overt expression of passive roles which might undermine his image of independence. He replaces this false start by a pseudo-transitive construction implying action, 'I + Verb + Object': 'I had a look round'. The semantic analysis of this transitive syntax agrees with our analysis of the preceding examples: 'Had a look round' conveys a mental experience, not a willed activity – contrast 'I explored the campus' in which he would be a real agent doing something active. So the self-correction transforms a syntax of manipulated passivity into a syntax which makes a claim of independent action but still concedes Brian's obligation not to be too pushy by *really* (in deep structure) meaning only 'I had a visual experience'. In this case, the linguistic presentation of a self not overly confident or feebly compliant requires considerable agility in the encoding of messages.

This candidate is not merely barbarously inarticulate (most people's speech looks like this when transcribed faithfully); he is making a complicated adjustment to his image of the required relationship with his interviewer; and he is doing this in an unfamiliar situation. How does he manage all this? For candidates, interviews are exceptional communicative experiences. Many universities select entrants on paper qualifications alone, and it is quite possible that this is the only interview that Brian Gentle has had. Interviewers, on the other hand, perform this task many times every year (usually, about twenty to thirty interviews annually, in our experience). Experienced interviewers are well aware that interviews are highly structured, conventional occasions. The same train of events is reproduced in each one that 'goes well' or is 'brought off': an opening sequence in which the candidate's identity is established, in which he is 'put at ease' (!) and in which the institutional role of the interviewer is clarified; a point at which the participants get down to business, make a deliberate transition to the substance of the interview; a sequence of questions and responses on (for the interviewer) predictable subjects; an invitation to the candidate to ask a few token questions; a dismissal sequence. These stages and transitions are linguistically marked in ways which we have not attempted to demonstrate completely in our analysis. And in addition to regularity of the linguistic format, there is a notable stereotyping of the social roles enacted by the participants through tone of speech, dress, posture, eye-movements, etc. (to the effect that Ir is informed, relaxed, dominant, non-committal, while Ie is innocent, formal, submissive, yet moderately voluble, and so on).

Our society sanctions 'experienced interviewer' as a valid social role, whereas the 'experienced interviewee', the perennial supplicant, is a taboo role. How could the 18-year-old university applicant, prepared only by a few bits of advice from his school, master the genre at his first attempt? The answer cannot be that he 'learns the genre'. It seems more likely that Ie's role in the performance of this genre is achieved through extension of patterns of linguistic behaviour that he practices and encounters regularly in his verbal transactions within social structure. Mary's 'could you send it off . . .' indicates extreme deference in her use of the past tense modal auxiliary 'could', a usage which she has doubtless employed in many previous verbal encounters (not necessarily job interviews) with persons of greater authority. Liz's 'we' confronts Mary with an expression of anonymous power which Mary has encountered in letters from the housing authority, from mail-order firms, and in editorial pronouncements in papers and magazines. Brian Gentle's delicate combination of experiential verbs with a pseudo-transitive syntax has been practised, in very diverse situations, with authority-figures such as his schoolteachers, his GP, his father. These usages do not encode the interview situation as such, but the materially based fact of power differential in interaction in general. The interview is a peculiar conversation in that it is an intense stereotyping of the power differences encoded in discourse generally. The linguistic structures for encoding are acquired in the individual's general history of socialization through linguistic (and other) experience. He meets them in less formal, less intimidating, contexts of discourse, apparently more open conversations at home, school, club, work. These interviews are only a specialized, institutionally validated, variety of the interactions revolving around power differences which go on all the time in our society.

5 · The ideology of middle management

BOB HODGE, GUNTHER KRESS and GARETH JONES

Ideologies are sets of ideas involved in the ordering of experience, making sense of the world. This order and sense is partial and particular. The systems of ideas which constitute ideologies are expressed through language. Language supplies the models and categories of thought, and in part people's experience of the world is through language. The categories of language may, like those of ideology, seem to be fixed and given, but both may be subject to constant change. In speaking, we establish, maintain, confirm and often challenge the categorizations of language, and of the ideologies which language expresses. The analysis of language is thus a necessary part of any attempt to study ideological processes: through language ideologies become observable.

In this chapter we look at how a particular individual, Mr Miller,[1] responds to ideological conflicts and problems, arriving at a set of ideas which generate an order of his social world. The ideological conflicts and problems he faces arise out of his social position; he is on a particularly fraught borderline, that between those who can unambiguously be defined as managers and the shop-floor workers. Through a close analysis of his use of language, one can understand the complexities of his situation and his difficulties in ordering a situation which is inherently composed of forces and processes in tension and opposition.

The text which we use here is part of a long interview, itself one of a series of interviews conducted by Gareth Jones. He was interested, as a sociologist, in the position of middle managers and the functions of management training courses as elements in the occupational socialization of such individuals. The long preceding section of the interview consists of Mr Miller's recounting of a specific course and his assessment of its utility. Here is the section we will analyse:

1 *Jones:* If I asked you to draw a line in this factory between managers and below-managers, where would you draw the line?
Miller: How do you mean, where?
Jones: At what level, where, beneath you?

5 *Miller :* Oh, I think that would be difficult. I think that would be difficult because, really, if you look at the management of our own division, it consists, really, of several people with a figurehead. That's as I see our management. It consists of people like myself, Frank Dyer, who is the Senior Planner, um Williams, – Frank Dyer

10 the Senior Planner reports to Mike, Williams, who is Chief of Progress reports to me, um, and Don Frankland I suppose, who reports to Mike and runs the shop, the workshop. But management, as such, really consist of those people. How can – if you have to draw a line through the whole Company, it would be a pretty thick line, you

15 know, it would have two edges, and there would be a fair number of people in it, contained in it.
Jones : Where would you be – above that thick band, or . . .
Miller : I don't think so, I'd be in the band – and there would be one or two figureheads on the outside – people like Mike, for instance, um,

20 and I suppose some of the other managers.
Jones : So what would you say is the kind of definition of a manager?
Miller : Well, our own definition is that he is a figurehead.
Jones : What do you mean by a figurehead?
Miller : Well, literally, he, – he's the face that is nailed at the front of

25 the ship, you know, but the ship is run by the group of people that's within it. Um, the people that fall outside the line will be Mike on the one side as a manager, because he's the figurehead, and all the direct operators at shop-floor, who are the crew. But um, it's officered, if you like, by people who form the management team. And

30 most of Mike's management decisions are made amongst that team, you know. And you find that um, some will lead the team from the front, and they all agree, that's the way we're going to go, yeah, others will lead it from the back, but that's the way they go anyway. And Mike normally sounds everybody and takes a – a pretty close

35 consensus of opinion before a decision is made, and the decision that's made is usually made amongst all of us, you know, we each of us decide. And I suppose that's one of the reasons why instead of now deciding this is what the division is going to do, and we do it, I don't do that, I call for Frank Dyer, and Fred Williams, or somebody

40 else, whoever's relevant to that, and we make it amongst us.

From a first and cursory reading we can see that the crucial area for Miller is *who is called what*, and that the way this is established is by *who does what*. The two seem to be mutually interdependent, so that the kinds of activities that individuals perform are crucial, and the kinds of labels they carry determine both the actions they perform and how these actions are viewed by others in the factory. Miller uses a number of terms for the various roles: 'management', 'our management', 'other manager', 'manager', 'the management team', 'management decisions', 'Senior Planner', 'Chief of Progress'. The interviewer introduces one other term, which is obviously not a recognized label: 'below-manager'. It is an interesting fact about English that there is no term readily available to describe the negative of manager. The same is true of 'worker'; there is no term 'over-worker'. For our purposes, it is important to note that Miller does not apply the label 'manager' to himself. He is part of 'our management' (8), and this category excludes on the one hand the operators at shop-floor level and on the other, Mike, who is a manager. It seems clear even from this brief analysis that the term 'middle management' is ambiguous. Miller is part of neither 'management' nor shop-floor: he is not a 'manager', indeed it appears that middle managers fall outside management. As far as the factory as a whole is concerned, 'middle managers' are in the middle between managers and the shop-floor. In this sense the term is as adequate a description as 'middle shop-floor'. Interestingly enough the term lower management does not have as much currency as upper or senior management. There are managers (of whom Mike is one) and presumably above him upper or senior management.

We need, therefore, to take the distinction between 'management' and 'manager' seriously. On first appearances the words have a great deal in common. However, there are a number of important syntactic differences. 'Manager' is concrete and human. As such it has a plural form in common use and can be the subject of any verb which takes a human agent. 'Management', on the other hand, is an abstract form, usually in the singular, and can therefore only be the subject of a limited class of verbs. To enable a clearer perception of this it will help to look at the syntactic constructions in which the two terms are used. First a list of constructions involving 'management'. On the left of the page are the terms in their syntactic context, on the right an explanatory analysis.

Construction	*Analysis*
6–7 the management of our own division consists of several people ditto 8, and 12–13	(a) The phrase 'management of our own division' points to a proposition 'some people manage our division'. Here the syntactic agent would need to be named; and it is significant that Miller uses a form which turns that proposition into a

noun, where specific names and relations are not recoverable.

(b) 'Consists of': the verb associated with 'management' is purely definitional. As we said above, this is part of the problem for a 'middle manager'.

29 people who form the management team

(a) 'Management team' as above, conceals a proposition: either 'the team manages', or, 'someone manages with (by means of . . .) the team'.

(b) 'People form the team'. 'People' appears as syntactic agent as though they are doing something, though the action, as before, is constituting the team.

28–9 it's officered by people who form the management team.

A passive; the active sentence would be 'people who . . . officer the ship'. 'Officer', the active verb, can be paraphrased as 'provide the officers' or 'act as officers do'. This expression is therefore also about position, role, but it is ambiguous, and again tells us nothing about actual management, who does what. It tells us 'who is what'.

30 Mike's management decisions are made amongst that team

(a) 'Mike's decisions' points clearly to 'Mike decides', (and implicitly, 'Mike's management' to 'Mike manages').

(b) The construction is again passive, so that the agent can be deleted: 'are made by whom?' is the question that follows from that deletion. We can infer that it is actually 'Mike', but the preposition 'amongst' allows the complicating possibility that the 'team' plays some part. Mike may make his decisions in much the same way as

> the manager of a football team
> makes his decision amongst his
> team, physically in the midst of
> them in the dressing room. Foot-
> ballers, however, can't talk of
> themselves as 'the management
> team'.

Mr Miller is part of 'the management team', but his use of this term tells nothing about his functions in the team. Rather it is used to disguise that he is not a manager. Let us now look at how 'manager' is used syntactically.

19–20 . . . Mike and some of the other managers . . . would be on the outside

Again this is a definitional statement, placing 'managers' in a *location* relative to 'management team', not attributing *action* to them.

26–7 Mike (as a manager) will fall outside

As above; the intransitive 'fall' deserves notice: not 'was pushed', or 'jumped', but without ostensible cause he 'falls'.

27 he's the figure-head

Again definitional, a classification (still with a spatial metaphor).

31–2 some will lead the team from the front

Here at last we have an action, an agent (this manager) and those affected by the action, the team.

33 others will lead it from the back

Ditto.

34–5 Mike normally sounds everybody and takes a – a pretty close consensus

(a) Though both clauses are transitive with Mike/manager as agent, 'sounding someone' is not transitive in meaning. Someone who has been 'sounded' is not different after being sounded to what he was unsounded. Nor does the sounder necessarily act any differently.

(b) The second clause has an overt marker of the editing which Miller performs: after 'takes a' there is a pause, and what has happened

85

here is that a word which Miller had intended to use has been suppressed. (For the same phenomenon in another interview involving the fraught relation between Dr Jones and Mr Gentle, see p. 78.) The resulting utterance is not well formed, for a consensus is 'established' (i.e. as the result of someone's action), or 'reached', not 'taken'. Here the suppression gives the appearance of the manager 'taking/receiving' what has been previously established amongst the group, lessening the effective power of Mike's action.

35 before a decision is made

A passive, a nominalization, and in both cases the agent deleted; again we ask of his decision and of 'made': 'by whom?'

35–6 the decision that's made is usually made amongst all of us

Passive; agent deleted; 'amongst all of us' is simply the location where the decision is made (by whom?)

36–7 we each of us decide

(a) As well as shifting the content of the discussion (he is presumably talking about different decisions now), 'decide' is used without an object. The verb 'decide' used intransitively is a different kettle of fish from the same verb used transitively:

'What do you do? I decide'
'What do you do? I decide the winner'

(b) Also note the switch from 'we decide', which is in line with the 'management team' view; to 'each of us decides', which is the individually responsible 'manager' view.

The shift from 'we decide' to 'each of us decide' signals Mr Miller's attempt to interpret his function in terms appropriate to the manager: 'I don't do that, I call for Frank Dyer'. Though even here the role or function interpretation prevails: 'whoever's relevant to that.' This is not well formed in terms of an 'everyday' use, for it is *things* which are relevant to something ('a consideration relevant to that', 'an objection relevant to that'), and not *humans*: we wouldn't say 'she is the wife relevant to that'. With the 'relevant to' construction we are tempted to use the 'that'-form 'that is the wife relevant to that,' showing the non-human character of the entity in the pronoun used, 'that' rather than 'who'. Indeed, throughout this extract the oppositions between animate/inanimate and human/non-human recur. Interesting here is Miller's use of 'figurehead' in the sentence 'he's the face that is nailed at the front of the ship'. The significance of this usage is related to a confusion of categories between animate and inanimate. In English, things take the pronouns 'it', 'which' and 'that', people take 'he', 'she' and 'who' or 'that'. It is ungrammatical to say 'the stone who came', or 'the man which came'. 'That' can refer to either animate or inanimate. The rules that Miller is breaking, then, concern 'he is a face' where 'he' refers to 'a figurehead' which is inanimate. If we think that 'he' refers to Mike as a human, not a non-human figurehead, then we have to confront the difficulty of the strong expression 'nailed'. Generally, Miller prefers the 'that' form, which blurs these distinctions. He says 'the group of people that's within it', where 'who', agreeing with 'people', would be more common. His 'that' agrees with 'group', and being in the singular it changes 'the people' into a single entity which is ambiguously human/non-human. Or in 'the people that fall outside', 'that' refers to the managers, who are called 'people' but given the ambiguous pronoun. In contrast to these usages, he uses 'who' for the 'direct operators at shop-floor', and in the 'people who form the management team', that is people like himself.

If we wish to draw out the 'rules' which Mr Miller applies in his use of linguistic forms, they can be stated as follows:

management (*team*)

(1) used in definitional utterances only;
(2) used as a 'location' for activities by the manager, not as an activity itself;
(3) real nature of activity concealed through the use of the noun formed from a full proposition;

(4) is classified as an inanimate, non-human collective;

manager(s)

(1) also used in 'definitional' utterances;
(2) occurs as subject/actor in transitive sentences (both those transitive in meaning and those not);
(3) 'occurs' frequently as the deleted subject(s)/actor(s) in passives;
(4) classified ambiguously: 'the face *that*'; 'people like Mike'; '*he* is the face'.

The spatialization of the ideological problem pervades the syntax. In the examples above it serves either to include or to exclude individuals in their *role*-capacity. Within the management team the concern is about the constitution of that unit. Whatever activity middle managers perform is concealed. Minor exceptions are Mr Miller's attempt, towards the end of this extract, to indicate actions – 'decide', 'call', 'do'; and earlier, where he points out the lines and the directionality of communication – (9–10) 'Frank Dyer reports to Mike'; (10–11) 'Williams reports to me'. But this indication of communication is primarily about directionality, thus about a unit conceived in spatial terms.

The recoding of activity in spatial terms, in terms of directionality and location, is effected through the syntax, and it is also a typical feature of the images and metaphors used. At the beginning of the extract the interviewer offers the image of a line, and with it a clear, two-dimensional view of management or shop-floor. The interviewee refuses to accept this metaphor, and significantly rejects it precisely in terms of his own difficulty: 'How do you mean, where?' If a line is to be drawn it will either definitively confirm one analysis, consigning him to the shop-floor, or confirm another quite different one, classifying him as part of the group that Mike and other managers belong to. The latter, it seems, is not the case, and he wants to avoid the former. So 'line' is inappropriate for his needs. In response to this initial difficulty he uses the term 'management', which he defines in such a way that it includes precisely the people who are in his situation, and excludes both upward and downward. 'Management' is thus defined as a *group* of individuals, who stand in a spatial and hierarchical relation to each other: 'X reports to Y'. It is impossible to draw a *line* through a group without destroying the cohesion of that group. Further, because he has defined it in positional and functional terms he has given an identity to that group.

His aborted 'How can' (you draw a line . . .) is a covert negative: 'you cannot'. 'Can' is usefully ambiguous here, meaning either 'in the nature of things', or 'it is not permitted'. Once he has established the internal complexity of the group, he is able to move on to reflect this in an alteration of the metaphor: the line thickens (14: 'it would be a pretty thick line'), and becomes two-dimensional (15: 'it would have two edges'), and then three-dimensional (15–16: 'there would be a fair number of people . . . contained in it'.

This is an illustration of the interaction of metaphor and language, in the service of a pressing ideological problem. It is an even neater illustration of the creation of the ideology and the linguistic forms in which it is carried, in actual speech. From the problem posed by the dichotomizing 'line', one participant has expanded this into a three-dimensional 'thick line' which contains people. The interviewer now plays his part by supplying the new term which then sticks, 'band', though he still uses it in a two-dimensional way (his problems are less pressing!): (17: 'Where would you be – above that thick band, or . . .'). The interviewer obviously hasn't quite understood the nature of the interviewee's problems at this stage; above or below a band, however thick, would be no better than above or below a line, however thin. Mr Miller does not want to give up this new metaphor, though he realizes that if his claims to middle management are to have credibility, then those outside will have to have their claims undermined. Hence, he reintroduces the image of the 'figurehead': they are on the outside, prominent, but not particularly functional. From here he moves easily to the image of the 'ship', composed of 'officers' and 'crew'. Here ideological and linguistic processes are at work, inextricably interacting, acting together, neither possible in isolation. The new metaphors, as they are introduced, open up the possibility of new kinds of syntactic potential for the middle manager. So the 'band' allows the form 'people contained in it'; the 'ship' permits a more active role 'people form the management team'. From merely 'being' (either above or below a line), the syntactic potential has been extended to 'forming a team'. As we have already pointed out, the last passage in the extract is much more active as far as the syntactic role of Mr Miller is concerned: 'deciding', 'calling', 'doing'.

Throughout the extract Miller subtly uses pronouns to negotiate his way in this ideological minefield. Here are some examples: 'our own division' (what would the manager say? 'my division'?); 'our management' conceals, as we have said, who does the managing;

'some of the other managers' refers to people like Mike, but is vague enough just possibly to include Miller; 'our own definition' – here things become tricky, for it is rather important who 'our own' refers to. Presumably Mike would have a somewhat different view of things. The 'our' might be thought to include Mike, just as it might in 'our management', but as Mike is unlikely to agree, 'our' excludes him. The use of pronouns is trickiest in the passage that follows: 'some will lead the team from the front, and they all agree, that's the way we're going to do it'. The progression is 'some' – 'they' – 'we'. 'Some' is clearly 'them', the figureheads who lead. 'They' is ambiguous: either the leaders all agree, or the leaders and the led agree. 'We' is clearly 'us', 'the people in the band', with the figureheads outside. Mr Miller has shifted power from the managers/figureheads to the management team/officers. Again it is the nearly covert nature of this shift which is the most important aspect. If he had real power he could openly assert it; as he hasn't, he must covertly attempt to gain it.

Related to the pronouns is his use of names. In referring to people in the band he uses first and last names 'Frank Dyer, Don Frankland' etc. In referring to the one person outside he uses first name only, and an abbreviation at that. The convention that we are familiar with (and which is documented in some research carried out in America, for references see p. 216, note 1) indicates that the first-name-only form of address shows familiarity and solidarity, and the first and last name convention indicates distance and formality. Miller neatly inverts this convention, suggesting solidarity with the figurehead, and formality with the people in the team.

Throughout the extract Mr Miller gives indications as to the degree of certainty with which he holds the ideas he puts forward. These 'modalities'[2] range from the use of the modal verbs, 'can', 'how can', 'would' ('it would be a pretty thick line') to the use of 'mental process verbs' ('I think that would be difficult') where the proposition is 'softened' by being preceded by a clause which in effect says 'This is only what I think'. It may be helpful to set this out in tabular form, with the linguistic forms on the left and glosses on the right.

Modal forms	*Expressions of degrees of certainty*
(a) *modal verbs:* 'can', 'would'	These express the speaker's ideas about ability, permission, obligation, etc.

(b) *mental process verbs:* 'think', 'suppose', 'see' ('that's as I see our management')

These soften the proposition, as they offer it as the speaker's opinion rather than as unmitigated fact.

(c) *hypothetical forms:* 'if you look', 'if you have to draw'

The second example gives a good insight into the actual function of this form. Miller starts 'How can' i.e. 'you cannot'. He changes to 'if you have to', i.e. in the face of an impossible situation, unreal, you can hypothesize this way.

(d) *modal particles:* 6, 7, 'really'

In the interview this 'really' has major pitch movement, thus is presented as a separate piece of information: 'this is what I offer as reality'.[3]

12 'management as such'

Dissociating the meaning which he wishes to use from that which may be the common meaning: 'I am offering you a new definition'.

14 'a pretty thick line', 15–16 'a fair number of people', 24 'literally', 29 'if you like', 34 'normally sounds', 34–5 'takes a pretty close consensus', 36 'is usually made'

(a) where the particle modifies the noun, it indicates uncertainty about the quantity, nature, extent, of the idea expressed by the noun;

(b) where it modifies a verb, it expresses similar uncertainty about the nature of the action. Overtly in both cases it attempts to indicate the opposite, i.e. certainty, magnitude.

21 'the kind of definition of a manager'

Used by the interviewer, who is beginning to sense the awkwardness which surrounds the definition of 'manager' (cf. pp. 75–6 above).

(e) *distancing devices: tense:* 'that would be difficult'

Placing the utterance in a 'remote tense', that is, a tense other than now. Has the effect of making the utterance less immediately applicable.[4] Note that it is the interviewer's preferred form here.

Pronouns: 6 'if you look', 13 'if you have to', 22 'our own definition'

In each case this permits the interviewee to shift from making a statement for which he would have to assume responsibility to an impersonal or collective form; so where Jones asks, 'what would *you* say is the definition of a manager'. Miller answers by using the anonymously collective 'our'. Note the shifts of pronoun in the last seven lines of the extract.

(f) *stalling and hesitation:* 3 'how do you mean', 5 'oh', 9, 11, 19, etc. 'um', 25, 31, 36, e.g. 'you know', 13, 34, e.g. 'pause with new start'. Also under this heading should be 'really', 'as such', etc., which have this function as well as their other one.

Though all of these forms differ in their precise meanings (see pp. 75–6 for a discussion), they have the function for the speaker of giving him time to think or change tactics. For the hearer they have therefore the inverse function of alerting him that an extra amount of editing was applied by the speaker to the bit of speech that follows.

Interestingly, the background against which these complex shifts of modality are set is one of present tense: 'consists', 'is', 'reports', etc. The meaning of that tense is predominantly one of certainty on the part of the speaker. So a revealing tension exists between the speaker's constant background assertion of certainty about his statements and the complex weaving of uncertainty in the fluctuations of the discourse. This linguistic equivocation mirrors the tension of the real situation in which he finds himself: a reality and actuality of uncertain status and function, with the need to gain certainty precisely about these things.

In this brief extract a number of important matters emerge. An ideological conflict, focused in the position of one individual (though he stands for a group), is, in the process of speech, turned into a still problematical but manageable resolution. The process is rough going and it involves not so much the creation of new labels (which is the solution one might have thought the more obvious) but a reclassification of the existing labels in two ways. First they are given specific content, so that 'management as such', 'management team', emerge with meanings which are specific to Miller and his fellow middle managers. In this reclassification the second step is made possible, namely the reclassification of the syntactic potential of these terms and of middle manager. In one sense then the process has involved the reconstitution of language and the rules of language at a very deep level. Where before middle managers simply *were*, or *constituted something*, through the reclassification process they *do*. Admittedly, they do a limited number of limited things, but the change is significant. In the same process power has been taken away from Mike, the manager. He *is* a figurehead. It may be that the changes which reclassify Miller and his fellow middle managers, in order to alter their capacities, also reclassify Mike, changing his.

Miller, through the linguistic changes illustrated in this interview, has arrived at an ideology appropriate to his position. The management training courses he has attended have been designed to provide for him an identity as manager, but the content of these courses, with their emphasis on job-enrichment and the devolution of routine supervisory tasks to the shop–floor, have robbed him of just those activities which demarcated him as a manager. Instead he has reclassified the workplace in the way we have described into 'figure-heads', 'management team' and 'shop–floor', assigning himself to an active management team. Finally, it should be noted that it would be a mistake to regard this process of reclassification as complete or finished. Changes in the organization of administrative and supervisory work may threaten the categorical security of Miller now, Mike later.

6 · Theory and ideology at work

TONY TREW

On Monday 2 June 1975 the front pages of newspapers all over the world carried reports of events in Harare, Salisbury, the previous day. At about 4.15 pm police fired directly for about 40 seconds into a crowd of unarmed people and killed five of them. In the hours of angry reaction that followed police killed another six people in surrounding neighbourhoods.

About all that can be said for this misleadingly sparse description is that it stands up to a close reading of the most detailed and circumstantial of the varied reports that were in the media that night and the following day. But unlike those reports it contains almost no explanation or interpretation, no connection of the shooting and killing with anything else. The contrast can be seen by looking at the beginnings of the reports from two British newspapers, with their headlines.

First, *The Times*:

RIOTING BLACKS SHOT DEAD BY POLICE AS ANC LEADERS MEET

Eleven Africans were shot dead and 15 wounded when Rhodesian police opened fire on a rioting crowd of about 2,000 in the African Highfield township of Salisbury this afternoon.
The shooting was the climax of a day of some violence and tension during which rival black political factions taunted one another while the African National Council Executive committee met in the township to plan its next move in the settlement issue with the government.

The *Guardian* report began like this:

POLICE SHOOT 11 DEAD IN SALISBURY RIOT

Riot police shot and killed 11 African demonstrators and wounded 15 others here today in the Highfield African township on the outskirts of Salisbury. The number of casualties was confirmed by the police.
Disturbances had broken out soon after the executive committee of the African National Council (ANC) met in the township to discuss the ultimatum by the Prime Minister, Mr. Ian Smith, to the ANC to attend a

94

constitutional conference with the government in the near future.

While these reports leave many questions unanswered, much seems to be explained. The shooting and killing is put in a context and in a network of causes. The descriptions contain many social concepts, something which is hardly present in my description.

Theoretical or ideological processes

To the extent that the concepts in a discourse are related as a system, they are part of a theory or ideology, that is, a system of concepts and images which are a way of seeing and grasping things, and of interpreting what is seen or heard or read.

All perception involves theory or ideology and there are no 'raw', uninterpreted, theory-free facts.

The terms 'ideology' and 'theory' are used to mark very important distinctions primarily and fundamentally in philosophical use, and also in indirectly related attempts to make a sociological distinction. There is no generally applicable *linguistic* distinction corresponding to either of these kinds of distinction. Which systems are imaginary representations of reality and which not, which are practical and which purely knowledge-producing, cannot be decided by reference to properties of the *language* in which the representations are expressed. In a particular case of opposing representations, there may well be a systematic linguistic difference – but there isn't a generally applicable one. Decisions about which systems of representation are correct and which are not can be taken only in the light of the relevant scientific and social practices to which the systems belong. Ideally a term is needed to present what it is in systems of representation that can be grasped linguistically, but there are none that are readily available.[1] I will sometimes use the clumsy phrase 'theory or ideology' and sometimes one of the two terms if the most common usage tends to make it rather than the other more expected in the particular context. But in terms of the linguistic ideas being developed, this variation will not express anything significant.

Commonly the term 'theory' is used for the clearly articulated 'models' that are part of the sciences – like the model of the atom as a structure of particles orbiting about a nucleus of particles, or of light as waves, or the model of society as a conflict between contending forces. The models are meant to represent the reality of things underlying what we perceive. They are used to locate the phenomena

95

we perceive in a network of causality whose laws and connections are those of the model, and to transfer by analogy the reasoning known to apply to the models to the field in question.[2] But in fact all description, and not only the kind found in scientific discourse, involves theory, that is, systems of concepts involved in explaining things, in connecting events with other events, in placing them in the context of patterns and structures and causes. This is most obvious when models of the kind just discussed are used in everyday discourse, like news reports. A striking example was the use of the military model in the reporting of events at the end of the 1977 Notting Hill Carnival in London – 'WAR CRY!' proclaimed one edition of the *Daily Express* on 30 August, right across the page, above another headline 'Chanting police go into carnival battle'. And those newspapers in which the military analogy was predominant in their perception of the events (and in which the police were not seen as the hostile force) drew the logical conclusion that the solution to the problem was a more powerful and resolute army (police, magistrates and judges) to defeat the enemy (variously described as 'hooligans', 'thugs', 'yobs' and the like).

But more straightforward descriptions also make connections. There may be an explicit causal linking, as there is in the description 'They were shot dead' as compared with 'They died': the first explains the dying as the result of some other action. And even the simplest, most basic description of a particular thing or event, any judgment about its nature, involves classifying it and registering its similarities and analogies with other things. It is judged to be one of a kind, and if the judgment is correct, then the particular fits into the network of connections that things of that kind have with things of other kinds. So the linking of particular events to a network of causal relations and to structures of objects or forces is a part of all judgment and perception. This idea is commonplace in philosophical and methodological discussion. But so much of that discussion is at a very general level and carried out in such abstract terms that it tends to leave readers with little ability to say or understand in what ways theory enters into perception. On top of that, these things are usually discussed in a way which makes it easy to think that the terms like 'interpretation', 'explanation', 'abstraction', 'generalization', 'judgment' and so on refer simply to theoretical relations or structures, and not to the theoretical *processes* of interpreting, explaining, judging and the like.

Dealing with awkward facts

Now there is one kind of situation in which the existence of these processes is manifest and their nature quite easily seen. That is when things happen in a way that does not seem to fit in with the way a theory would lead one to expect them to happen. In that case the event seems anomalous – and as long as it remains so, it stands as a challenge to the correctness of the theory according to which it should not have happened. It is in responses to this situation that the theoretical processes in question can be seen most easily.

Anomalies constantly face scientific theories. If they are minor, and can be seen as peripheral, then they can be set aside in the belief that they will be dealt with in time and fitted in, or they can even be denied and written off as the result of mistaken observations. But if they are serious, or if minor cases accumulate beyond a certain point, then there has to be a resolution of the conflict either by changing the theory or by reinterpreting the event so that it appears after all to be just the kind of thing to be expected.[3] Not only scientific theories are faced by anomalies. So too are the systems of ideas of a more familiar kind, such as the ideologies forming everyday perceptions of the world (whether social or 'natural'). In the case of political and social ideologies, the challenge posed by anomalies has a particular urgency. They occur in the context of an ongoing conflict between alternative ideologies that is a direct part of generally antagonistic social conflicts. And the gap between reality and theory is so great that there is a continual stream of 'awkward facts' which opponents will exploit if they are not successfully denied, suppressed or reinterpreted. Above all social ideologies are essential to the legitimation of a social order and their acceptance is essential to the maintenance of that order. Glaring anomalies are a challenge, therefore, not simply to the ideology but to the legitimacy of the order. The option of abandoning the ideology is, therefore, unthinkable, and the challenge has to be resolved in the terms of the ideology itself, whether by denial and suppression or by reinterpretation.

This need calls for particular kinds of discourse. The proceedings of law courts are one kind. Another kind is the government courts or committees of enquiry that are called into being when the legitimacy of some state practice is challenged in a direct way.[4] But it is in the media that we find the most common and familiar kind of discourse

97

which presents the social in terms of given ideologies and repairs the breaches opened up by the intrusion of what is not supposed to happen, since it is the media which present information about what is happening, including the very events which give rise to the need for reinterpretation. Often one can see over a period of days a sequence in which something happens which is awkward from the point of view of the newspaper reporting it, and this is followed by a series of reports and comment over the succeeding days, perhaps culminating in an editorial comment. By the time the process is finished, the original story has been quite transformed and the event appears as something very different from how it started. This change involves the theoretical processes I referred to above. Because the processes involved are linguistic as well as theoretical, linguistic theory can be used to study them.

Now, the shooting and killing of unarmed people described in the reports from *The Times* and *Guardian* was an event of this kind. Let us see what happened to the reports over the days that followed. Take the headlines and the first sentences:

The Times:

RIOTING BLACKS SHOT DEAD BY POLICE AS ANC LEADERS MEET

Eleven Africans were shot dead and 15 wounded when Rhodesian Police opened fire on a rioting crowd of about 2,000.

Guardian:

POLICE SHOOT 11 DEAD IN SALISBURY RIOT

Riot police shot and killed 11 African demonstrators and wounded 15 others.

There are three linguistic points I want to make about these reports: (1) An obvious difference between the reports is that *The Times* report is in the passive form, and the *Guardian* one in the active, although the content is very similar in the two cases. The contrast is repeated in the headlines. Using the passive form puts the (syntactic) agents of the killings, 'police' in less focal position.[5] By itself this may not seem very important – but as the first step in a process that goes further the next day, it does become important. In fact there is an indication of how this could develop further, in *The Times* report. Not only is it in the passive, but the syntactic agent is deleted ('11 Africans were shot dead by . . .') and is identified only weakly by implication through the temporal conjunction with the police opening fire ('when police opened fire on a rioting crowd of about 2,000'). Looking at this in purely syntactic terms, with the deletion of the agent there is no longer any direct reference to who did the action and there is a separation of the action from whoever did it. This is something that can only happen if the description is in the passive form or some equivalent. (The headline contains the complete passive form, including the agent.)

(2) Both newspapers describe the circumstance in which the shooting took place as 'riot'. One headline has POLICE SHOOT 11 DEAD IN RIOT and the other RIOTING BLACKS SHOT DEAD BY POLICE. This establishes a framework for explaining what happened. It is also a description which legitimizes police intervention, because riot is by definition civil disorder requiring police action.

By itself it doesn't legitimize 'armed' intervention, or killing – but it is a step which opens a way to justifying it. Note how in *The Times* 'riot' is attached to those who were shot, in the phrase 'rioting blacks'. Given that the report focuses on the ones shot rather than the shooters (by use of the passive), attaching 'rioting' to 'blacks' simultaneously makes 'rioting' the focal action, and also makes those shot responsible for the situation which is both the context of the shooting and a partial explanation of it.

(3) Note the ways in which the various participants in the reported processes are characterized. Looking at the pieces first quoted, the agents are 'police' when they are mentioned (and sometimes also 'riot police', or 'Rhodesian police'). The victims are categorized as 'Africans', and also 'blacks', and are described as 'rioting' and 'demonstrating'. 'Africans' and 'blacks' are basic categorizations which describe the participants in terms of qualities that are unchanging and stable, while the descriptions 'rioting' and 'demonstrating' refer to qualities that are not permanent but which the participants sometimes have and sometimes do not. These facts are recorded in Table 1. The linguistic terms in the top row derive from Halliday. Note that they are linguistic concepts and that linguistic processes or participants need not coincide with the real processes and participants.

The table overleaf shows both the similarities in the reports and the differences.

In *The Times*, then, the effects of the linguistic facts pointed out are a tendency to shift the focus away from those who did the shooting and onto the victims, who are categorized as 'Africans' (or

Table 1

	Agent	Process	Affected	Circumstance
The Times		PASSIVE		
Headline	police	shoot dead	rioting blacks	(as) ANC leaders meet
		PASSIVE		
Report	—	shoot dead	eleven Africans	(when) Rhodesian police opened fire on a rioting crowd
Guardian		ACTIVE		
Headline	police	shoot dead	11	(in) Salisbury riots
Report	riot police	shoot and kill	11 African demonstrators	—

'blacks'). The *Guardian* likewise uses the category 'African', and, like *The Times*, firmly locates the events as occurring in a context of 'riots'. The agents, who did the shooting, are categorized as 'police'. Although they are formally separable, these features are linked with each other and with other features, in ways that will become clearer when we look at the news and comment of the following day.

On the second day the focus of the news shifted as the extent of the differences within the African National Council became public. But the events of the previous day are still reported, presented as the context of the further developments. And there is a continuation of those processes which began with weakening the expression of causal links between the shooting and shooters, and with making 'riots' the explanatory context. Here is the beginning of *The Times* report on 3 June:

SPLIT THREATENS ANC AFTER SALISBURY'S RIOTS

After Sunday's riots in which 13 Africans were killed and 28 injured, a serious rift in the ranks of the African National Council became apparent today.

The report continues with descriptions of the 'split' as well as statements about the events of the previous day. The headline doesn't say 'AFTER SALISBURY'S *KILLINGS*' which is what might have been expected, as the killings were the focus of the news the day before. On the other hand the way it is put in *The Times* might seem reasonable if what is described as 'riots' and 'split' have the same causes. And the reports in both *The Times* and the *Guardian* clearly do suggest this, as they report the 'riots' as the outcome of 'clashes between rival black political factions' (*The Times*) and 'rival youthful gangs from ZANU and ZAPU' (*Guardian*). But even so, the exclusion of the 'killing' from the headline is striking.

In *The Times* report itself there is a reference to the killing, but in a way that is significant. It is in this clause:

After Sunday's riots in which 13 Africans were killed.

Once again, it is in passive form, and the agent is deleted. But more than this, the description is changed from 'shot dead' to 'killed' so that any reference to the manner of death is deleted. The new description gives no hint of the agent or the manner of death – there is only a suggestion of a cause resulting from the way the 'riots' are made focal and made the context of the deaths. Similar processes, carried a little further, occur in the *Guardian* that day.

FACADE OF AFRICA'S UNITY COLLAPSES IN THE RHODESIA RIOTS

The divisions within the African Nationalist movement deepened today as police announced that the number of dead in yesterday's riots in townships on the outskirts of Salisbury had risen to 13.

Note how the events of the day before are summarized:

The number of dead in yesterday's riots is 13.

There is no reference here to the agents, no reference to the manner of death, no reference even to there being any causes of death (it is 'dying' rather than 'killing'), and from this report by itself it is impossible to tell if there were any agents. For this reason, placing deaths in the context of 'riots' (quite literally, using the locative preposition 'in'), suggests even more strongly that 'riots' were the cause of death. There isn't even a description of the victims, who are referred to only in terms of the effects of whatever process brought about their death – all we learn about the dead is that they died.

In other ways, things are linguistically very like the day before. This is not surprising, because basic categorizations – like 'Africans', 'riot', 'police' – are unlikely to change from day to day. The use of the term 'AFRICA' in the *Guardian* headline is characteristic – and yet it might also seem strange if you were to read the whole report (not reproduced for lack of space): you would find there no reference to anything outside the borders of 'Rhodesia'. So why then are we told that 'THE FACADE OF AFRICA'S UNITY COLLAPSES'? This will be explained later.

By this stage, what happened on 1 June has come to be reported as a process – killing and dying – with no stated causes. Because it is presented in a context of 'riots' a cause is vaguely suggested, but only vaguely, and in any case the 'riots' themselves are ephemeral events that themselves need explaining in terms of deeper causes. *The Times* leading article on that same day (2 June) provides the missing explanation.

THE RIOTS IN SALISBURY

The rioting and sad loss of life in Salisbury are warning that tension in that country is rising as decisive moves about its future seem to be in the offing. The leaders of the African National Council have ritually blamed the police, but deplore the factionalism that is really responsible. The brawling between supporters of Zanu led (from abroad) by the Rev. Ndabaningi Sithole, and the hench-men of Zapu, led by Mr. Nkomo, both nominally under the control of Bishop Muzorewa, recalls the vendettas between the two nationalist parties in the early days of the Smith Government and before. It will certainly give fresh life to the whites' belief that African politics is based on violence and intimidation.

Leading articles can serve various purposes – but one thing that can bring them into being is the existence of an anomaly that needs resolution, the kind of situation discussed at the beginning of this chapter. *The Times* leading article completes the reinterpretation of the events of Sunday. Sunday's events are summarized in the heading which announces the theme of the article, 'THE RIOTS IN SALISBURY'. Reference to the originally newsworthy aspect of the events – 'shooting dead' – is completely absent. Instead, what was the context, is now the topic. The article itself does refer to the original event, in 'Rioting and sad loss of life'. But even in doing this it puts the event in a subordinate position to 'rioting', and by rewording 'kill' to 'lose life', it changes to a description that is appropriate to death caused by natural disaster or by carelessness of those who died, rather than to deliberate killing. By the conjoining of 'rioting' and 'sad loss of life', a nominal expression is made which describes a situation whose occurrence needs to be explained. It is now given an explanation in terms of more general causes than those figuring at the start ('police'). It was, says *The Times*'s editorial, using yet another nominal, 'factionalism which was really responsible'. The way it is put leaves unclear exactly what the 'factionalism' is supposed to be responsible for, the 'deaths' or the 'riots' – but the conjunction of these two, and the construction of the sentences, suggests strongly that 'factionalism' brought about the generally distressing situation that includes both things. What is clear is that the account of the events is by now using a number of words to describe what happened – 'rioting', 'loss of life', 'factionalism' – all of which, in the sequence of reports being considered, have a common syntactic agent, namely 'Africans'. No mention is made of the 'police' except as those 'ritually blamed' – and note how even in this one reference the syntax has 'Africans' as agents and 'police' as affected participants (the victims of blaming!).

Despite this systematic presentation of the events as stemming from the actions of 'Africans', the article still contains symptoms of the original threat of anomaly. This is shown in linguistic features of a very different kind from those so far discussed, and which I will only illustrate in this one case; a proper treatment would involve going into the extremely important area of the linguistics of modality.[6] That the police were held, by authoritative figures, to be responsible for the killing had to be recorded, but it is done in a way that at the same time actively rejects that view and devalues it, by calling it 'ritually' blaming. This may seem to dispose of the threat, but it also involves an acknowledgment of the unwanted fact and, by introducing the overt judgment involved in 'ritual', seeks to block any request for investigation which will let the 'facts speak for themselves'. In a very similar way, the word 'really' in the phrase 'really responsible' involves both an acknowledgment that appearances suggest different causes, and an active rejection of the truth of that suggestion – but in neither case is any evidence given for judgments of *The Times* article.

It is time to take stock. Table 2 is a summary of the series of linguistic transformations traced so far in *The Times*.[7] The arrows are used to show some of the most significant switches in position, selections, rewording and dilution of expressions of causality. (The sentences written in lower case are inserted to break up the explanation into simpler steps.)

The content of this transformation is to present a new cause, 'factionalism', for the original events. Now we know from these and other reports that the demonstrations were caused by political divisions within the African National Council (differences over whether to negotiate with Smith or not). But what turned the demonstrations into a 'riot' has not been established yet.

Police statements and other reports make clear that what sparked the 'riot' was not a conflict between 'rival groups of demonstrators', but conflict between police and demonstrators, especially after police dogs were brought in. (During a subsequent trial of some of the demonstrators, charged with 'public violence', a police inspector was reported in the *Rhodesia Herald* (11 July) as saying that 'the riot

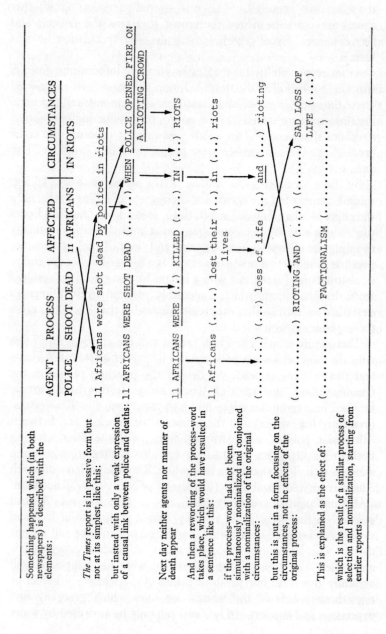

	AGENT	PROCESS	AFFECTED	CIRCUMSTANCES
	POLICE	SHOOT DEAD	11 AFRICANS	IN RIOTS

Something happened which (in both newspapers) is described with the elements:

The Times report is in passive form but not at its simplest, like this:

11 Africans were shot dead by police in riots

but instead with only a weak expression of a causal link between police and deaths: 11 AFRICANS WERE SHOT DEAD (......) WHEN POLICE OPENED FIRE ON A RIOTING CROWD

Next day neither agents nor manner of death appear

11 AFRICANS WERE (..) KILLED (.....) IN (...) RIOTS

And then a rewording of the process-word takes place, which would have resulted in a sentence like this:

11 Africans (......) lost their (..) in (...) riots lives

if the process-word had not been simultaneously nominalized and conjoined with a nominalization of the original circumstances:

(.........) (....) loss of life (..) and (....) rioting

but this is put in a form focusing on the circumstances, not the effects of the original process:

(..............) RIOTING AND (....) (........) SAD LOSS OF LIFE (.....)

This is explained as the effect of:

(..............) FACTIONALISM (..............)

which is the result of a similar process of selection and nominalization, starting from earlier reports.

started when a man was bitten by a dog and the crowd surged towards the police'.) On top of that, on the day of *The Times* leader the *Guardian* reported: 'The unanswered question is whether agents provocateurs incited the crowd to attack the police'; and the *Financial Times* reported more detailed speculation on this theme.

As for responsibility for the deaths, the only information given is that the police killed the dead. (During the same trial mentioned above the same inspector said that before the demonstration 'general instructions were issued', to the police 'from some high authority' to 'shoot if necessary'.) In another newspaper covering the court proceedings the instructions were summarized in a headline ('Use guns not gas').

By, first, weakening the linking of the agents with the killing, second, eliminating the agents and their action of killing so that only the effect of what they did is left, third, focusing on 'riots' and putting to one side all questions about what caused them, and finally coupling the abstract nouns 'rioting' and 'loss of life', it becomes possible to move to a new explanation at a higher level of generality or abstraction. Taking this with a judgment that the 'riots' resulted from demonstrations which undeniably resulted from differences described as 'factional', it may seem reasonable that *The Times* gives the explanation which it does.

The picture which *The Times* presents in the end is right in line with the view which has been used to justify white rule in Africa – and this is some of what lay behind the puzzling phrase in the *Guardian* about 'the façade of Africa's unity'. In this leading article in *The Times* there is a constant contrast between the 'Rhodesians' (evidently the whites) and the 'Africans' or 'blacks', and between 'Rhodesian politics' and 'African politics', with the latter referring both to black politics in Rhodesia and also at times to something wider as well. This shares the view white 'Rhodesians' have in which Angolan or Mozambican ('African') politics and 'Rhodesian' ('African') politics are easily taken as one. The view of 'African politics' in this ideology is, roughly, that it is the site of factional division determined by tribalism, and based on violence and intimidation, with the whites concerned merely to promote progress, law and order. *The Times* editorial says that what has happened 'will certainly give fresh life' to 'those beliefs of the whites'. Whether or not 'those beliefs of the whites' are ones which generally find expression and support in *The Times* can only be answered by wider study. In any case *The Times* editorial on Salisbury aligns itself with those views in what it says next.

Whether there is a connection between this outburst which seems to have been envenomed by Matabele and Shona tribal feelings and the recent killings among the Zanu freedom fighters which is supposed to be mainly an internecine Shona struggle, remains to be seen. The killings in Zambia were expected to have repercussions in Rhodesia.

'Seems' to whom and 'supposed' by whom and 'expected' by whom are not explained. With no evidence, without asserting anything, the category of 'tribe' is laid down as the primary category of nationalist politics. The picture is of a vast, homogeneous social group, the 'Africans', whose underlying 'natural' unity is overlaid with tribalism. That is why political differences are automatically classified as 'factional', a term for division within a unity. It is of course a term which has its proper uses, and if the ANC had been a unity it might have been in place on that occasion. But it is also a term deeply embedded in the ideology of white racialism, and is often interchangeable with 'tribal' (for example, conflicts believed to be 'intertribal' are often known in this ideology as 'faction-fights').[8]

One part of the picture in question is that 'Africans' have to earn freedom by behaving like whites. To maintain this view it is necessary to ignore the real nature of the conflict, whether in Angola or 'Rhodesia'. This requires a suppression of the fact that the white regimes apply violence and intimidation, and suppression of the nature of the exploitation this makes possible. It requires that the regimes and their agents be put constantly in the role of promoters of progress, law and order, concerned to eliminate social evil and conflict, but never responsible for it, and only killing unarmed people when forced to do so by those people themselves. All this is so far from the truth that only a powerful grip on the press and information and the diligence of the media in resolving the flood of anomalies which they report are adequate to preserve the pretence that the press is truthful. For a pretty pure expression of this ideology, look at this *Rhodesia Herald* leading article, 3 June:[9]

TRAGIC SUNDAY

As has happened so often in Africa, a political clash has led to death and injury. The rioting in Salisbury townships on Sunday, and the shooting by police, were typical of dozens of such incidents which have disfigured the political scene in this part of the world for so long.

Everybody will deplore the loss of life. After that however there will no doubt be the usual differences of opinion.

Overseas some observers will see the shooting as a fresh example of official savagery in Rhodesia, and the riots as a natural reaction to repression and discrimination. It will probably be overlooked that the police were sent there to protect the townsfolk from their own excesses.

In Rhodesia, on the other hand, rioting will be seen as a strange way of expressing political maturity – even if, as is usually the case, it is perpetrated only by a relatively small number of thugs and troublemakers.

What is equally disturbing is the further evidence that rival (and banned) factions of the ANC are still very much alive and kicking. To those militants the ANC no doubt provides merely a legal umbrella under which to persist in their skirmishing.

This can only add weight to the argument that no matter how conciliatory a line the ANC takes, developments beyond that will inevitably be dictated by tribalism.

What we saw in *The Times* is an example of what has to be done repeatedly to maintain this ideology. White police shooting unarmed Africans expressing political differences by demonstrations is an anomaly – rioting and sad loss of life caused by factionalism is just what is expected by those who hold this kind of view. When the original violence occurred, it could not be ignored or kept from the readers of newspapers. But the work of transformation following a path shown by the ideology produces finally a version of events fitting in with that ideology. Of course divisions *do* weaken opposition to the regime, and the divisions are not all politically determined. But put in the terms and in the context of a racist ideology of white rule, these things have a different sense and different implications from what they have in the context and the concepts of a struggle for liberation. Here, as an illustration of the contrast, is a very different leading article from the *Tanzanian Daily News*, on 3 June, the same day.

COMMENT

Rhodesia's white supremacist police had a field day on Sunday when they opened fire and killed thirteen unarmed Africans, in two different actions in Salisbury; and wounded many others. Their pretext was that the men had been rioting. . . . Nobody will buy the statements from the Salisbury propaganda machine, that in fact all the [non-fatal] ways [of crowd control] were used. Rather knowing the blood-thirsty nature of the illegal regime, it is much more conceivable that if any of the non-murderous methods were employed, they were merely a quick formality abandoned without valid reason, in order to rush to the 'real thing'.

For the ANC and Africa it would be wrong to imagine that this is only an isolated act, or that the regime will stop here. A correct analysis of this latest outrage fits it in a pattern of acts of provocation against the people of Zimbabwe with the view to intimidating them so that they can slow down their tempo in demanding their rights.

It is a follow-up to the other relatively less violent acts of provocation which preceded it – the arrest and detentions of the ANC leaders and the continued imprisonment of political prisoners.

Zimbabwe nationalists must reckon with the fact that in their desperation, the illegal rulers of their country have now embarked on wanton use of the bullet on unarmed men to instill fear and despondency.

It is a phase which calls for greater cohesion in the liberation ranks, cohesion which will make it impossible for the enemy to divide the people for his benefit.

We appeal to our brothers of Zimbabwe to be extra vigilant so that they can correctly anticipate and interpret the enemy's machinations aimed at provoking them into a situation and taking advantage of it to murder the people.

The processes abstractly considered

I want now to look in a more abstract way at the processes of transformation which occurred in *The Times*. They involve both theoretical and linguistic transformations. The theoretical change has aspects which are of a very general kind. It starts from a description of a process giving an agent or cause, and then weakens or removes that attribution of causality by selecting or abstracting the effects of the process, and then explaining these effects by reference to causes of a higher degree of generality or abstraction than the one that figured at the start. An event presented as having a cause is reinterpreted by locating it in a context which gives it a more general and less immediate cause than the one it was originally presented as having. Each specific case of reinterpretation will vary in form depending on a number of factors, including the nature of the actual events being described. Each specific transformation is not only a theoretical one, but also a linguistic one, and it will already be clear from the case study that there is some kind of close relationship between them. That relationship is seen again when we look at those aspects of the transformations that do occur more generally.

Table 3 is an attempt to set out one kind of sequence of linguistic changes which has the effect of a reinterpretive explanation of the event described in the original statement. (The illustrative sequence

Table 3

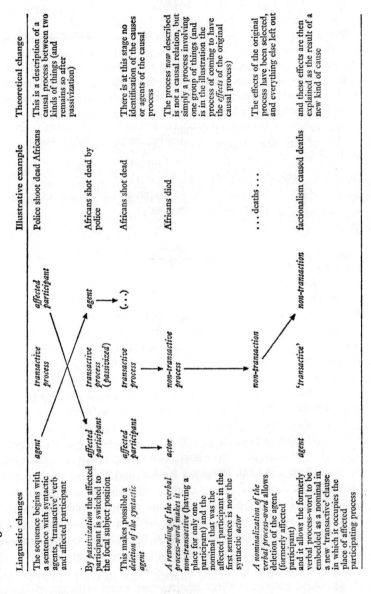

Linguistic changes				Illustrative example	Theoretical change
The sequence begins with a sentence with syntactic agents, 'transactive' verb and affected participant	*agent*	*transactive process*	*affected participant*	Police shoot dead Africans	This is a description of a causal process between two kinds of things (and remains so after passivization)
By *passivization* the affected participant is switched to the focal subject position	*affected participant*	*transactive process (passivized)*	*agent*	Africans shot dead by police	There is at this stage no identification of the causes or agents of the causal process
This makes possible a *deletion of the syntactic agent*	*affected participant* → *actor*	*transactive process* → *non-transactive process*	(. . .)	Africans shot dead	
A rewording of the verbal process-word makes it non-transactive (having a place for only one participant) and the nominal that was the affected participant in the first sentence is now the syntactic *actor*	*actor*	*non-transactive process* → *non-transaction*		Africans died	The process *now* described is not a causal relation, but simply a process involving one group of things (and is in the illustration the process of coming to have the *effects* of the original causal process)
A nominalization of the verbal process-word allows deletion of the agent (formerly affected participant)		*non-transaction* →	*non-transaction*	. . . deaths . . .	The effects of the original process have been selected, and everything else left out
and it allows the formerly verbal process-word to be embedded as a nominal in a new 'transactive' clause in which it occupies the place of affected participating process	*agent*	*'transactive'*	*non-transaction*	factionalism caused deaths	and these effects are then explained as the result of a new kind of cause

109

is an artificial one, a variation on the one from *The Times* and differing from it in missing out a stage and in having 'die' in place of 'lose life' and 'caused' in place of 'was responsible for').

In the table a distinction is used between transactive and non-transactive process terms.[10] Roughly, transactive process words can combine with two linguistic items, syntactic agent and affected participant (and a sentence with a transactive verb represents a causal process in which one thing – or group of things – affects another). Non-transactive process words combine with only one item (and sentences with non-transactive verbs represent events as processes with only one participant).

One of the most important subsidiary processes in this sequence of linguistic changes is the one in which the effects of the event as originally presented are selected by deletions and rewordings. One way of representing it is given in Table 4 (with the missing step, changing 'shoot dead' to 'kill', inserted):

Table 4

	Agent	Effects	Affected	Instrument
Police shoot dead Africans	√	√	√	√
Police kill Africans	√	√	√	Deleted
Africans die	Deleted	√	√	(Deleted)
The deaths . . .	(Deleted)	√	Deleted	(Deleted)

One thing that stands out about this selection is the smoothness of the change. This goes both for the theoretical aspect (there is simply a gradual lessening of information given) and from the linguistic point of view (the deletions and rewordings cause no need for any other changes to the text or its grammar. Other kinds of changes have more far-reaching effects).

The actual sequence in *The Times* had 'loss of life' in place of 'deaths', and that, I noted above, involves a rewording that goes beyond mere selection. Even so, it is a mild shift compared with some more radical and abrupt changes that occurred in some other newspapers. For example the *Tanzanian Daily News* carried a report very similar to that in *The Times*, and which on the basis of comparisons seems to be basically a *Reuters* report. But its headline was

RACISTS MURDER ZIMBABWEANS

The headline writer has made a much more substantial change on his raw material than did the editor of *The Times*. The rewording of 'shoot' to 'murder' like that of 'die' to 'lose life' is one of a different kind from the change of 'shoot' to 'kill' or 'die'. The rewording introduces new restrictions on the range of participants – agents and affected – which can go with it, whereas the second kind of rewording does the opposite, actually widening the range of possible participants. The change is therefore a complex one affecting many aspects of the text and not just the verb. The change which includes the rewording of 'kill' to 'murder' also involves changing 'police' to 'racists' and 'Africans' to 'Zimbabweans'. Had the report itself been completely rewritten in terms of the ideology expressed partially in the headline, a large number of detailed and systematically related changes would have been made, because it would have meant a radical ideological shift.

This contrast leads to a distinction between two kinds of rewordings. One kind of rewording remains within the terms of the given theory or ideology, while the other kind may involve a shift from one theory to another (and must occur if any shift takes place). In the one case there is maintenance or reproduction of ideology, and in the other ideological transformation.

Formulating things in this more abstract way makes it clear that the concepts have a wide and general application, and provide some basic terms with which to describe theoretical processes and linguistic processes and to formulate questions about relations between them. The basic configuration of a system of ideas representing reality is made up of the kinds of things it presents as existing, and the kinds of interactions and relations in which they are involved. What is linguistically relevant in the discourse are the patterns of categorization of participants, and the relations of transitivity (that is, the representation of causality in the process words and clauses). This side of things I have only briefly touched on so far, and will develop further in the second study.

What I looked at in the first part were various theoretical or ideological processes, that took place in discourse. Processes like interpretation, selection, abstraction are logical processes which can be characterized by the logical relations between starting point and end product. The processes are effected through a series of linguistic changes, like agent deletion, rewording, nominalization and embedding. No simple one-to-one correspondence can be set up between the linguistic and theoretical processes, because the latter are structured sequences of the former, and can occur in various forms and because individual linguistic changes can occur in different kinds of sequence. A single linguistic transformation – like passivization –

does not have a fully determinate theoretical significance. But if it stands as the first in a sequence of changes that include deletion of agents, selective rewording, nominalization, and embedding, as in our example – then that single linguistic change belongs to a structured sequence of changes, which as a whole has determinate theoretical or ideological significance. Because each of the transformations making up the sequence is one of a number of changes known to be possible at that point, and because the structure of the sequence is determined by the requirements of theoretical transformation, it follows that the theoretical or ideological patterns in any consistent and systematic transformation of texts are apparent in a complete linguistic description of the change.

It goes with another major point illustrated by this case study. The theoretic and linguistic processes are material processes that take place within discourse and are transformations of discourse. They are not merely abstractions, nor merely relations between propositions, nor are they just postulated processes in the human mind which are unobservable or only observable by psychological or neuro-physiological study. The material reality of linguistic processes as transformations in discourse is sharply at odds with the picture presented in the debate surrounding Chomsky's formalization of transformational grammar. The approach in this article is closer to the original formulation of transformational grammar in the work of Harris. The contrast between the approaches can be illustrated by looking at one phrase that occurs towards the end of the process studied in *The Times*: 'rioting and . . . loss of life'. Chomskyan transformational grammar would propose that this is the surface realization of an abstract structure containing dummy noun-phrases, NP_1 and NP_2, as the subjects of 'riot' and 'lose life:[11]

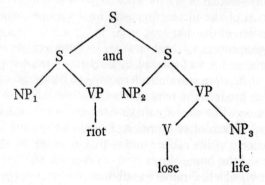

But in fact, as we have seen, the phrase occurred in a sentence which was the result of transforming other *sentences*, with actual specific noun-phrases as subjects of 'riot' and 'lose life'. It is precisely the disappearance of the deleted material, and its non-recoverability, that is significant for an analysis of the ideological or theoretical characteristics of the material. The Chomskyan theory tells us at most what *kind* of sentences were transformed, but it abstracts this kind and posits the abstraction as the real start of the transformational process. Furthermore, in doing this the theory has nothing to say about rewording, about the transformation of systems of *words* (relexicalization as Halliday calls it).[12] Words can appear only as the realization of lexical items, a consequence of lexicalization. *Re*-lexicalization has no place in this theory's conception of language. On this 'Chomskyan' approach, then, choice of words is always just insertion of words, and never rewording, transformation is always production of sentences and never transforming sentences, and discourse is a set of single unconnected sentences.

Reproducing ideology: the question of power

Returning finally to the newspapers, if in general the original material is not recoverable by a linguistic analysis of the final product, then comparison of initial and final material is significant. It is because there are linguistic options in handling the original, that it is not recoverable. Which option is used can be explained in part as the effect of ideological determinations.[13] The distinction between transformations of discourse which reproduce ideology and those which involve substantial ideological shifts gives a way of establishing formally whether or not the ideology present in news reports is a reproduction of the ideology present in the source material or a transformation of that ideology.

All the elements in the final view in *The Times* were present in the first reports, and it was reached by a relatively smooth process of selection, abstraction and shifts in focus. The editor did not have to do much to produce the reinterpretation of the killing of unarmed demonstrators. The ideology shaping the end result was present in the original system of categories including and relating 'Africans', 'riot', 'faction', 'police'. The same system of categories are used in the reports of the *Inter-African News Agency* (IANA), the Rhodesia news agency, which, through its link with *Reuters*, was the source of many of the newspaper reports, and was also the source of this report by the *Rhodesian Broadcasting Corporation* on 1 June 1975 (1600 GMT) (recorded by the BBC Monitoring Service):

Here is a later item just received. IANA says that 5 Africans were shot dead and 8 injured when police opened fire on a crowd of about 2,000 rioting Africans.

Whether or not this had the same source as *The Times* report of 2 June, the similarity of this sentence to the opening sentence of the first *Times* report is striking, and the similarity of concepts almost total. A study of the available material, including reports of various press statements by the police and interviews of police spokesmen by journalists, and reports of court proceedings involving trials of demonstrators charged with 'public violence', shows that what is produced here, and in the news-columns and editorial of *The Times*, is a view which is basically the same as the one expressed in the judgments and categories of the police, the agents of the state in the maintenance of 'civil order', and which was confirmed by other agents of the state in the courts. Just in case there might be a thought that the case studied was an isolated one, compare this summary, from the *New York Times Index* of 1976, of the events of 16 June 1976, when South African police massacred unarmed school students staging a peaceful demonstration and sparked the sustained uprising that followed. Here it is, *in full*:

At least 6 people are killed when demonstrations by 10,000 black students against instruction in Afrikaans language turn into riot in Soweto; deaths come only wk before S. African Prime Minister John Vorster is scheduled to meet with Kissinger in West Germany; trouble reportedly began when students gathered to protest Government regulation requiring use of Afrikaans as language of instruction for some subjects; regulation has provoked sporadic student strikes for mo. with up to 2,000 pupils boycotting classes.

The perception of the protest, resistance and political struggle as essentially civil disorder received its confirmation in the courts. In the year after 16 June the uprising was suppressed and more than 20,000 people were prosecuted, and most of them convicted, under laws which officially conferred on their actions the descriptions of *public violence, unlawful and riotous assembly, sabotage, inciting or promoting racial unrest, arson, malicious damage to property*.[14] The police were not prosecuted. (To make sure no one did bring a case against the police, an Indemnity Act was passed to protect them, defining their actions as legitimate and lawful. A similar Act was passed in Salisbury in September 1975, not long after the events whose report I have been analysing.) And now, two years after Soweto, the same perception is reproduced in a news bulletin on BBC 1, reporting church services held in Soweto on 18 June 1978, to 'commemorate those who died in the riots two years ago, on the anniversary of the disturbances'. In the indexes of newspapers, in the labels on files, in the phrases by which the events are recalled, the residues of those original reports reproduce the perception of agents of the state in the maintenance of order and control, and reproduce the invisibility of their own actions – a view confirmed and sanctioned in the repression itself and in the law courts.

The ideology I have been examining is rooted in the practices of its society. The order, which the organs of the state maintain, will be expressed in the 'official manifestation' of the society through an ideology which legitimates the maintenance of that order. To the extent that journalists are dependent on official and officially approved sources, that will be the view expressed in their sources. Some degree of dependence is inevitable – the police have special access, and control the access of others, to many kinds of events. Where this dependence is almost complete, as in Southern Africa where it is secured by various controls on information and movement, the options other than those open to the (illegal) organs of an underground movement seem to be reproduction of the official view or transformation of it in newspapers beyond the control of the regimes, as in the case of the *Tanzanian Daily News*. But even this second option still involves dependence on the international news gathering system, and there is a great difference between translating a report involving an alien ideology, by altering a few key words (as did the *Tanzanian Daily News*) and having reports expressing an alternative ideology. A genuine alternative view is obtainable only by relating to the movement to transform the social order, and this is an option not immediately or easily accessible to journalists in the conditions obtaining in Southern Africa. But it is possible outside the borders of these countries, and it is something for readers of newspapers to remember. The nature of the situation and the relation of the British media to it means that the voice of that movement is not heard, except at a remove and marginally. This is one reason why reports of the Salisbury event expressing an alternative ideology were not widely available. But it is far from the whole explanation of why the British media generally reproduce the official view. Liberation movements and solidarity organizations do make available to newspapers much that they do not use or do not value as information. A complete understanding of the ideological nature of the coverage in the media must in the end be based, not only on an understanding of what the sources of news are, and their relations to the state and other powers, but also on an understanding of the engagement of the newspapers and other media in social relations and processes. Linguistic analysis cannot provide that understanding, but I hope that this first study has shown that it can be used not only as a means of revealing ideological processes in the production of discourse, but also in pointing towards the questions that need to be asked, even if it cannot answer them.

7 · 'What the papers say': linguistic variation and ideological difference

TONY TREW

A word or two can often tell you a lot about how a person thinks about things, or about the ideas you will find in a book or a newspaper. 'We weren't speaking the same language' is a familiar remark that is often heard when negotiations break down. TUC General Secretary Vic Feather said it as he emerged from negotiations with Prime Minister Edward Heath over the jailing of the five dockers who defied the Industrial Relations Court in 1973; Joshua Nkomo said it when negotiations with Ian Smith broke down in March 1976. In one literal sense it is false – everyone was speaking English. But differences in thought are expressed in linguistically describable forms. When the differences are fairly comprehensive and systematic, and about things that matter, then the linguistic differences are comprehensive, systematic and stable enough to lead people to speak of 'different languages'.

It is in such cases that a few words can tell so much. The differences between 'terrorists' and 'freedom fighters', between 'Rhodesians' and 'Zimbabweans', mark, each one of them, a comprehensive, systematic kind of difference in thinking about specific matters. There are more subtle cases than these instantly recognizable differences of names. Phrases like 'the British people' and 'the people of Britain', between 'hooligans' and 'hooliganism' might at first sight seem to differ only in form and not in content. But they are as firmly integrated in systems of thought as the first examples, in ways that will be illustrated.

Sometimes a difference in wording is significant only in very specialized or restricted discourse. Some systems are so comprehensive and universally used that their existence is scarcely noticeable. But sometimes, above all in discourse about social processes involving conflict, there occur fairly comprehensive, well-articulated and often sharply differing systems of ideas.

This chapter, like the preceding one, is an investigation of examples of the presence in newspaper discourse of some of these more visible systems, and the part they play in perception of social matters.

Although the illustrations are from newspapers, the linguistic ideas can be applied to any form of discourse.

The examples were chosen for what they could show about the linguistics of ideological or theoretical processes, and this is one of the main reasons why they are concerned with perceptions of social violence. When social norms are infringed or the legitimacy of the institutions of control is challenged, there is commonly a response in the media that tends to show most visibly the existence and effects of specific – and often differing – ways of perceiving things. Whereas chapter 6 started from the response in a newspaper to 'awkward facts' in its own reports, this one is concerned with ideological processes involving reports that are not 'anomalous'. It shows the scale on which the processes work, shaping 'on-the-spot' reports, connecting news and comment, extending over several themes and issues and working cumulatively to link events of various kinds under the same stereotypes and headings and to express the perceptions as those of specific social forces or groupings. The material is from the coverage in the English national daily press of events at the end of the 1977 Notting Hill Carnival, in London. After a detailed comparison of the news reports in two contrasting newspapers, and their relation to the editorials in those papers, I examine two processes. One is the transition from news to editorials, involving aspects not present in the material of chapter 6, and the other is the process, covering some weeks, by which links between a number of specific events, expressed in the editorials, were established. The results of the work on these two papers are considered in a brief comparison with reports in the other dailies. I use the material to try to develop more systematic ways of isolating ideology in discourse, to illustrate further aspects of the linguistic expression of the relations of newspaper and ideologies to social processes, and to show a bit more of the linguistics of ideological processes and ideological conflict. The end of the chapter is a summary of some of the uses and limitations of linguistic theory in the study of ideology.

Notting Hill Carnival, 1977: the headlines

Every year since 1965, over the August Bank Holiday weekend, a carnival has been staged on the streets of Notting Hill, a part of inner London. 'In 1974 the Carnival assumed grandiose proportions', according to a press statement (on 5 June 1978) from the

Carnival Development Committee, one of the two main organizing committees in 1977:

From hundreds the crowds grew to a quarter of a million. The Carnival from its tentative beginnings had arrived. It is now a prominent institution in the social and cultural life of the United Kingdom . . . 1976 was a critical year for our Carnival. Besieged by police officers on all sides, rent by internal conflict, Carnival 1976 exploded in violence between spectators and police.

In the months and weeks preceding the 1977 Carnival there were frequent reports of predictions and fears that there would again be violence. There was, and the press responded with these headlines on 30 August.

'INTO BATTLE! Riot shields out as police storm Carnival mob!' (*Sun*)
'Police move in on Carnival gangs. OUT COME THE RIOT SHIELDS' (*Daily Express*)
'RIOT SHIELDS AT CARNIVAL. Police charge with truncheons as rioting mobs pelt them with stones and bottles' (*Daily Mail*)
'RIOT CRAZY Aggro kids in bid to wreck the Carnival' (*Daily Mirror*)
'Dozens hurt at Carnival. RIOT FLARES IN NOTTING HILL. Gang fury hits police and black officials' (*Daily Telegraph*)
'POLICE MOVE IN AS GANGS SPARK CARNIVAL VIOLENCE' (*Guardian*)
'Riot shields used at Carnival' (*Financial Times*)
'VIOLENCE AND TENSION MAR END OF CARNIVAL' (*Times*)
'FIGHTING MARS END OF CARNIVAL AFTER A DAY OF PEACE' (*Morning Star*)

The response was even more varied than these headlines suggest. The headlines varied from two-inch capitals right across the front page of the *Sun*, to inconspicuous lower case lettering in a side column of the *Financial Times*. It was on the front page of all papers, but the lead story only in some. Photographs ranged from pictures of the procession in the *Morning Star* ('Just some of the quarter of a million revellers') to close-ups of the conflict in the *Sun* ('Punch up in the Portobello Road'), and pictures of 'Victims of the violence' in several papers.

Two on-the-spot reports

Words alone cannot capture all that is put over with words, pictures, layout and type all together. But there is much more expressed in the words than might seem to be the case. To show this, and how the different forms of words express different frameworks of interpretation, I will analyse the reports in two of the newspapers whose headlines are listed, the *Sun* and the *Morning Star*. There are many differences between these two papers. The *Sun* is now the largest circulation daily in Britain, the *Morning Star* the smallest. The *Morning Star* is the official organ of a political party, the Communist Party of Great Britain, while the *Sun* has no formal relationship with a political party. But they are chosen in this study for the contrasts between their treatment of the one event, the last hours of the 1977 Notting Hill Carnival. It will turn out that other newspapers contrast in the same way, even if not quite so clearly and sharply. It will also turn out that the differences are not simply differences between these reports alone, but that they are aspects of differences of a more permanent nature both in the reporting in the newspapers and in their social relations. Here are the reports, each presenting an account of what happened and who did what to whom.

Sun 30 August 1977
INTO BATTLE! Riot shields out as the police storm Carnival mob
Two hundred police carrying riot shields and truncheons last night charged a rioting mob of black youths at London's Notting Hill Carnival.

More than 70 policemen were injured, one stabbed, before the Special Patrol Group officers cleared the trouble spot at Acklam Road – flashpoint of last year's riot in which 600 were injured.

The 10-minute riot began when youths charged a police cordon. Hurling bottles and bricks they burst through the thin blue line.

Police reformed the line and

Morning Star 30 August 1977
FIGHTING MARS END OF CARNIVAL AFTER A DAY OF PEACE
Police observers hovering in a helicopter above the huge crowds at London's Notting Hill Carnival yesterday estimated between 200,000 and 250,000 people were taking part.

For most of the time and for the majority of the people it was a happy, peaceful occasion.

But by 9 p.m. some streets in Notting Hill had become a battle-field, with the police mounting a massive operation to clear them.

The trouble started about 8 p.m. at the top of Portobello Road, near

Sun 30 August 1977 (*cont.*)
counter-charged with truncheons, but the weight of the crowd
was too much for them.

Scotland Yard's Deputy Assist-
ant Commissioner David Helm
gave the order that Carnival organisers had been dreading: Bring out
the Special Patrol Group and the
riot shields.

The Group, held out of sight
during the two day carnival, met a
barrage of bottles and bricks.

An eye-witness said 'At one
point the police were pinned down.
The mob stoned them and they
used their riot shields to protect
themselves'.

The riot began when Carnival
organisers asked black youths running a mobile disco in Portobello
Road to close down for the night.

A gang of eight youths immediately started stoning the organisers.
[What follows is from a second
report on the same page.]

One of the stab victims – 21
year old Morwean Hatom of Cambridge Gardens, Notting Hill – was
critically ill in hospital last night.
He was knifed in the chest as he
left home to watch the carnival
procession.

The stabbed police officer, PC
Fred Bibby, was later said to be
not seriously ill.

The violence started early in the
afternoon when small groups of
youths used the gaiety of the Carnival for an orgy of crime.

They beat up people in lava-
tories for the small change they
were carrying. Girls were attacked,
beaten to the ground and their
handbags stolen.

Morning Star 30 August 1977 (*cont.*)
Westway. A scuffle erupted into
the police cordon.

Police, using plastic riot shields
and goggles, charged down streets
using truncheons under a hail of
stones and cans.

The two sides sparred amid a
hail of missiles, and from there on
the police adopted streetfighting
tactics. However, until 10 p.m. at
least, part of the Carnival festivities
did continue in the streets around
Notting Hill.

Dozens of police coaches were in
the area and groups of police were
standing on every corner, though
they were subjected to a hail of
missiles said by witnesses to be
more violent than the Lewisham
incidents.

They seemed determined in
numerous street charges to even
the score.

When they broke into one shop
from where missiles had been coming, those inside were knocked
about by truncheons.

There were reports last night
that a man of 21 was in a critical
condition with a stab wound. A
policeman was also reported to
have been stabbed in the stomach.

As the sun began to go down the
crowds were in a happy mood despite packed streets – even by 5
p.m. it was impossible to move
down Portobello Road and other
main routes.

But generally the atmosphere
was very lighthearted and good
humoured.

The only incidents I noticed
occurred when crowds moved
suddenly as groups of youngsters

Sun 30 August 1977 (*cont.*)

A gang of youths attacked a group of press photographers. Cameraman Barry Beattie was kicked to the ground and badly beaten up.

At Ladbroke Grove Tube Station several hundred youths hurled bottles and bricks at a police cordon. They scattered as a police bus drove towards them with its lights flashing . . . .

Before the violence began, laughing happy crowds followed steel bands through the streets. They danced for joy as West Indians and whites mingled peacefully together. . . .

And the cry went up from the Carnival stewards: 'Stay cool. We want another carnival next year.'

Everyone listened except the thugs.

Morning Star 30 August 1977 (*cont.*)

started running down the street.

The great gay surging carnival of music, dancing and singing got under way smoothly in blazing sunshine. . . .

[The rest of the report is a description of the Carnival procession earlier in the day]

There are a number of parallels between these reports, in terms of the information given and the incidents mentioned. But there is one striking difference between them. In the *Sun* report there are several references to those in conflict with the police – 'rioting mob of black youths', 'youths' 'the mob', 'a gang of eight youths', 'a gang of youths'. But there are none in the *Morning Star*, except to a 'a group of youngsters running down a street', in a report of an incident earlier in the day. The contrast is distilled in the two headlines:

Sun – 'INTO BATTLE! Riot shields out as the police storm Carnival mob.'

Star – 'FIGHTING MARS CARNIVAL AFTER A DAY OF PEACE'
In the second are just words for processes and relations between processes. But the *Sun* headline refers to three categories of participants, with 'police', 'mob' and 'riot shields'. This contrast goes right through the reports. On a crude frequency count there are seven words for every mention of a participant in the *Star*, and only five in the *Sun*.

More significant than the *frequency* of references to participants is the *distribution* of those references and the distribution in particular of references to participants as agents or affected, as active or passive in processes of causal transaction. These matters are at the heart of the expression of ideology. To establish what the distribution is and to analyse it, we need a reliable way of getting at the patterns or structure in a text as a whole. This means we need a way of systematically applying to a text or discourse a theory like Halliday's which analyses clauses in terms of how they present agency and transaction. I will illustrate one way of doing this, giving enough detail to explain it and to allow readers to test its usefulness on other texts or sequences of texts.

The first part of the two-stage procedure involves a sorting of the terms of a text into categories of process and participant and then using this as a basis for abstracting the distribution of agency and interaction amongst participants. There is perhaps a need to say a little here about the distinction between process and participant. The term 'process' is used by Halliday as 'covering all phenomena to which a specification of time attaches'[1] whether they are events, relations or states. Although processes are primarily expressed with verbs, this is not always so, and the basic test of whether a term is a process term is to look at its relations with the various linguistic systems for the expression of time and duration, including such matters as the beginning, continuation, repetition and ending of events. 'The riot began' shows that 'riot' is a process term, even though it is in nominal form. Similarly, 'the violence ended suddenly' marks 'violence' as a process term even though it has no corresponding verb form. The term 'participant' covers in the first instance the entities involved in processes, not themselves subject to the same modifications of time (and it is in this sense that I am using it, possibly deviating a bit from Halliday's use). Terms for participating entities are typically in noun form, and never in verb form. Process words can, as has just been seen, occur in noun form. As such they can occupy the place in a clause for 'participants' in the representation, say, of relations between processes, and might then be said to represent a 'participating process' (see the last stages of the development shown in Table 3 on p. 109 of the previous chapter). In this case the process term has the surface of a term for a participating entity, a fact which can give the term a dual function that may be ideologically significant. It is important to note that the category to which a term belongs may not be fixed for a language. As we shall see, there is a case for saying that what appears primarily as a participant term in one discourse (e.g. 'hooligan') may appear primarily as a process term in another (e.g. 'hooliganism').

Bearing these distinctions in mind, the terms in the two Notting Hill reports can be put into grammatical categories of participant and process (and circumstance and modifications of process), using a standard format illustrated in Table 5. In recording a transactive clause[2] (representing a process involving two participants, one the active causer and the other merely involved or acted on) the term for the causer (actor or agent) is put in the first participant column and the term for the affected participant is put in the 'second participant' column. With a non-transactive clause (any clause presenting a process as involving just one participant and involving no causal transaction) the term for the participant is put in the 'first participant' column. That is done whether the clause presents the participant as active ('the youth ran') or as merely involved ('the youth fell'). Causal transactions are understood here as covering ones that may be physical ('hit') 'mental' ('frighten') or speech acts

Table 5

First participant	Modification of process	Process	Second participant	Circumstance
two hundred police				
		carrying	riot shields and truncheons	
		charged	a rioting mob of black youths	
				last night
				at London's Notting Hill Carnival
			more than 70 policemen	
	were	injured		
			one	
		stabbed		
				before
the Special Patrol Group officers		cleared	the trouble-spot at Acklam Road	
		the riot		
	began			when
youths		charged	a police cordon	

('threaten'). The table should be read going down the lines one by one, reading each line from left to right. The first few sentences of the *Sun* report, and a later sentence in the report, are analysed in Table 5 (the analysis of the clause containing 'cleared' is a bit uncertain).

When this has been done for the whole report, a second stage must be carried out to extract just the information needed to find out the distribution of agency and interaction amongst the participants, ignoring information in the table that may be needed for other aspects of a fuller analysis of the ideology in the text. (This includes information about the thematic structure, recorded by preserving the original sequence of the words, and much that is relevant to modality, mainly in the 'modifications' column (see later on p. 140 for the relevance of modality).) This second stage is explained in two steps for the purposes of this illustration. In the first step you take from Table 5 just the information about processes and participants, ignoring the original sequence of the text, and the various modifications and circumstances. Table 6 is the result of this operation on Table 5. Where there was pronoun or ellipsis in the original text the original term expressing the participant or process is inserted, and where a process is presented as involving a participant which is nevertheless not identified, this unidentified participant is indicated by ****.

Table   6

Participant	Process	Participant
two hundred police	carry	riot shields and truncheons
two hundred police	charge	a rioting mob of black youths
****	injure	more than 70 policemen
****	stab	one policeman
the Special Patrol officers	clear	the trouble spot at Acklam Road
****	riot	
youths	charge	a police cordon

Just for the record and just for illustration, Table 7 and Table 8 show the results of carrying out this operation on an analysis of most of the rest of the *Sun* report and most of the *Morning Star* report. A few sentences have been left out where dealing with them requires complicating the format of the table – the two-fold distinction between transactive and non-transactive clauses used in this illustration cuts across the more delicate distinctions needed for a fuller and more adequate analysis. The kinds of complication needed to take in more clause types is illustrated in the tables. For instance, the complex speech act clause in Table 7 has its three parts tied with the bracket on the side of the table, and the fact that the unidentified participant is the same in each part is marked by (x). In the analysis of the *Morning Star* report it was necessary to recognize the existence of another type of clause, the *attributive* clause – in analysing one of these, like 'the crowds were happy', the attribute 'happy' is put in a column of its own, the process being expressed by 'were'.

Table 7

Participant	Process	Participant
youths	hurl	bricks and bottles
youths	burst-through	the thin blue line (of police)
police	form a line	
police	counter-charge	youths
Cdr. David Helm	order	**** (x)
**** (x)	bring out	the Special Patrol Group
**** (x)	bring out	riot shields
****	held out of sight	the Special Patrol Group
bottles and bricks	barrage	the police
an eye witness	says	
****	pin down	the police
the mob	stone	the police
the police	use	riot shields
the police	protect	the police
****	riot	
carnival organisers	ask	black youths
black youths	close down	a disco
black youths	run	a disco
a gang of eight youths	stone	the carnival organisers

Table 8

Participant	Process	Attribute	Participant
police observers	hover in		a helicopter
police observers	estimate		
200,000–250,000 people	take part in carnival		
most of the people	are	happy	
****	battle		****

the police	operate		
the police	clear		some streets
****	trouble		
police	use		riot shields and goggles
police	charge		
police	use		truncheons
stones and cans	hail (on)		police
the two sides	spar		(with each other)
missiles	hail (on)		the two sides
the police	streetfight		
dozens of police coaches	are	in the area	
groups of police	stand		
missiles	hail (on)		the police
witnesses	say		
the police	break into		one shop
truncheons	knock about		those inside the shop
missiles	come		
****	report		
a man of 21	is	in a critical condition	
****	stab wounds		a man of 21
****	stabs		a policeman
the sun	goes down		
the crowds	are	happy	
****	pack		the streets
****	move		
****	are	light-hearted and good-humoured	
I	notice		
crowds	move		
groups of youngsters	run		

Incomplete as they are, and containing some problematic analyses, these tables could be used even as they stand to give an indication of the distribution of agency in the texts. Running one's eye down the columns confirms the impression of the initial reading of the two reports – more participants and more transactions in the *Sun* report, with more non-transactive clauses in the *Morning Star* report (including attributives as non-transactives). But a more reliable way, and perhaps the most economical way of summing up the information that is wanted about the text as a whole – which could be quite extensive – is to use a matrix. (This is a method that lends itself very well to analysing sequences of texts of the kind studied in the previous chapter.) This is how they work. The terms on the side of the matrix represent the causers or agents in *transactive* processes, and the ones along the top the affected participants. The occurrence of a transactive clause in a text is recorded with a T in the square against the causer and under the affected participant. The occurrence of a *non-transactive* clause is recorded with an N on the diagonal for the participant involved, that is on the square which has the term for the involved participant both at its side and above it. Taking two participants 'Youths' and 'Police', we can record the transactive clauses 'The youths hit the police' and 'The police hit the youths', and the non–transactive clause 'The youths ran', in the matrices (a), (b) and (c) respectively:

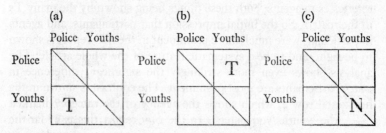

To deal with a wider range of clauses or even to indicate more of the content of process words, more letters can be used. It is necessary to add a category of unidentified participants, and a category for any other groups of participants which the text presents as being involved. In the two news reports different terms are sometimes used for the same participants, and they are grouped together in one category for this analysis. For instance 'police', 'policemen', 'officers' are grouped as 'police' and 'people', 'crowds', 'the public' are grouped as 'people'. Several participants may be grouped together in the texts as a significant category. 'Bricks', 'bottles', 'cans' are collectively referred to as 'missiles' or 'weapons'; and goggles', 'truncheons' and 'riot shields' as 'equipment'. They are grouped together for the matrices in the same way. All the unidentified participants are taken together, not because they are assumed to be the same, but simply for their relevance to this analysis. There is one group of participants for whom there is no term common to both reports. The *Sun* report contains 'black youths', 'gangs of youths', and the *Star* 'groups of youngsters'. This is a divergence whose significance will become clearer as the analysis proceeds, and to mark this the category is not given a label but is marked by . . . . This may be a bit awkward, but the reader can try filling it in with a term that is neutral with respect to the two reports. The matrices are given in Table 9 with the occurrence of each clause in the whole reports (not just the bits in the Tables 7 and 8) recorded by either T or N in the appropriate square.

A record like this contains much more information than can be used in a short space, even though it also leaves out relevant things, as I have indicated. The frequency of occurrences of transactive clauses should not be interpreted as somehow proportional to the power of the agents involved. But the analysis does show some things very clearly. There are many more transactive clauses in the *Sun* report, that is expressions of causal interaction, and many more references to agents, both these things being shown by the many Ts in the matrix. So the initial impression that participants, and agents in particular, were much more prominent in the *Sun* report is shown to be right, and to be a systematic feature of the whole article. The analysis shows even more strikingly the significant difference in *which* participants are most prominent. The contrast is shown in the horizontal row 4, which shows the agency of the category marked '. . .', the 'youths/youngsters'. In the *Sun* report this is by far the most active category, acting on every other category. In the *Morning Star* report there is only one reference to a transaction in which they are involved. And if anything the matrices understate the contrast. (That one reference in the *Star* is from the clause 'the two sides sparred' and, as there is no identification of those sparring with the police, this is perhaps really a case of 'unidentified participant'.) On top of that, in the *Sun* report there are three transactive processes analysed as having unidentified agents (from the sentence 'Girls were attacked, beaten to the ground and their handbags stolen') which perhaps should have been analysed as having 'groups of youths' as the agent. The sentence follows immediately after one saying that 'small groups of youths used the gaiety of the carnival for an orgy of crime', and this sets up a cohesion between 'crime' on the one hand, and 'attack', 'beat to the ground' and 'steal' on the other, which makes the agent of the first the agent of the others.

Although the police are mentioned equally often in both reports, given the absence in the *Morning Star* report of reference to those

Table 9

Sun

	unidentified	people	police	...	organizers	equipment	weapons	
1	NNNN TN	TTTT T	TTT		T			unidentified
2		NNNN NNNN NNNN	T					people
3	TT		NNNN N	T		TT		police
4		TTT	TTTT	NNNN	T	TT	TT	...
5				T	NNNN			organizers
6			T	T		N		equipment
7								weapons
	1	2	3	4	5	6	7	

Morning Star

	unidentified	people	police	...	organizers	equipment	weapons	
1	TNNN NNN	T	TT					unidentified
2		NNNN NNNN NN						people
3	TTT		NNNN NNN	T		TTT		police
4			T	N				...
5								organizers
6		T				N		equipment
7	T		TT				N	weapons
	1	2	3	4	5	6	7	

they are in conflict with, they are presented in the *Morning Star* report as the most prominent active participants, the initiators of action. But at the same time their activities are presented in that report as directed either at unidentified participants or their own equipment. Otherwise processes are expressed at a level of abstraction which requires participants to be inferred (again the headline is characteristic: 'FIGHTING MARS CARNIVAL AFTER A DAY OF PEACE'). Note, too, the number of clauses in which inanimate participants are presented as active (truncheons knock people about, bricks and bottles hail on the police). The reports differ, then, in at least two ways in how they present things. In the *Sun* the processes are presented explicitly as interactions between identified groups of people and objects, with the 'groups of youths' the most prominent initiators and actors, followed by the police. In the *Morning Star* report the processes are what is focal, they are not so much processes of interaction, and the participants tend to be on the edge of the picture except to some extent for the police. The second big difference is in the way one group of participants is described. It is referred to only once in the *Morning Star* report with the phrase 'groups of youngsters'. But the *Sun* has 'youths', 'mob of black youths', 'gang of youths', 'black youths', 'thugs'. So there are 'gangs' and 'mobs' versus 'groups' (a difference highlighted in the sentence in the *Sun*: 'a gang of youths attacked a group of press photographers'), and 'youths' and 'thugs' versus 'youngsters'. These lexical variations – differences in wording – are repeated in the terms for the processes in which this group is most centrally involved ('riot' versus 'trouble', 'hurl' versus 'hail', 'charge' versus 'run'). On the other hand, in describing the other groups of participants, the same words are used in the two reports. The meaning of these differences becomes clearer when the news reports are related to the editorials that followed, and to the way that such matters are routinely handled in the two newspapers.

Two editorials: our language and theirs

The editorials, as in the Salisbury case, put the event into a wider network of relationships, giving an interpretation that explains what happened and producing a call to action based on that explanation. The news reports and editorials differ in the degree of abstractness of language, in the breadth of context to the events, in the use of language, that is the explicit language of judgment and exhortation (attributives, equatives, imperatives). However, the call to action is so bound up with the interpretation and explanation, and so intrinsically linked to the original reports, that it is impossible to distinguish the reports from the editorials as fact, on the one hand, and comment, evaluation or prescription on the other.

In the editorials the day after the news reports, some of the original categories of participants are present, others not, and amongst those that remain there is a shift in relative prominence. (This could be shown by doing causal matrices for them; and comparing them with those for the report.) Original categories that remain prominent in the editorials (in different ways) are 'people' and that other category with the disputed title, which the two editorials only agree in describing as a 'small' group. New participants enter the picture – the 'authorities', and very prominently in the *Sun*, the 'courts'. All the categories are used in a general sense with only a little specific reference to those involved in Notting Hill. What I want to focus on is the language used to describe that small group and its activities, and to describe the 'people', and also the ways in which links are laid down between Notting Hill and other specific events. These two things are central, and they are inseparable from each other, and from the views about what is to be done.

Sun 31 August 1977

IT'S UP TO THE COURTS
The violence which erupted in the wake of the Notting Hill Carnival has provoked a reasonable and respectable public demand for action.

The question is: What kind of action?

It would be appalling if the vicious outrages perpetrated by the small, but dangerous, thug element became the cue for a wave of official repression.

That would damage the rights of the peaceful majority and feed propaganda to those who cry 'Police state' every time the law tries to defend the rights of the

Morning Star 31 August 1977

BACK THE CARNIVAL
No one yesterday was crazy enough to suggest abolishing sea fronts, banning summer holidays or making it illegal to turn up in Margate.

But in the Kentish resort on the bank holiday Monday several people were stabbed, a good many more arrested and holiday makers disturbed by gang fights and violence.

The Notting Hill Carnival, though, has become an immediate target for the law and order brigade.

Many more than last year turned

Sun 31 August 1977 (*cont.*)
citizen against the excesses of the hooligans.

What Notting Hill has shown yet again is that violence in the streets is not a case of black against white or rich against poor.

It is the Yobs against the rest of us.

That is true not only in Notting Hill but in Lewisham, in Lady-wood and in the turmoil that engulfed the Grunwick dispute.

The same goes for the louts who disrupt soccer matches and smash up railway trains.

It is not society which is on trial in any of these cases. It is the effectiveness of justice to defend the ordinary peaceful man.

Already there are cries for the banning of not only events like the Notting Hill Carnival but even of political demonstrations and meetings which a lunatic fringe might use as an arena for their political savagery.

There is – as yet – no need for wholesale bans or the introduction of mandatory 20-year prison terms for assaulting police officers.

The answer lies with the courts. And they must not let us down.

Magistrates and judges do not lack the power to stamp out violence.

Tomorrow, with the introduction of the new Criminal Law act, even the lower courts will be able to impose fines of £1,000 and prison sentences of six months for hooliganism.

What the public has a right to demand is that the courts will not be too wet to exercise their responsi-

Morning Star 31 August 1977 (*cont.*)
up for the carnival, the biggest event in the Caribbean calendar in Britain.

They added up, on the Sunday alone, to pretty well three-quarters of the total number of people who came to watch all the Test matches of the current enthralling series.

So what was the most important thing – the carnival or the violence? Was it the dancing, music and enjoyment of the tens of thousands or the thuggery of what, both police and organisers agree, was a very small minority?

Already Tory Deputy Leader William Whitelaw is saying that the carnival must not be allowed on the streets again.

Earlier in the month he was advocating 'glasshouse' detention centres based on 'the old idea of providing a short, sharp shock treatment' for young 'thugs'.

His solution to both issues is not only unreal, it is guaranteed to make them worse.

Rather than seek to restrict the carnival the authorities should be giving it, and every other event of its kind in the country, the financial support it deserves and so urgently requires.

Penny-pinching attitudes and demands for more police action are not the way in which the frustration and alienation of young people – black or white – in Britain today can be overcome.

Whether at Margate, Acklam Road or on the football terraces, the violence and hooliganism has its causes.

Those causes need tackling.

Sun 31 August 1977 *(cont.)*
bility.

Those properly convicted upon reliable evidence must pay the price.

Those who rob with violence carry offensive weapons or attack the police and the public are guilty of grave offences.

THEY MUST GO TO JAIL

And the police must get the official backing, the equipment – and the wages – they need to sustain their efficiency and morale.

The way to make the streets safe for the law-abiding is to make them unsafe for the thugs.

Morning Star August 31 1977 *(cont.)*
And one way to help is to see that community events of unity and joy like the carnival are given full backing by the authorities both local and national.

This time last year in the aftermath of the 1976 carnival and the police clashes which marked its end the Star urged that this 'deeper sickness' behind the violence be made a priority for government action.

It would be good not to have to repeat the message in 1978.

One final point. It is odd to see those who rush to stop any ban on National Front racist marches demanding, without a moment's hesitation, that the Carnival be stopped. Or is it?

In the *Sun* article there is a rich variety of terms for that small minority: 'the small but dangerous thug element', 'hooligans',[3] 'louts', 'thugs'. In the *Morning Star* the only terms for the people involved are 'young people' and 'young "thugs"'. The occurrence of '"thugs"' in the *Star* article is right at the heart of the process I am examining. It is both an acknowledgement of the existence of the ideology expressed in the *Sun*, and at the same time a rejection of it which presents the term as one without application. This is not just expression of ideology, but explicit engagement in ideological conflict. The quotes put the term at a distance, declaring it a term of the enemy. The *Morning Star* article does not have, and rejects, any special terminology for classifying the people involved in the processes which the article discusses, the people for whom the *Sun* article has a special and rich vocabulary. In the *Star* article they are presented as part of the group of 'young people', themselves a part of the category of 'people', to whom the article is addressed.

What about the terms 'hooliganism' and 'thuggery' and 'gang fights' that occur in the *Morning Star* article? They are words for processes, not participants, and this is a crucial difference. The activities are marked out with a special vocabulary, but not the people involved. The difference is immensely important, because it leads to different forms of explanation of what has happened. All 'yobs' are violent, but only some 'young people'. Events presented as the actions of 'yobs', 'thugs' and 'hooligans' need no explanation – they were done because of the nature of the people who did them. But when presented as acts of unauthorized violence done by 'young people', they need explaining. As the *Morning Star* editorial says 'the violence has its causes', it is the effect of 'the frustration and alienation of young people' which the editorial presents as part of a '"deeper sickness"' which regular readers of the *Morning Star* will know to be the effect of social deprivation and various social conditions. In this specific case, too, the causes include inadequate public financing of the carnival.

From these different forms of classification and their implicit explanations, flow, with all logic, different remedies; 'punish them,' says the *Sun* editorial – 'improve the conditions,' says the *Star* editorial. 'These people are our enemies,' says one, 'it's the yobs against the rest of us.' 'These young people are our young people,' says the other, 'we must remove the causes of their anger.' To deal with an enemy you need a powerful and resolute army, courts with the power and the will to exact the price, police with the power and the equipment to defeat the enemy in battle. To deal with the deprivation of some of our people, resources are needed and the will of the authorities to release them.

There are two opposing sets of theses here, expressed not only by what is overtly said but by the systems and forms of classification used to present the central processes and participants. There is some room for play and variation, and some of the terms used in a system can be directly taken into another with little effect on meanings. But there is no possibility of this in the key terms which register the focal areas of overt ideological conflict, and which, through their place in the systems can by themselves virtually express a whole ideology. This conflict can focus on almost any aspect of the language, but the terms categorizing central participants are often the most charged with ideological significance, because the way people are categorized may involve attributing socially significant causal powers to them, as we have seen, and a place in social relations. In such cases the set of terms that are used in the different discourses form what might be called a 'dispute paradigm', a set of words which are the options available for use in that situation, each of which marks an alternative ideological position. This is one important form of several kinds of expression of ideological conflict. The variation in the case of the classification of this one group (and correspondingly in the case of 'people') contrasts with agreement in the terms for other groups, and much of the significance of the variation lies in this contrast.

Alongside the use of different terminology there is also explicit rejection of the terminology and theses of others, expressed in various forms of negation and modality – like the use of quotes ('"thugs"', '"police state"') or negation ('It is not society which is on trial').

There is variation, it should be noted, not only between the articles, but within the *Sun* editorial itself, which has the proliferation of terms, 'lout', 'thug', 'yob' and 'hooligan'. This seems to be a case of what Halliday calls 'over-lexicalization'.[4] He explains it as an aspect of language used in transforming social relations – to the extent that this is a use of language to change attitudes, the 'interpersonal' aspect of language tends to be prominent. Whether or not that explanation fits this case each of these words, which differ only slightly in meaning, are categorizations embedded in, and expressing, a system of discourse about different forms of violence presented as manifestations of violent natures. Each lends itself, in the way we have seen, to a campaign, to shift social practices and relations towards 'deviants' in the direction of more control and coercion. They draw together the slightly different but related attitudes of hostility to those involved in violence. Coming all at once in one short text they are almost like an incantation and have a kind of axiomatic, tautological effect that forecloses all discussions. The effect is like that of the remark by a senior police officer reported in the *Sun*: 'Hooligans are hooligans', with which he prefaced a statement about the necessities of containment.

Besides the differences in categorizations of participants, the other difference that stands out is how the events at Notting Hill are related to other specific events. Grouped together in the *Morning Star* editorial as events similar to those at the end of the Notting Hill Carnival are disturbances of summer holidays, football matches, cricket test matches and community events of unity and joy in general. The end of the 1977 Notting Hill Carnival is presented as a case of alienated young people disturbing the communal leisure activities of thousands of people. Grouped together in the *Sun* editorial along with the end of the Notting Hill Carnival are Lewisham, Ladywood and Grunwick, as well as disturbances at football matches. These are all presented as cases of disruption of lawful activity, a challenge to the rule of law and a threat to the rights of citizens. The processes by which these events are presented as being linked together in this way will be analysed. For the moment the close connection between the linking of events, the primary categorization of the central participants, and the call for action can be seen condensed in these passages at the heart of each editorial.

Sun

What Notting Hill has shown yet again is that violence in the streets is not a case of black against white or rich against poor.

It's the yobs against the rest of us.

That is true not only in Notting Hill but in Lewisham, in Ladywood and in the turmoil that engulfed the Grunwick dispute.

The same goes for the louts who disrupt soccer matches and smash up railway trains.

It is not society which is on trial in any of these cases, but the effectiveness of justice to defend the ordinary peaceful man.

Morning Star

Penny-pinching attitudes and demands for more police action are not the way in which the frustration and alienation of young people – black or white – in Britain today can be overcome.

Whether at Margate, Acklam Road or on the football terraces, the violence and hooliganism has its causes.

Those causes need tackling and one way to help is to see that community events of unity and joy like the carnival are given full backing by the authorities both local and national.

These are fairly pure and sharp examples of two opposing approaches to a number of issues involving social conflict and violence, organized around opposing theses about the cause of conflict. It is not just a question of ideas; each set of ideas expresses an existing form of social *practice*, and the conflict of ideas expresses attempts to advance one form of practice against the other. This is clear enough from the two editorials. It is made even more explicit almost daily in the continuing 'law and order' campaign. For instance, in May 1978 the *Guardian* reported Sir Keith Joseph, a leading Conservative, as saying, 'Socialism has taught that it is deprivation, not delinquency that lies behind crime and violence' and arguing that 'consequently socialists had legislated to take juvenile crime "out of the hands of lawyers and magistrates and into the hands of social workers"'. This was just a few days after the chairman of the Police Federation had, according to the *Daily Mirror* (16 May) attacked 'do-gooders who were reacting timidly to the alarming upsurge of violence in Britain', citing as an example the view that 'soccer hooligans are victims of inner city deprivation'. And in July, Scotland Yard's Metropolitan Commissioner called for 'punishment before welfare' in the 'treatment of young offenders' (BBC Radio 4, 9 July). But at the same time the opposing practice continues as well – the '£1 MILLION PLAN TO CURB SOCCER VIOLENCE' reported (with a slightly misleading headline), in *The Times* in May, is an allocation of money to provide sport and recreation facilities in inner-city areas and to finance schemes to involve supporters in their clubs.

These examples illustrate the nature and the implications of the contrast between the editorials that has been highlighted so far by the analysis. But having said this, it is important not to leave the matter there, or to simplify the ideological process by abstracting from the editorials just these 'pure ideologies of crime' and their bases in the news reports. It is necessary to examine more closely the specific ideological formation at work here, and in doing so it will be seen that some important matters have been missed in the analysis so far. To get at these things it is necessary to think now not just of the texts or articles, but of some of the processes out of which they came. Two (interacting) processes can be distinguished. One is the process by which the news reports are assimilated within the broader system expressed in the editorials, discussed in the next section. The other is the process of formation of that broader system and its effect on the way news is reported. This is of course a permanent and ongoing process, but what is immediately relevant to this analysis are the developments in the months preceding Notting Hill, when the events mentioned in the *Sun* editorial occurred. This is discussed under the heading 'Linking events'.

Appropriating an event: mediators

The analyses of the news reports and editorials showed a strong conformity between the ideologies extracted from the editorials and the systems of categorizations of participants and processes in the news reports. The focus on agency of the 'youths' in the *Sun* and the emphasis in the *Morning Star* on processes and relations between processes which are not attributed to the agency of people, made for material that could be assimilated without much work into the terms of the editorials – indeed to a large degree the terms are already present and structuring the reports. The work of appropriation and assimilation involves processes of linguistic transformation of the kind illustrated in the Salisbury study. But there is another kind of process that I want to highlight here that shows a great deal about the relations of newspapers, ideologies and social forces.

The news reports and the editorials were in fact just the first and last in two sequences that contained intermediate texts. (The articles stand in a sequence in the sense that ones 'later' in the sequence use, refer to, or depend on ones that are 'earlier' in the sequence.) In the *Sun* there was on the first day, beside the lead story news report 'INTO BATTLE!' also a second item, part-report, part-assessment, reporting responses to the events described in the lead story, and headlined 'IS THIS THE LAST ONE?' Next day there was more assessment, on a page labelled 'INQUEST'. The main item was headlined 'THE RENEGADES: POLICE SAY GANGS CAUSED VIOLENCE'. Another fairly prominent one, headed 'GIVE 'EM 20 YEARS' reports a demand for stiff jail sentences from Conservative MP Rhodes Boyson. The sequence culminates with the editorial 'IT'S UP TO THE COURTS – THEY MUST GO TO JAIL'. The three part sequence in the *Morning Star* goes from the report 'FIGHTING MARS END OF CARNIVAL AFTER A DAY OF PEACE' to assessment and reported comments the next day, headed '"DON'T STOP CARNIVAL" PLEA BY ORGANISERS', and then the editorial 'BACK THE CARNIVAL'.

The opinions, assessments and comments reported are strikingly similar to the views in the editorial in the same newspaper. Where opposing views are reported they are given no prominence, and are distanced by quote marks or other forms of indirect quotation. Although each newspaper reports the views of a carnival organizer, they are from rival committees. Disagreements after the 1976 carnival, partly over relations with the police, had produced two organizing committees, the Carnival Development Committee and the Carnival and Arts Committee. The *Morning Star* interviews the director of the Carnival Development Committee, whose views are almost word-for-word those in the editorial. The *Sun* reporting comments of the chairman of the other committee, stated that 'members of the Carnival's organising committee have been pressing for a local – not a national or international – event. Mr. Louis Chase, the Committee's chairman, said the Carnival had grown too big for Notting Hill'. The existence of two committees and their differences were too well known for it to be ignorance that explains the failure of both newspapers to mention the other committee, or the inaccuracy of the reference in the *Sun* to '*the* organising committee'.

There are many points of contrast, both in terms of the selection of the views of people quoted in both papers, and in the choice of people quoted. The police are quoted in both papers, but in different ways. For instance the Commissioner, commenting on crime statistics, is reported in both as saying it was only a minority involved. But his further comments are differently reported in the two papers. He was reported in the *Morning Star* as adding that 'it was not as bad as some people had feared', and in the *Sun* as saying 'But hooligans are hooligans. When they are in that mood they cannot be contained without injury'. But apart from the police, almost all the other views are from people reported in only one of the papers. While the *Sun* quotes the director of the Carnival and Arts Committee, an eye-witness ('the mob stoned the police'), a victim of the violence ('police stayed on the fringe'), and local shopkeepers ('the carnival must leave Notting Hill'), and Rhodes Boyson ('Give 'em 20 years'), the *Morning Star* reported the views of the Director of the Carnival Development Committee, the Welfare Officer of the West Indian Standing Conference, and Chairman of the Commission for Racial Equality.

The editorials are clearly not discrete and self-contained meditations on the events – they are a continuation and expression of social processes in which the newspaper is engaged. The framework of interpretation and selection which characterizes the ideological position of a newspaper is more than a set of terms for report and comment – it involves the valuations of different sources, different connections and links with institutions, groups, campaigns, movements and so on. The newspaper itself is not a self-contained institution, but a site at which the views of various combinations of social forces and practices are articulated, an organ which different forces have different degrees of access to and different degrees of influence or control in the determination of the terms in which information is formulated and social reality represented. This is a two-way process. The newspaper expresses certain forces – but at the same time the credibility of the newspaper with its readers also depends on which forces it gives expression to, or more formally which organizations and institutions and public figures it takes as valuable sources of information and comment. The linguistics of modality is particularly relevant here, with its ways of expressing agreement or disagreement, adoption or rejection of the words of others. The papers do not speak directly to the readers, but rather through the groups and organizations to which the readers belong, the institutions, movements and sections of society they identify with or support or respect. The representatives and spokespersons of these groups and institutions play a crucial part in the processes of 'mediation of perception' in which the 'media' themselves, as usually understood, are just one aspect. They could be called 'mediators', for this reason. The interpretation of events in terms of the ideologies expressed in editorials – and reports – is through a process that simultaneously effects the assimilation and authenticates it.[5]

Linking events

Taking this one incident, then, and approaching the treatment of it in the two newspapers in terms of linguistic analysis, we find that the ideological processes involved in the presentation of the event are complex. This complex ideological formation does not just come into existence with the one incident – and its development should be understood, not just for its own sake, *but because of its contribution to the meaning of the result*, a contribution expressed in, and partly effected by, various linguistic aspects of the editorials. The development is a continuous process of using and modifying already existing formations, involving on each occasion various forms of abstraction, mediation and so on. The resulting appropriation of an event can itself become material used in the presentation of events yet to happen. The editorials in the two newspapers refer explicitly to events in the months preceding the Notting Hill Carnival and it is the treatment of these events that will be examined in this section, to recover the meaning of some of those references and to understand the nature of the links that are made. At the same time, there are references to issues that have been preoccupations for many years, such as 'youth', 'race' and 'crime'. The meaning of the editorials on Notting Hill Carnival 1977 is also partly constituted by the past treatment of these issues in the newspapers and other media, to the extent that it is either recoverable from the articles themselves or has affected the meaning of the words and the readers' understanding of the words. There are relatively stable ideological formations, but they change. The processes in which specific events and issues are appropriated in terms of an ideological system are also ones in which the system develops through this deployment in social experience. This is part of the process of linguistic change, and it involves linguistic processes, but it is also more than that. This is something for a fuller and another kind of investigation[6] but there is one prominent phrase in the *Sun* editorial which illustrates this and which needs to be understood, since it is presented as the theme of the article. The phrase 'violence in the streets' has a very specific meaning that would not be found in a dictionary, for instance. The *Sun*'s long concern with that theme and some of the nature of its preoccupation is shown in an editorial on 13 October 1972 headed 'TAME THE MUGGERS':

WHAT *are the British people most concerned about today?* Wages?
Prices? Immigration? Pornography? People are talking about all these
things. But the *Sun* believes there is another issue which has everyone
deeply worried and angry: VIOLENCE IN OUR STREETS. . . .
Nothing could be more utterly against our way of life, based on a
common sense regard for law and order. . . . If punitive jail sentences
help to stop the violence – and nothing else will – then they will not only
prove to be the only way. They will, regrettably, be the RIGHT way.
And the judges will have the backing of the public.

An image and a set of terms is established, condensed in the phrase, 'violence in the streets', which provides a basic model which can be deployed again and again as the organizing theme in a cumulative shaping of social perception. Against this background, let us see how a series of events and issues, starting in June, were collected in the discourse in the *Sun* under the same heading as the events at the end of the 1977 Notting Hill Carnival in late August – 'Lewisham', 'Ladywood', 'Grunwick' and 'football violence'. Comparison with the *Morning Star*'s treatment of those same matters will show much about both newspapers, and about the linguistics of ideological processes.

In June 1977, when the Grunwick strikers had been picketing the entrances to the firm for nine months over their claim for trade union recognition and reinstatement, mass picketing to support them began. On 14 June a report in the *Sun* headlined 'FURY ON THE PICKET LINE' describes 'one of the worst scenes of violence outside a British factory gate', the initiators of which were 'a squad of flying pickets', 'left-wing "rent-a-mob" agitators', 'a mob' bent on 'intimidating' by 'mob-rule', 'those inside the factory', 'outsiders'. A 'mediator' of this perception is George Ward, director of Grunwick, quoted as describing the events as involving ' "rent-a-mob" ' set on mob-rule'. The editorial defines the issue as one of a minority of trouble-makers threatening peaceful activities: 'The disgraceful punchup outside Grunwick laboratories was predictable ... a number of agitators who had no connection with the union or with Grunwick decided to join in ... a challenge that makes a mockery of the whole concept of peaceful picketing.'

On 20 June the definition is sharper. An editorial titled 'THE RIGHT TO WORK' contains this: 'What the strike is now about is the duty of the forces of law and order – and that includes the government – to uphold the rights of the people in this factory.' The threat is said to come from 'rent-a-mob' (no longer in quotes), 'the Fascist Left' and 'Bully boys' who need to be faced by 'the Law' and 'forces of Law and Order'. An editorial two days later speaks of 'LABOUR'S TWO FACES' the one of 'moderation and responsibility', the other the one 'seen amongst the seething mob at the Grunwick barricades'. Four days later still sees the editorial statement that 'the explosion of violence at Grunwick gets more frightening'.

'It is one of the most alarming breakdowns in law and order for many years' and is brought about by 'demo-merchants' and 'arrogant union militants'. A couple of days later there is a photograph of a policeman, with a report headed 'VICTIM OF THE PICKETS' (24 June). In the same week prominence is given to a report of a call by Rhodes Boyson, (who recurs as a mediator in the *Sun* treatment of Notting Hill), 'for the sacking of Shadow Employment Secretary' [his own party] 'for refusing to condemn the "lawless anarchy"' (30 June). This is followed two days later by an editorial on 'STANDING UP FOR THE LAW'. After more clashes, there is a report headed 'THE BATTERED BOYS IN BLUE' (2 July) (referring to the police).

The essence of the situation as presented is that a group of self-determined trouble-makers, outsiders, are threatening the rights of ordinary people by challenging the rule of law. The forces of law and order have a duty to end this by using their powers and enforcing the law. The basic categorizations used are 'people' (some of whom are in the factory), 'forces of law and order', including 'police', who are presented in a defensive position. The industrial participants are 'pickets' and 'Company Chiefs'. The most prominent and active participants, the ones who have initiated the violence, are a group with no fixed description, but with a number of descriptions which present them as alien, aggressive and violent in nature – 'agitators', 'rent-a-mob', 'outsiders', 'riot-pickets', 'bully-boys', 'seething mob', 'squalid extremists', 'demo-merchants', 'arrogant militants'. (Note again, the proliferation of terms focusing on the one group of participants.)

The full meaning of this appropriation of the events within a 'law and order' framework involves its relation to a very different kind of presentation, an example of which occurred in the *Morning Star*. The contrast is if anything even greater than in the Notting Hill case, an effect of the very different relations the two papers have with the trade union movement. The start of the mass picketing was reported in the *Morning Star* on 14 June with the headline 'POLICE WAGE WAR AGAINST PICKETS' and second head 'Grunwick strikers won't give up fight', and a report with the lead-sentence: 'Police yesterday tried brutally and systematically to destroy the first mass picket in the week of action in support of the Grunwick strikers' struggle for union recognition'. Another report had the headline 'WE WON'T BE INTIMIDATED' and carried a statement from the Grunwick Strike Committee, speaking of the police action as 'a partisan attempt to intimidate trade unionists carrying out their lawful right to picket' and of 'open collaboration between the police and the employer'. It ended with a call for 'maximum solidarity for the mass picketing', and the statement that 'this strike has become a key issue of trade union recognition for our movement, and every worker should do his or her utmost to help the strike to a speedy and victorious conclusion'. There is also a letter from the chairman of the London Area Council of the union APEX calling for support for the Grunwick Picket Line. The next week, when the *Sun* editorial called for 'the forces of law and order' to be asserted, the *Morning Star* reports, 'all out support for the Grunwick picket line was called yesterday after company boss George Ward side-stepped an offer of talks' (20 June). There is a photograph showing evidence of 'GRUNWICK SOLIDARITY' and an editorial saying 'STEP UP SUPPORT'. The day the *Sun* editorial speaks of 'Labour's two faces' the *Morning Star* front-page lead story has the headline 'THUGS! 8 MP'S BRAND POLICE RENT-A-MOB', with the second head 'Close Grunwick say strikers', and a report starting like this:

Eight Labour MP's yesterday denounced police outside Grunwick as thugs, after seeing for themselves the treatment given to pickets. After one of their number, Mrs. Audrey Wise, was arrested, Mr. Martin

Flannery accused the police of provocation – 'The police acted like thugs – I think they were the rent-a-mob here' he said after meeting the Home Secretary to demand an immediate halt to the brutal tactics of the police. (22 June)

The contrast between the papers is very great, and shows in a number of ways. The 'mediators' in the *Sun* are the director of the company, and a right-wing MP, while those in the *Morning Star* are the Grunwick Strike Committee, Labour MPs supporting the picket line, trade union officers. The systems of terms used are correspondingly at odds. On the one hand the participants are 'police', 'pickets', 'people', 'the Law', 'Company Chiefs', 'outsiders' and 'agitators', on the other, they are 'police', 'strikers', 'trade union movement'. The term 'rent-a-mob' is fixed into one system when the director of the company applies it to pickets and it is taken over in this use in the *Sun*. Then in language of extremely complex modality, this use of the term, along with the term 'thugs' to categorize people amongst the pickets, is rejected by the MP supporting the strike who uses it to characterize the *behaviour* of the police – and taken over in this use by the *Morning Star* (as a '*branding*' rather than a categorization). The one set of terms underlies the call 'to enforce the Law to protect the rights of the public', while the other set underlies a demand for 'solidarity with a trade union struggle'.

There are then a number of related contrasts – different systems of classification, opposing calls to action, engagement with different and opposing social forces, and, a very important contrast, the difference between presenting the events as part of a trade union struggle with specific aims on the one hand, and, on the other hand, abstracting the conflict from the particular content of the struggle and also presenting the events as incidents of violent threat to law and order.

There is a similar abstraction from the specific content of a struggle in the treatment in the *Sun* of Lewisham and Ladywood. Lewisham was the scene of an attempt by anti-racists and anti-fascists to stop a National Front march called 'to let the Reds, their mugger friends and above all the Multi-Racialist authorities know that the NF will never back down in defence of the White British People'.[7] Attempts by the police to ensure that the march went ahead led to violence (and riot shields were used for the first time in England, which is why they were still so newsworthy two weeks later at the end of the Notting Hill Carnival). Before the march the *Sun* in an editorial on 2 August, does refer to its racist nature, speaking of the National Front as 'racist demagogues' and of its 'march of hate'. But in the same editorial it marks out as the fundamental distinction the division between the 'innocent citizen' on the one hand and on the other both the National Front 'racist demagogues' and 'the extreme left-wingers', 'the lunatic left' (here again, a case of over-lexicalization). The 'innocent citizen' is threatened by these others who are the source of 'the danger ahead'. In reporting the march afterwards and the violence that occurred, the focus in the *Sun* is on conflict between these groups, without reference to the issue of racism. And while the *Morning Star* has a report headlined 'POLICE PILE IN' ('to crowds of anti-fascists') WITH HORSES AND RIOT GEAR' and speaks of the police 'protecting the "right" of the National Front to peddle its racist propaganda', in the *Sun* the police are described as 'the heroes in the middle'. Ladywood, a similar incident on a much smaller scale in Birmingham a few days later (17 August), confirmed both views for those who held them. While the *Morning Star* called for a ban on National Front marches because of the racist nature of the movement, the *Sun* first headlined the Home Secretary's refusal to do this: 'I WON'T BAN THE FRONT MARCHES', and then gives prominence to a call from a leading conservative for 'TOUGHER CURBS ON DEMO-THUGS', for 'a hardhitting plan to hammer political bully boys at street demos' (18 August).

The problem, in this presentation, is not racism, but the threat to the innocent citizen which is posed by a minority of aggressive people '(demo)-thugs', 'bully boys', a threat to be met by a more powerful police force and a determination to enforce the law.

The final element in the chain is the beginning of the new football season. On 12 August, ten days before the season started, the *Sun* had carried a feature article headed 'WAR ON THE SOCCER YOBBOES' covering an interview with the Home Secretary reporting measures he had announced to deal with violence at football matches, a series of penalties and controls aimed at those involved in violence. 'SHAME OF THE BIG KICK-OFF' was the headline of the report on 22 August, of the day the season started with the second head, '200 arrests as football fans go on the rampage'. The report begins: 'Britain faces the threat of another season of shameful soccer aggro. For hooligans went on the rampage as the new league season kicked off.' The report uses the terms 'hooligans', 'soccer thugs', 'soccer hooligans', and leads logically to the editorial cry 'SMASH THE YOBS' which expresses the hope that magistrates will use new legislation which will enable them 'to jail the violent thugs for up to six months'. The *Morning Star* only reported the fines imposed by magistrates on those arrested. But in an article in the *Morning Star* a month or two earlier, the following views had been expressed, under the heading 'LAW AND ORDER' DANGER:

All these [proposals for harsher penalties and controls] carry general dangers for young people. They sweep the problem under the carpet. Jailing and fining football vandals will not make the causes of the problem go away. . . . Football cannot eradicate the poverty, the bad housing, the poor education, the boring jobs, the life of society's no-hopers, many of whom turn to thuggery as the only form of expression. (April 13)

The themes and the contrasts are now familiar.[8] Each of these events is presented in the *Sun* in the same way, as being essentially a threat to the 'peaceful majority', 'the innocent citizen', 'the ordinary person', emanating without reason from the actions of a minority of people, violent by nature, whose existence necessitates the strengthening of the 'forces of law and order'. In the *Morning Star* the terms of the interpretation are totally different.

It was necessary to make this retracing of steps to avoid simplifying the issue between the two treatments of the end of the Notting Hill Carnival as one of two ideologies of crime. There is that, but there is more as well, because in the *Sun* it is not only the Carnival that is brought under this ideology as a problem of public order, but also one of the major trade union struggles for some years, and the struggle against racism. In each case there are similar ideological formations comprising a number of themes and movements. The editorials fit in a continuous process and their part in it is linguistically expressed, in the names given to events and in other references and allusions whose meaning is only recoverable through knowledge of earlier stages of the process, in the negations and rejections of alternative ideology, in the proliferation of terms for one group of participants, focusing on them as both the manifestation and the cause of the 'problem' and as the objects against which action is to be directed, collecting and binding together perceptions of, and attitudes towards, a number of phenomena. It was necessary to retrace the steps because the steps were part of the process constituting the meaning of what was being analysed. And retracing the steps throws light on the linking, in the *Sun* editorial, of the end of the Notting Hill Carnival, Lewisham, Ladywood and Grunwick, and 'football violence'. The link was not effected retrospectively or arbitrarily by this one editorial – the events were already linked by each being appropriated in terms of the same ideology, one which foreclosed all understanding and explanation of the various conflicts other than in terms of the violent and aggressive nature of some people and the insufficient power of law enforcement agencies to contain them.

The language of the news: linguistic variation and ideological difference

We need to look at these matters in order to assess the analysis applied to the original news reports, an analysis that looked for the expression of agency, causation and interaction, and patterns of classification. If we now go back to those original reports and their analysis, we see how the contrast between the editorials is similar to the contrast between the reports. Not every feature of the editorials is there, of course, because the editorials place the events in a wider system than the report. But much is already there. Each report is consistent with its editorial – and discrepant with that of the other newspaper. The contrasts between the reports which the initial analysis pointed to, in the way summarized in the causal matrices, are consistent with the contrast between the editorials. The differences were in the presentation of the processes, both in terms of their origins or causes, and in terms of the classification of both processes and participants. In the *Sun* processes have participants as their initiators, pre-eminently the 'gangs of youths'. They are presented as the source of violence through their syntactic position as agents, through their classification as 'gangs', 'thugs'. And in the description 'rioting mob' they are presented as a problem of public order to which the police action is presented as a response, and a necessary and legitimated one. The prominence of 'riot shields' in a principal thematic position expresses both the theme of control and the fact that the increased level of police armament is still newsworthy.

The *Morning Star* report, on the other hand, presents the processes without participants, in particular those that were the occasion of the police action. This fits easily into the scheme in which the causes of such violence are social conditions, as easily and smoothly as the *Sun*'s report fits into its scheme.

It is hardly surprising that there is this conformity between reports and editorials. Although with each even there is a sequence running through news/assessment/editorial, each type of text is a permanent feature of the means for producing items for the newspaper, and a general tendency to conformity of ideology expressed at each stage, on any given subject, is to be expected.

So, despite the limitations and qualifications, the analysis of initial reports yields a great deal of information. There is in fact more that was revealed than has been discussed, since I have not paid attention to the expression of other themes which are present, such as youth and race, having concentrated on the dominant themes.

How representative were these two newspapers of responses to what happened at the end of the 1977 Notting Hill Carnival? Let us look briefly at the opening sentences of the reports in the other daily newspapers on 30 August (relying on the journalistic convention whereby these sentences summarize the 'essentials' of a story).

Daily Mail

Police with riot shields and drawn cudgels charged rampaging mobs of drink-crazed youths at the Notting Hill Carnival last night. They were met with a hail of missiles – beer bottles, cans and bricks – as they fought to clear the packed street.

Daily Mirror

Rampaging teenage gangs turned London's Notting Hill Carnival into a bloody riot last night.

Running battles broke out through the carnival area as the wreckers pelted police with bricks, stones and bottles.

Lines of officers, protected by riot shields, charged the mobs while frightened revellers cowered behind walls, sheltering little children from missiles raining down.

Daily Express

Police went into action with riot shields last night as London's Notting Hill carnival ended in fury.

Main centre of trouble was under the Westway motorway.

Police squads, after a day of keeping a low profile, made a pincer movement to round up gangs of toughs.

A fist fight turned into a running battle.

Daily Telegraph

Notting Hill's West Indian Carnival, plagued by muggings and sporadic street fighting throughout yesterday, erupted into an ugly all-out battle between the police and West Indians last night.

In the Portobello Road we saw West Indian youths – even some white youths – ripping up pavement stones and smashing them against walls to use as missiles against the police who were trying to defend themselves with riot shields.

Guardian

The violence which had been predicted and feared at the Notting Hill Carnival finally spilled over last night. Police moved in in force to the area round Acklam Road under the flyover after most of the revellers had left the Notting Hill streets.

Bottles and bricks flew throughout the air and crashed against police coaches as they tried to force their way through. Lines of police with riot shields and dustbin lids drew up in hasty formation behind their shields as they tried to dodge missiles.

Financial Times

Police resorted to riot shields last night at London's Notting Hill Carnival as sporadic incidents of violence developed after a comparatively calm day.

The Times

Tension and sporadic violence clouded the end of the Notting Hill Carnival last night.

After the violent scenes of Sunday night, when black youths looted shops and attacked white passers by, the festivities began peacefully enough, but by early evening the area . . . had again begun to simmer.

Here again there is a combination of linguistic uniformity and variation. There is near uniformity in the way most of the participants are described. But, in a way that is now familiar, the reports vary widely in the way they categorize those in conflict with the police, and the processes they are involved in. This variation is summed up in Table 10 below, with terms from the headlines (on page 119) in parentheses. Where participants involved in a process expressed in the clauses analysed are not identified, this is recorded with, ***. The newspapers can be divided into two groups, the first five in contrast to the last four, according to the patterns in their presentations of agency and classifications of processes and participants, as will be explained.

The processes involving the bottles, cans and stones are expressed in two ways: 'pelt', 'hurl', 'use as missiles' present their movement as the effects of the actions of those attacking the police, while 'hail', 'rain', 'fly' describe their movement with no reference to any external

Table 10

	Terms for the 'principal' participants	Terms for the 'focal' process	Terms for the processes involving the 'weapons'
Mail	(mobs) mobs of drink-crazed youths	(riot) rampage	( ) missiles hail
Mirror	(aggro kids) teenage gangs wreckers	(riot, wreck) bloody riot battle	( ) pelt rain
Express	(gangs) gangs of toughs	( ) running battle fury	( )
Sun	(mob) mob of black youths youths	( ) riot charge	( ) hurl
Telegraph	(Gang) West Indians West Indian youths white youths	(fury, riot) all-out battle	use as missiles
Star	(***) ****	(fighting) trouble battle	( ) hail
Guardian	(gangs) ***	(violence) violence	( ) fly
The Times	(***)[9] ***	(violence, tension) tension, sporadic violence simmer	( )
Financial Times	( ) ***	( ) sporadic incidents of violence	( )

cause. Where both forms occur, the transactive form is dominant, occurring either in a headline, or in an earlier sentence than the non-transactive form. The papers divide into two groups. In the *Mail, Mirror, Telegraph, Sun* and *Express,* the objects are described as being directed against the police by those in conflict with them (the *Express* uses 'fusillade' in the sentence following the quoted passage). In the *Guardian, Morning Star, The Times,* and *Financial Times* they are, if mentioned at all, presented as moving without external causes (in the only reference in *The Times* later, cans 'bounce off vehicles').

There is variation in several dimensions in the way the main processes are presented, and their participants. 'Tension', 'violence', 'sporadic violence', 'sporadic incidents of violence', and 'trouble' in *The Times, Financial Times, Guardian* and *Morning Star* (the same four as before, note), are terms which neither give information about the specific nature of the processes, nor have any linguistic place for mention of participants. Where the *Morning Star* uses terms involving participants – 'fighting', 'battle(field)' – participants other than the police are unidentified. The other papers have more specific descriptions of the violence, with some diversity. They draw basically on two paradigms. There is the paradigm of military conflict, with 'battle', 'charge' and 'fight' in the *Mirror, Sun, Telegraph* and *Express*, (and also the *Morning Star*) and one of uncontrolled disorder with 'riot', 'bloody riot', and 'rampage' in the *Mail, Mirror* and *Sun*. These last three newspapers are the ones in which 'mob' is used, the term for people beyond control of the civil authorities. The term 'gangs', a less specific term, can occur with a wider range of processes, including conflict as well as disorder.[10]

Apart from these themes, linguistically the most prominent, paradigms of 'race' and generation are also present in the categorizing of participants. One contains West Indian/coloured/black (adjective)/ black (noun) and the other youths/teenagers/youngsters/kids/schoolchildren/young. The relative prominence of themes alters a bit if we consider the effects on interpretation of the text of the photographs, some focusing sharply on race, and of the history of Notting Hill as the site both of black resistance to white racism in 1958 and of the yearly Carnival. While this shows a limitation of the analysis, it also underlines the ideological dominance in the verbal texts of the theme of conflict/disorder started by 'a small minority', taken still further in editorials. The full meaning of this dominance and its relation to massive state intervention in a mass black cultural event,[11] would emerge if the analysis of variation were complemented with the kind in the last chapter. So the reports are ideologically complex, showing an intersection of three basic themes – order, generation and race. It turns out that the linguistic and ideological contrasts which stood out so clearly in the *Sun* and the *Morning Star* are repeated to varying degrees in the news reports of the other daily newspapers, in a way that shows the dominance in the reporting of the one complex theme and the existence of two very different options in handling it. Although the table recording the analysis lists the terms under three separate headings, the three divisions into the same two groups of newspapers are interrelated, because the words are bound together in systems. It was this systematic nature of linguistic variation, underlying the idiom of 'speaking different languages', that was the starting point of this study. In these reports, as in the cases of the first two, the linguistic variation is neither simple nor total – it is a complex of variations expressed in a complex of 'languages', and it affects the representation of only some of the processes and participants. This complexity is important to take stock of. The grouping of the newspapers was specifically with reference to the presentation of one event, in terms of the most general concepts involved. The grouping cannot be expected to hold in the case of other events or issues – to take an obvious example, over the dispute at Grunwick the grouping was quite different, with the *Morning Star* differing radically from all the others. Second, even within the broad groupings in terms of this one theme, there were differences, because each 'event' involves the intersection of a number of aspects each perceived in different ways in different papers. These differences are already shown even in these opening fragments of the reports, and they develop with the editorials and features that followed. But this is not to lessen the significance of the grouping in the press response to this occasion, and the dominance of the one theme in organizing the perceptions.

Whether or not the editorials in the other newspapers, with their various analyses and calls to action, have that close relationship to their news reports which existed in the *Sun* and the *Morning Star* would have to be discovered by investigations of a similar kind. So too with the question of which forces and groups have their views expressed in each paper and which not. The investigation would in the end be much wider than that illustrated. Notting Hill Carnival is an annual event, but it is a subject of newspaper discourse throughout the year, with reports of negotiations over funding, organization and policing, reports of court proceedings, statements and discussions about the nature of the Carnival and anything that happens during it, including the question of relations between the police and the black community, hardly touched on in the dailies with their focus on the one weekend's Carnival. All this can interact with discourse about almost anything else that news is made of, as we have seen. Analysing the cycles and processes would show a great deal about the part the newspapers play in their society. But an adequate investigation would have to be wider still and of a different kind if it was to lead to an understanding of, say, why specific ideological formations are expressed in the newspapers, and of why certain themes are dominant in a given period. It would have to look into the ways in which forms of discourse in the newspapers are maintained, and at the relations of newspapers with other institutions and practices. Amongst other things it might help explain why the *Morning Star* has the lowest circulation of any daily newspaper, and why the *Sun* has the highest, why the combined daily circulation of the four papers which in the reporting of the events at the end of the 1977 Notting Hill Carnival expressed a predominantly 'liberal ideology of crime' is only 810,979 in the first half of 1977 and that of the other five daily newspapers is 13,949,768.[12]

Although these investigations go far beyond the scope of the analysis used in this study, we are directed to them by that analysis. At the same time the wider investigation shows the meaning of the linguistic variations and the modalities, as expressions of ideological difference and conflict, and expressions of engagement in social processes.

Summary

This chapter, like the preceding one, is a record of attempts to develop ways to apply linguistic theory as an aid to studying the ideological character of newspaper discourse. It is very much a case of work in progress.

Linguistic theory can be used in such work, because discourse[13] is a field of both ideological processes and linguistic processes, and because there is a determinate relation between these two kinds of process.

One of the premises from which such analysis begins is that social ideology or theory involves the representation of the social in terms of social entities engaged in relations and processes of action and interaction. Such representations constitute the ideological determinations of social discourse and effect a perception of the social. It is for these reasons that a linguistic analysis aimed at presenting the ideological character of discourse must be based on a linguistic theory in which the categories of process and causation are central. While any single linguistic characteristic of the presentation of process, taken by itself, does not have a determinate and unique ideological significance, there is a limit to the kinds of significance and to the sets of relations it can have with other linguistic features. The ideological character of a discourse consists in the systematic patterns and organization of linguistic characteristics of the relevant kind, including, in particular, the systematic patterns of classification of process and participants and the presentation of agency and interaction.

A second premise was that ideology is best understood not by analysis of given texts, such as articles and reports, but by analysis of the processes of which the texts are a part. Ideological or theoretical processes come into play when discourse contains material which needs explaining, interpreting, appropriating, suppressing, translating and so on. The field of analysis therefore contains sequences of texts and related discourses, representing discourse in progress. The implications of this premise include the need to make use of transformational linguistic theory, understood in a way that involves both transformations of sentences in discourse, and transformations of wordings (relexicalization). The implications also include the need for a linguistic theory of modality as an expression of the evaluation of other discourse which enters the process, and the need for a linguistic theory of textual structure in which the cohesion of a text with other discourse is expressed.

A final major premise is that ideological difference does not consist simply in variation, with the existence of separate texts and discursive practices expressing distinct ideologies. It involves also ideological conflict of various modes, which have a wide range of linguistic expression. This includes variation in wording – 'lexical variation' – because even this involves the occurrence of one option and a rejection of known alternative options. It includes the extremely important case of the *same* word being used with different meanings because it is embedded within different linguistic systems expressing different ideologies or theories. But there is also overt ideological conflict which is manifested linguistically in ways that mark terms as unacceptable, in various forms of negation and modalities of rejection and distancing. So together with the means for a linguistic description and understanding of linguistic variation, there is a need, once again, for a linguistic theory of modality taken in a wide sense which comprises all linguistic expression of attitude to, and valuation of, enunciations and their sources.

The two studies have illustrated how ideology and ideological processes are manifested as systems of linguistic characteristics and processes. At the same time it is important to remember the limitations as well as the uses of linguistic theory in this kind of work. As representations of social reality, ideologies may be inadequate to a greater or lesser degree – that is not something that linguistic analysis can determine. This was part of the reason for not making a distinction between ideology and theory within the terms of this linguistic analysis. And then while the analysis of a single report or article shows it clearly to be a part of a process, and provides pointers to directions of investigation for the understanding of those processes, it can only be a part of the research into those processes. In the cases of reporting of events like those in the Salisbury study, it is not difficult to establish if newspapers are reproducing the views of the agents of the state engaged in maintaining the existing order. In a case like the Notting Hill Carnival it is a much more complex matter needing much research to establish which combinations of forces and institutions find expression of their views in the newspapers, which have the power to make their terms stick, and the extent to which the newspapers read by most readers reproduce the official ideology of the dominant forces and play a part in the maintenance of the order of that society. Newspapers are only a part of the ideological institutions of a society, a part whose specific nature involves the fact that they are primarily concerned with making public information about what is happening (even if that is not true of all 'newspapers'). It is precisely because they have the role of providing information that they also have a major ideological role, both because all information involves theory or ideology, and because the information itself creates a constant flow of material which needs to be ideologically processed. It is for the same reason that they are sites of, and give expression to, conflicts over the terms in which information is to be formulated and social reality represented. But the part that newspapers play in their society is only partially – and often misleadingly – expressed in the discourse of newspapers.

What the linguistic analysis does offer is a reliable grasp of the ideological determinations of discourse, and it shows the marks of its engagement in social processes and of some of the dynamics and stages in the reproduction and transformation of ideology. The language used in newspapers expresses a lot more than is consciously grasped when it is read simply for information or comment. Some aspects of this have been illustrated in these studies.

8 · Newspapers and communities

BOB HODGE

The study of newspapers and other mass media involves the study of a set of interrelated communities. There is the community constituted by the act of communication, those who produce the paper and those who read it. There is also the community which the newspaper transmits or creates; the world that it records, the images of social relations and events involving people in its pages, and the community implied by this content. Finally there is what we can call the real world, the world of people and actions which are recorded, accurately or inaccurately, or ignored by the paper concerned.

Newspapers inevitably give only a partial version of the world. They select, reorder, transform, distort, and suppress, so that the final product is recognizably that paper and not another, whatever happened on the day in question. The buyers of the *Sun* know in advance what they are buying. Readers of *The Times* similarly have expectations which the paper is able to confirm, irrespective of what the world chose to do the day before. This, the real commodity that keeps the readership loyal, is more than a distinctive style of presenting common material. It is a structure that pre-exists the specific content. This structure causes systematic bias of content, but more importantly it is itself a content. Each individual copy confirms a version of the world, or demonstrates a capacity to assimilate events which could challenge that version.

Analysis of newspapers needs to take account of the three kinds of community involved. The paper contains a version of the social world, but we can only understand the significance of this world if we can relate it to the world it claims to refer to, and if we know whose this version of the world is, and whom it is for. If we restrict ourselves to mass-circulation newspapers in England, we can make an initial distinction between the so-called quality papers and the popular press. Both kinds of paper are owned by members of the same class, and journalists who work for both are predominantly middle class, but the quality papers are aimed at readers in the higher categories of the registrar-general's scale, whereas the popular dailies find their readers more from the lower end of the scale. So we can hypothesize that the world offered in the qualities is internal to a class, written by members of the class for members of that class, while the world of the popular press is sold to members of one class by members of another. We shall see that this hypothesis has to be modified in light of the complexity of the social relationships involved, but the distinction it makes remains well founded.

There are three basic ways of arriving at the underlying structure or ideology of a paper. One would be to ask the editor what he thought it was, and hope that he told the truth and nothing but the truth; or look at the instructions or guidelines that maintain the editorial policy in practice. Another would be to start from the world of events, and trace the process of transmutation stage by stage to its final form in the paper. The third starting point for analysis would be with the finished product, the newspaper itself, attempting to work back to the underlying categories.

In chapter 6 the starting point was the original event, tracing its fate over time in different newspapers. In this chapter I will mainly explore the third strategy, which starts from the text of the paper itself. A simple form of analysis along these lines consists of content analysis, counting the occurrences of individual words or kinds of item. This kind of analysis allows quantitative treatment of the data, which can be extremely convincing. However, content analysis on its own tends to pick up only surface qualities. The structures at issue can be realized by particular surface forms, but they are essentially abstract, often unstated and unconscious. The class of content they project may only be recognized as a class after the nature of the structure itself has been grasped.

As a first account of the structure of the presented world of a paper, we can take the main categories of item in the two kinds of paper. The *Sun*, as a typical example of a popular paper, has news (home and foreign, concerning public and private figures), advertisements, editorial and cultural comment, letters to the editor, cartoons, jokes and comics, and sport. *The Times* has a greater range of news items, with more foreign news, including West European and Overseas, and a business section. It has no jokes or comics. Otherwise its categories appear to be the same.

In spite of this similarity there is an important difference in the mode of existence of these categories. *The Times* gives many headings for classes of items: Home news, Overseas news, etc. The *Sun* has items in these categories, but generally does not refer to the categories themselves. Sport is clearly labelled. Otherwise the different kinds of item are intermingled on a page, with no formal indications as to how they are categorized. This means that the structuring principle is invisible in the *Sun*, where it is overt and visible in *The Times*. So the categories are demonstrable and conscious in the quality paper, but implicit in the popular paper. There is one important exception to this rule. Popular papers normally distinguish between editorial and other material: quality papers do not. The *Sun*'s editorial is headed *The Sun says*. *The Times* has no distinct heading for its editorial comment. The other quality papers follow *The Times*'s format here, while the other popular papers are like the *Sun* (*Mirror comment, Daily Mail comment, Daily Express opinion*, with the Communist *Morning Star* following the same style, *We say*). The fact that the distinction does not appear on the surface implies one of two contradictory situations: either that the distinction does not or may not exist for at least some readers, or that it exists so strongly that it need not be mentioned. Conversely, the fact that it does appear could imply that at least some readers would not be able to distinguish between fact and opinion without this help. *The Times* can do without a heading *The Times says* because it can trust its readers to make the necessary distinction.

The world that is offered by a newspaper as an adequate image of the real world is what it includes in the category of news. There is a marked discrepancy between the *Sun*'s and *The Times*'s coverage of events. The *Sun* prints a claim that its coverage is comprehensive by definition: *If its news it's in the Sun if its news it's*. . . . However, there is no distinct section for foreign or overseas news, and only a low number of items of either kind, compared with *The Times*. The stories that do appear usually involve an explicit mention of a British interest, often embodied in particular individuals who are participants in the event. Taking the *Sun* of 30 August 1977 as a representative example, there are only three stories that refer to events outside Britain (or England): an attempt to steal Elvis Presley's body from its mausoleum, a story about Ian Smith's rejection of Dr Owen's peace proposals, and a story on how *Spanish spivs sting British tourists*. For the *Sun* reader, the world outside Britain hardly exists, except in the columns of the sporting pages.

The Times, in contrast, has a large and differentiated category of news. It distinguishes between home news, West European news and overseas news, each section containing more items than the total news coverage of the *Sun*. The reader of *The Times* lives in a

Britain which is part of a large and complex international community in which events can be of significance to British readers even if they do not directly involve Britons as participants. The majority of the stories in the overseas and foreign news sections do not mention Britain or individual Britons.

A representative sample of foreign news coverage in *The Times* is page 4 for 30 August 1977. The stories, with their country of reference where necessary, are:

1 French ready to tackle their problems again after six week holiday.
2 Bonn concerned at its image abroad.
3 Friuli inquiry into corruption allegations (Italy).
4 Industrialist's wife seized and villa looted (Italy).
5 RAF team wins Rhine raft race.
6 Anarchists end hunger strike (W. Germany).
7 Three dead and 50 wounded as Italian hunt opens.
8 Tension over deputies' cancelled trip to Potsdam (W. Germany).
9 Whites and blacks differ radically on reason for Rhodesia conflict.
10 President Tito wants troops out of S. Korea.
11 Treason trial Ugandans all admit guilt, Kampala says.
12 Philippines wary of foreign interference.
13 Peking pays late tribute to victim of radicals.
14 Mr Kruger denies threat to close African newspaper.
15 Moscow–US accord on stopping bomb test.
16 Attempt to steal Elvis Presley body.
17 Mother wins back son in US court.
18 Georgia trial raises issue of racial oppression.
19 100 countries to discuss plan for desert dwellers.

Only one of these stories, the Presley item, appeared in the corresponding issue of the *Sun*. Eleven of the nineteen stories come from agency sources, which the staff of the *Sun* must have had available to them. Their absence from the *Sun*, then, has followed an editorial decision not to include them, which is equivalent to suppressing them for readers of that paper.

The sentences quoted are especially significant for the analysis of the basic structures which constitute the form of the newspaper concerned. These are headlines which attempt to concentrate the essence of the story that follows. The language of headlines has some conventions of its own, and there are some systematic discrepancies between what is said in them and what is possible in the body of the article. Even so, the structure of these sentences is one definitive image of the structure of the presented world.

Events typically consist of actions and participants, the participants being active or passive in relation to the action. Corresponding to this structure of the event is the typical structure of a sentence about events in English, which consists of verbs, plus nouns which refer to actors or affected participants. From a scanning of the sentences quoted, a number of generalizations emerge. The sentences are predominantly active (seventeen active, two passive). The active form typically keeps the focus on actors rather than those affected. This is a world where actors are in the foreground. The events described are either public acts, involving public persons, or persons who are only known because of the newsworthy incident they are involved in. In these sentences, the examples of public actions involving public figures predominate (fifteen to four). All items imply conflict, antagonism or violence. However, the verbs or words which indicate actions are mostly not physical process verbs, but speech acts or the expression of attitudes through speech. 'Bonn *concern*', 'Philippines *wary*', '*tension* over deputies' cancelled trip', 'President Tito *wants*', become news as a result of an official statement. 'Mr Kruger *denies threat*', 'Ugandans all *admit* guilt, Kampala *says*', '100 countries to *discuss* plan', 'Peking pays late *tribute*', 'Moscow–US *accord*' are all speech acts which are regarded as newsworthy.

We can summarize the basic rules of this world as follows.

1. Public persons say and tell, they do not otherwise act and are not acted on.
2. Private persons only exist if they are the subject or object of violent action, but what they say or feel does not exist as news.
3. The world outside Britain is unrelievedly a world of conflict, usually between states, or within states, or between governments and subversive forces, such as traitors, guerillas, anarchists, or (purged) radicals. The conflict is sometimes resolved, temporarily at least, but is more usually the motive for the reported action.
4. Since they are mediated through public persons, conflicts exist mainly through statements and attitudes.

5 Since public figures predominate over private, words and feelings predominate over actions.

There is one interesting class of agent that we have not yet considered. This is the syntactic form whereby a town or country acts as subject for a verb of saying or feeling: Bonn, Kampala, Moscow, Peking. This is not simply the old rhetorical figure of personification, since in all cases there is an identifiable human source of the statement, an individual spokesman or a group issuing the communiqué. Where the country or city is given as agent in the headline or first paragraph, there is often a named spokesman later in the story. This is a substitution process, whereby a certain kind of individual can be replaced by nouns referring to larger abstract entities. The effect is to identify official representatives totally with the state they represent, giving an image of the state as a single individual who acts through these representatives. The basis of the transformational process is an ideological construct, a model of the power structures of all such states. The capital stands for the whole country, as though there is a total identification of interests between the administrative centre and the different regions under the control of that administration. The government similarly is conceived of as a collective entity, which can be fully embodied in nominated spokespersons, as though there is no conflict within the government structure, and no opposition outside to take account of. Both these simple ideological versions of political reality are then related by analogy, so that the relation between capital and country is equivalent to the relation between spokesman and government.

This complex analogical structure must be understood if the reader is to translate the verbal formula. Consequently, an ideological structure is a precondition for interpretation of particular stories cast in this form. This structure strongly emphasizes consensus. However, the form can be used when the reality reported implies conflict. Headline 11 has 'Kampala says' and 'Ugandans admit guilt' in the same headline. The story refers to the trial of Ugandans opposed to the Amin regime, an indication of conflict. At the time, relations were strained between the British and Ugandan governments, but the Ugandan government is given an ideological form which implies its identification with the country as a whole, whereas the opponents of the government are in the plural, 'Ugandans'. In other cases, a similar opposition exists but less starkly. The reader of such reports gets a compound image containing both conflict and consensus, where consensus prevails totally within a government collective which engages as a single entity in conflict with forces outside itself.

The reader of *The Times* is made aware of a broad world which contains many countries. Events and news from these countries are collected together on a single page, with no explicit causal links to relate the stories or countries. With political stories, the link is a common structure, relating a class of agents to a class of actions. The unity of the presented world is given through analogy, a common structure which is replicated endlessly in story after story, day after day, a narrative of confrontations between supra-individual entities and a hydraheaded opponent, which is waged through language acts; communiqués, statements, accords, threats, denials, discussions.

If this is the world of *The Times* reader, we can ask what its relationship is to the reality of their social existence. The readers of *The Times* belong primarily to the managerial and professional strata, the AB categories in the registrar-general's scale. These are 'top people'. However, they are in general not as important as the people whose words and feelings are reported in *The Times*: prime ministers, presidents, cabinet ministers, judges, etc. The readers have economic power, but the main criterion of importance in the world of the overseas news section is political power. Where persons they could identify with are mentioned in the sample quoted, as in items 1, 4 and 7, they are slightly ridiculous (the French bourgeoisie and the Italian hunters), or a victim, or as in item 4 the husband of a victim. The presented world, that is, disconfirms the value of people like themselves, offering instead images of highly cohesive state power locked in inconclusive struggle with a protean enemy. It is not an encouraging picture. In outline it is reminiscent of the staple media product in *1984*, with its bewildering repetition of heroic struggles and infrequent victories.

If we asked what, as 'top people', they could gain from such coverage of world affairs, the answer must be: ideology. The major source of news items is from statements by official spokesmen. Naturally these will be giving the official view, what the government, department or agency would like people to think. Any one who based his judgements about what has happened or will happen on this material alone would often be misled. To take just one example from this page, 'Mr Kruger denies threat to close African newspaper'. Kruger's denial was presumably a fact, but within weeks of this announcement there was, as another fact, the announcement of the closure of the paper which Kruger had denied would occur. The public statement on this occasion was a reliable guide to what would happen only for the reader who realized that it indicates the opposite. The headline contains both 'denies' and 'threat'. The shrewd reader would realize that if Kruger denies a threat, people must have suspected him of making one. So the headline, and the accompanying story, is a contradiction with two meanings, one for the naive reader, who might take Kruger's denial at its face value, and the other the inverse for the reader who sees through the official statement to the disguised indication of official attitudes. In both cases the primary activity for the reader is an ideological exercise. In the first, the reader is taken in by the ideology, in the second the reader is set the task of decoding an official pronouncement to guess at the underlying reality. For someone who can do *The Times* crossword the task would present no great difficulties.

Page 2 of the *Sun* for 30 August contains almost all the domestic and foreign news in the paper, apart from the coverage of the Notting Hill 'riot' which is the main page 1 story. The headlines on page 2 are:

1 Smith kills off Owen bid
2 Airports face shut down over a lockout threat
3 Riddle of cut-price butter
4 Spanish spivs sting British tourists
5 Two stabbed on waterfront
6 Slash VAT to create jobs, says union boss
7 Cheers! Ron is back

On the same page is the editorial 'The Sun says: these sick doctors chill the spine', referring to Soviet psychiatrists. Three of the news items refer to overseas affairs, four if we include the editorial. Only one refers to the kind of political event that provides *The Times* staple. Domestic news predominantly involves conflict between labour and unions (items 2, 6 and 7) but there is also the report on the waterfront incident. The number of items is too small to establish any positive generalization, but is large enough to show what distinctions do *not* apply. In this case, there is evidently no distinction made between public and private, foreign and domestic.

The style of these headlines, and the articles that follow, is recognizably different from that of *The Times*. This style is often referred to as 'sensationalism'. We can see what linguistic processes are involved by analysing the first headline, 'Smith kills off Owen bid'. The article itself expands this, describing a statement by Ian Smith, prime minister of Rhodesia, which the report claims is a response to a proposal that Dr Owen, the British Foreign Minister, was going to make. So the headline is a translation into a vivid, sensational style of a sentence like 'Smith rejects Owen's proposed scheme in advance'. Similarly VAT is to be 'slashed' and British tourists are 'stung'. The two youths who were stabbed on the waterfront, as reported on this page, were linguistically in good company.

The key to this style is a systematic transformation of speech acts into physical acts of a direct and often violent kind. There is considerable loss arising from this process of transformation. In this case, 'in advance' could not be represented at all. The original sentence, which was presumably in front of the *Sun* editorial staff, involved a complicated relationship between two acts which occurred at different times and places. In place of this, the *Sun* has a single physical event which occurs at the one place and time. In *The Times*, the reader is presented with a world composed largely of speech events, but these events are reported directly, and they proceed from people or institutions with real power, who can make things happen. So the world of speech acts and the world of physical actions is causally related, by a complex chain. In the *Sun*, a small selection of these speech acts is presented, but transformed into analogous physical acts, thereby destroying the complex relation of these speech acts to each other and to the world of physical action.

This involves doublethink in two ways. The surface form, with its image of simple violence, is interpreted by most readers as equivalent to the cooler, more rational sentence 'Smith rejects Owen's bid', but the reader is still insistently given both versions. A common syntactic form is used for the two kinds of action, the actions of prime ministers and other public figures, and the criminals whose exploits are reported on the same page. In this form, public individuals and institutions are shown wreaking mayhem and havoc on entities like 'bids' and 'VAT'. On its front page in this issue, the *Sun* had deplored violence at the Notting Hill carnival, yet the habitual forms of the language it uses when reporting political news express extreme violence, directed by privileged political figures against abstract entities. This leaves the political figures ambiguous. What are we to think of Smith the killer, or slasher Basnett, the union leader of item 6 ? Do we deplore the violence, or identify with the violent ? After all, the violence is not real. No one seems to have been hurt. Feelings of anger and frustration that are felt by many workers in the face of bureaucracy and management seem here to be given a legitimated expression, transposed onto these figures from public life. Where the main agents in the world of *The Times* are ideally powerful and responsible, the agents in this world are presented as ideally violent and irresponsible.

The bulk of the stories in the *Sun* and other such papers are human interest stories. The majority of these involve sex and violence, often death. The relationships between the persons described are usually amoral, and often violent, involving an aggressor and a victim; 'Nurse raped in hostel terror', 'Towering inferno "fiend" kills boy', etc. The participants usually include a victim and an aggressor, and often the police. The society imaged is the society of the police courts, a society of maniacs, perverts and victims, sometimes but not invariably reduced to order by the law, but only after the event. It is this basic structure which provides the syntactic models for stories about both political and domestic events, except that the law will not arrest Smith for killing Owen's bid.

We can ask, as we did with *The Times*, what is the relation of this presented world to the typical social experience of *Sun* readers? These readers are spread across the social range, according to market surveys, but are predominantly law-abiding citizens, workers and housewives. To use Freud's terms, *The Times* is a world of super-ego figures, where the *Sun* is a world of figures from the id, gratifying primitive impulses without restraint, though not always without punishment. The socially weak can gain brief fame or notoriety and occupy the same page as the great by repudiating the norms of society. People of the same socio-economic status as the majority of readers of the paper, who follow the same code of behaviour and with whom they could identify most directly, appear only as victims. One effect of this is to make political understanding unthinkable. The formula continually invokes habitual mechanisms of self-repression, since the impulses indulged in by the inhabitants of this world are what must be repressed by adults in their normal social relations at work and at home. This gives psychological force to two valuations, a strongly negative judgment on illegitimate expressions of these impulses, and an intense identification with expressions which have been legitimated. The result is a highly charged form of false consciousness, a split consciousness where solidarity is felt towards amoral ruling class figures, and morality is concentrated against aberrant members of the general public.

The split consciousness is particularly clear with the page 3 pin-up.

This is usually a bare-breasted girl, with a punning caption and brief article. Attached to the picture on 30 August is the heading 'Janet is a home lover', with a description below of how Janet likes to go for walks near her home in Kent. The article is carefully trivial, reinforcing the innocent interpretation of 'home lover', so that the erotic interpretation exists only in the mind of the reader, who can pretend he has not seen it. A split in the consciousness of the reader corresponds to the split between picture and text. A split of this kind is repeated in the relationship between this item and what surrounds it. The pin-up, picture plus article, is on the same double-page spread as the main foreign news coverage and the editorial. The reader becomes a voyeur pretending to be a serious student of world affairs, or a serious student trying not to be distracted by irrelevant sexuality.

The same principle applies on a minor scale to the relationship between headlines and first paragraph and main text. The first paragraph typically translates the headline into more elaborate syntax. For example

POLICE PROBE THE FATE OF TOP TORY'S PETS

Police are investigating the agonising deaths from poisoning of three pet dogs owned by Tory Shadow Minister Michael Heseltine and his family. (*Sun* 13 Jan. 1978)

The language of headlines in papers like the *Sun* has a number of rules. The tense is the universal present – the past tense is never used with main verbs. The singular is used whenever possible ('fate', for 'deaths', and 'top Tory' for 'Heseltine and his family') and the sentence is simple, with one main verb and no participial phrases or subordinate clauses. This linguistic form necessarily filters out all complexity from the presented world. But the reader of the *Sun* has two versions of the world offered: the world of the headlines, and the world of the article, which is more complex though still simplified compared to *The Times*.

These two versions coexist on the page, but we can ask whether it is certain that they exist equally for all readers. Most people interpret the content of newspapers as though everything in them is read by a single reader with perfect comprehension. In practice, a paper will have many kinds of reader with different levels of reading ability, habitually reading different parts of the paper. The language of *Sun* headlines is much simpler than the language of the articles that follow them. The different kinds of text could correspond to different kinds of consciousness in the same reader, or to the consciousness of different readers. The page, and the paper as a whole, is stratified in a way that potentially mirrors a stratification in the readership. However, any such stratification among the readers is concealed by the fact that all kinds of text are included within a single copy of the paper, which could be read by a single reader. This becomes a persuasive ideological image of social harmony, since the coexistence of different kinds of text in a single community can be seen directly, unlike the diversity of acts of reading among five million readers.

The *Sun* and *The Times* aim at different readerships, and this affects the worlds they present and the way they present them, but both are examples of the capitalist press, owned and written by members of the same class. To test how far a real alternative is possible we need to consider examples of the radical left-wing press, papers like the *Morning Star* and *Socialist Worker* which express the viewpoint of the Communist Party and the International Socialists respectively.

The world presented in these papers is smaller than *The Times* with fewer items of foreign news. Like the *Sun*, they essentially present an image of English society to English readers. Within this world the relationships are typically of an antagonistic kind. Most items report some confrontation or contradiction. The confrontation normally entails at least one group, which is undifferentiated, its members without individuality, but acting as a single entity. One linguistic signal for this is the use of plural subjects with verbs that refer to a single action. One typical story from *Socialist Worker* of 4 September 1976 is:

Scroungers: the ones they ignore . . . and the one they hounded to the grave. Alfred Slim was just the sort of man impartial British newspapers love to get their teeth into.

Another is

Shamin will stay, say 2000 Asians

The front page story is:

P.M. Jim Callaghan was given what a Glasgow newspaper called 'his roughest ride yet' last week.
He couldn't move without coming face to face with angry workers.
Hoping for a quieter time, Sunny Jim travelled to Edinburgh.
There too, crowds of unemployed workers demonstrated against him.

We can make some initial generalizations about the syntactic forms here.

1 Plural nouns are typically the subjects of active transitive verbs (e.g. 'they ignore', 'they hounded', 'newspapers love').

2 Verbs with a plural subject imply a single action (e.g. 'they hounded', 'say 2000 Asians').

3 Singular nouns in sentences describing actions are the object of the action in transitive forms (e.g. 'the one they hounded', 'teeth into (Alfred Slim)', 'Callaghan was given'). Only intransitive sentences have singular subjects (e.g. 'Shamin will stay', 'he couldn't move').

4 The actions described are predominantly non-physical, as in *The Times*, but the surface forms often present these as physical actions of a violent kind, as in the *Sun* (e.g. 'hounded', 'get their teeth into', 'roughest ride').

5 The transitive sentences all describe antagonistic relationships, in which the antagonists come from a different class.

This is a world where groups are cohesive entities which are the main source of effective action. Individuals are passive or affect no one but themselves, even if they are prime minister. The underlying form for sentences and stories is given by a proposition about the class war, which has the ruling class fighting the working class. Particular forms of story and sentences are then generated by particular substitutions. Individuals or groups can substitute for one of the contending classes, with individuals able to fit in to the structure only as objects, never as agents. The struggle can be waged through speech acts, through newspaper campaigns, petitions or demonstrations, with direct physical actions simply re-inforcing the message.

This rudimentary grammar corresponds closely to the radical ideology of a paper like *Socialist Worker* and the strategy forced on a revolutionary workers' party in Britain if it is to remain within the law. The version of society it transmits is not dissimilar to that of *The Times*. Both are concerned with groups rather than individuals, seeing a cohesive ruling group permanently locked in struggle with a group challenging its power. In *The Times* the particular struggle can be within the ruling group, or between competing ruling groups, whereas the two classes are totally cohesive in *Socialist Worker*. As a matter of emphasis, *The Times* focus is more on the actions/pronouncements of ruling groups, where *Socialist Worker* more often reports the activity of militant workers, and presents attitudes on both sides as more aggressive and destructive.

The rhetorical style of *Socialist Worker* has more in common with the *Sun* than *The Times*, especially with regard to two features. Both translate speech acts into equivalent violent actions, and both focus on individual instances. However, the *Sun* claims to deplore actual violence although it exploits it as a major source of stories and style. Physical violence for *Socialist Worker* is continuous with other forms. It is equivalent to the legal violence exercised by management against workers, and a natural expression of working class anger and frustration, so the rhetorical feature expresses a basic commitment in a radical analysis of social relations. And though *Socialist Worker* gives individual cases, the individual is always clearly identified with a group involved in conflict with another group, and the political basis of the struggle is made evident, whereas in the *Sun*, political relations are represented as personal relations between irrational individuals. In *Socialist Worker*, the larger explanation is ever present, in the *Sun* it is disguised and made inaccessible.

In all three kinds of paper, the particular item of news is unimportant compared to the ideological structure realized through it. The details reported may be accurate – life is diverse enough to provide incidents which could support a range of stereotypes – and ingenious inventions like Winston Smith's creation of Comrade Ogilvy will usually be unnecessary. Within a day or two the details will be forgotten anyway, and all that will remain is the underlying form, reinforced by countless examples seeming to guarantee its truth.

The *Socialist Worker* ideology would be called radical not only because it insistently interprets actions and events in terms of a class struggle. The ideology also involves a set of values, a commitment to the working class and a repudiation of capitalism. There are a number of words in English as in other languages which carry strong positive or negative associations. We might expect *Socialist Worker* to rely heavily on these. There are some of these, but typically they do not simply underline the message. Take the article about Alfred Slim. 'Scroungers', 'hound', and 'get their teeth into' are all negatively charged words. 'Impartial' is positively charged. However, in the article, 'scroungers' is used to refer to tax-dodgers among the wealthy and to Alfred Slim, a worker who was called that because he was unable to work owing to an undiagnosed illness. 'Impartial' refers to the newspapers which have shown obvious partiality in their judgments, according to the article. 'Hound' and 'get their teeth into' are used of the press, their negative implications not challenged in the text.

This sounds arbitrary and confusing, but the text itself would not give a confusing impression to regular readers of the paper. They would understand that Alfred Slim was to be seen as an innocent victim of a press campaign, with the rich tax-dodgers and the press as the real villains. 'Scroungers', and 'impartial' would be interpreted sarcastically, but 'hound' and 'get their teeth into' are straightforward in their implications. The selective inversion of valency relies on two cues. Particular individuals (e.g. Callaghan) and types of institution (e.g. the major newspapers) and anyone identified as a capitalist or right wing, or as a worker, carry automatic valuations. Second, there is a set of value terms which is associated with the enemy as their distinctive vocabulary. These words are treated as quotations from a hostile group whose valuations are to be interpreted in the light of that hostility. With 'impartial', the process is relatively simple. They call themselves 'impartial', a claim which can be simply inverted. 'Scrounger' is used twice. Applied to Slim, it is as exactly wrong as 'impartial': Slim was not a scrounger in any sense, he was a sick man, according to the article. Used of the wealthy tax-dodgers, it works differently. It accepts the basic meaning plus evaluation, that people who receive money from the state and do not work for it are contemptible, but it applies it to a kind of person who would not be described as a scrounger, because working class (and not managerial class) is part of the meaning of the word as normally used.

The two kinds of cue plus the content of the article are complementary, so that only one set of evaluations will work for the article. The process of decoding is not entirely dependent on previous or even present sympathies. The article would not make much sense unless the necessary inversions are carried out. However, a general grasp of the two kinds of cue is probably indispensable for easy comprehension of the article. Since these cues are not always indicated on the surface but are indispensable to interpretation, they have to be activated by the reader, continually reinforced in the act of reading. The two actions performed by the reader are an invariable classification of all participants into the two categories, ally or enemy, and an ideological reprocessing of an alien vocabulary, in effect a training in how to see through the language of the enemy. In keeping with this aspect of the language is the frequent use of quotation. One example is the quotation attributed to an unnamed

Glasgow newspaper. The device here has the effect of reinforcing the judgment, not inverting it, since 'a Glasgow newspaper' is understood to be a hostile source which would therefore be likely to understate Callaghan's discomforture. The process of quotation, actual or putative, is pervasive. It is a possible strategy because the community of readers of *Socialist Worker* can be relied on to be sufficiently cohesive to be able to apply the right judgments and resist the wrong ones.

A paper like the *Sun*, with its large and diverse community, cannot make as many assumptions about the judgments its readers will bring to bear. When it wishes to communicate a judgment, it has to do it explicitly, using enough value-laden terms to make its point of view inescapable. For instance, in the issue of 4 September 1976 there is a front-page report of a speech by Tony Benn, the left-wing Labour MP, which included some comments hostile to the BBC. This speech is referred to in the report as 'an astonishing attack', 'his extraordinary charge'. Although Benn is normally reported in a hostile way in the *Sun*, the editors cannot rely on that as an implicit judgment. As well as the evaluation included in the report, there is an editorial comment alongside the article, saying:

The Sun says
What a load of Benn bunk.
From Mr Tony Benn, Bachelor of Bunkum, comes the maddest attack yet on the freedom of the B.B.C.

This judgment has had to be made so insistently because the community of readers of the *Sun* is not constituted by a set of common values as is the case with *Socialist Worker*. Nor is there a recognizable opposing community whose existence helps to define and sustain the boundaries of the paper's community.[1] *The Times* relates to a more cohesive community, and can leave its judgments more implicit than can a popular paper. But neither paper quotes an antagonistic community as frequently as does *Socialist Worker*. *The Times*, when reporting industrial matters, typically does not quote non-standard English. Words like 'black' as in 'black bans', which are marked as the language of unions, are usually given in inverted commas, to indicate that they are not assimilated into the language used by the paper, and are to be associated with a particular source, with all that that association implies. This trait is similar in function, though on a reduced scale, to the persistent use of implicit or explicit quotation by *Socialist Worker*.

The relation of papers like *Socialist Worker* and the *Sun* to their respective communities of readers is different, but in both cases it is a dynamic relationship. *Socialist Worker* takes for granted a set of commitments which it reinforces through practice, and tries to make the reader more actively involved in the movement. There are frequent imperatives addressed to the reader: 'Join the march', 'Join the lobby', 'fight racialism' etc. The *Sun* uses imperatives also, in the paper itself (e.g. 'Vote! vote! vote! for your TV star of the year', which was opposite the Benn article on the front page) and in advertisements: 'Rush your order now!' or 'Act now! Post today to . . .' or 'Examine it free for 10 days', etc. With imperatives, there are always two kinds of act, and two sources of activity. Both papers issue imperatives, where the agency for the action remains in the control of any reader who chooses to perform the action, to become the deleted 'you' left blank by the paper. But the nature of the command is different between the two papers. The *Sun* reader will be rewarded for obedience by possessions. The *Socialist Worker* reader is required to become part of a collective social agency, rather than an individual private agent who can perform the required action from his or her own home.

An analysis of the kind done in this chapter may seem condemned to triviality, emphasizing as it does style over content, habitual forms over actual lies, and a phantasmagorical world over the real one. But style carries a content that is more potent for seeming trivial and being habitual. Reading is a complex act which relies on a set of assumptions and attitudes working automatically and unconsciously, the preconditions for interpretation which are continually being reinforced. The truth or falsity of particular items is not as important as the kind of consciousness the paper forms, the version of social reality it mediates, and the community it creates to incorporate its readers. In *1984* Winston knows that the state-controlled media engage in massive falsification, but the point of that enterprise is not to evade particular facts that would be damaging to the rulers. No fact would be damaging enough or not assimilable into the predetermined structures of the ideology. The main function of the media is to unite the citizens of Oceania into a cohesive community that will be unable to contemplate a challenge to its rulers. The media are stratified to correspond to divisions in the society, and each stratum is offered the version of the world which contributes to its inability to perceive its real condition and fundamental interests. Britain is not a totalitarian society and its press is not organized from a single centre. Papers like *Socialist Worker* exist to focus an alternative community and articulate an alternative ideology. But the basic premises of Orwell's satire still apply. The structure of society is the key to the structure of the media, and media distortion is most debilitating when it affects the grounds of political and social thinking.

9 · Birth and the community

BOB HODGE

---

*The sex impulse was dangerous to the Party, and the Party
had turned it to account. They had played a similar trick
with the instinct of parenthood.*

(1984)

Winston here is indignant with what he sees as the Party's perversion
of the natural impulses of sexuality and parenthood, as though all
previous societies had respected the sanctity of these ties, and never
presumed to intrude into this most sacred of relationships. But the
1984 vision of total penetration of the family unit by the Party is only
an extreme and melodramatic version of what the majority of
societies have always done, our own society included. Social control
of sexuality and parenthood is ubiquitous. Society normally assumes
the right to determine the conditions of the major biological events
in an individual's life, birth, copulation, procreation, death. Typically, societies have ways of representing these biological turning
points in the lives of individuals to give them a social meaning, as a
way of asserting social control.

Birth is the first such turning point in the life of an individual. The
birth of a child is an important event for itself, but the infant is
beyond the reach of language. Social recognition and representation
of birth, bestowed by language and by other signifying systems, is
primarily concerned with the significance of this event for others.
There are rituals associated with this event in earlier societies.[1] Even
in our own secular society there are ritual-like acts associated with
this event, as with the other major turning points in human life. One
such act is the registration of the birth. In Britain, every child is
required by law to be registered in the Register of Births. This is not
merely a symbolic act. The Register is an instrument of control, an
assertion of society's legal responsibility for the individual. With
this public record of the birth, infanticide or the elimination of the
individual becomes more readily detectable. A copy of the relevant
entry is often required as proof of identity in later life.

The act of registration seems minimal and the form itself sparse and without significance. However, even the bleak impersonality of it communicates a meaning, and its particular features densely code a whole set of assumptions about social relations. Analysis of the form can reveal these assumptions in their full complexity.

The document which can be obtained for every birth is B. Cert/ R.B.D. This is a sheet of paper which has three distinguishable kinds of print or type on it. Most of the form is printed in a red ink, and applies to the whole of the United Kingdom. Blanks are left for the Registration district and sub-district, where a stamp is generally used. Blanks are also left for the details of the child, which are typed in, and there is space for a signature, in ink, by the Registrar. The different kinds of print demarcate a three-tier structure which is an image of social relations in Britain. The largest unit, determining the form generally, is the nation, the United Kingdom. The next level down, totally determined by the larger unit, is the district and sub-district. The next level is the family, consisting of the child and its parents, which has a fixed and predetermined place in this whole structure. The greatest scope for individuality is the right of the Registrar, whose signature is as personal and idiosyncratic as he or she wishes.

The syntax of the form is typical of government forms generally, but is no less significant for being so representative. There are only three full sentences:

1 I, [blank] Registrar of Births and Deaths for the sub-district of [blank], in the [blank] do hereby certify that this is a true copy of the entry no. [blank] in the Register of Births for the said sub-district, and that such Register is now legally in my custody.
2 Witness my hand this [blank] day of [blank] 19 [blank].
3 Any person who (1) falsifies any of the particulars on this certificate, or (2) uses a falsified certificate as true, knowing it to be false, is liable to prosecution.

Sentences with main verbs are the most direct way of representing events in English. In the language of this certificate, there is only one kind of action that is represented in full sentence form, actions associated with the function of the Registrar. In sentence 1, the Registrar is the sole agent. In the second, he issues a command to the witness. In the third, there is reference to two other categories of person, the falsifier, who is essentially an anti-registrar, someone who registers (but inaccurately and without authority), and the user of this hypothetical falsified certificate. So, for the person who receives a certificate, the only way to become an active agent in the language of certificates is to become an accomplice of the falsifier.

The bulk of the certificate consists of entries in ten columns, each with a heading. Many of these headings are nouns which have been transformed from verbs, which in turn come from full sentence forms in which various acts of people are described. What has happened is that these actions have been turned into the basis for classification of the child, who performs no act itself except to be classified. The entry contains the following headings:

No.

when and where born

name, if any

sex

name and surname of father

name, surname and maiden name of mother

occupation of father

signature, description, and residence of informant

when registered

signature of registrar

name entered after registration

Even here, many of the actions that have been turned into nouns are associated with the act of registration: signing, informing, registering, signing by the registrar, entering a name after the registrar has registered. The first seven categories are concerned to classify the child, to fix its identity, but the last four in effect classify the classification.

The first entry is the number, which is sufficient guarantee of the child's individuality. This, of course, is the number of the entry, not of the child. The next category gives 'when and where born'. This order departs from the normal English preference for indicating place before time. The formula for letters is to put address first, then date. Newspaper articles referring to foreign news follow the same convention: 'Salisbury, 13 Jan', 'New York 20 Feb', etc. But with birth, it is more important to be precise about time than place.

The next five categories give what are the sufficient classifications of the child. We can assume then that they are the decisive categories for this society. First, but optionally, is the first name. Later the child will refer to this name as 'his' (or 'her') name, as though it was its own, but the certificate acknowledges that the assigning of a name is the right of the parents. This is the handle by which the individual will be appropriated and controlled by his or her immediate society. The 1953 act could have required parents to make a decision on the name at the same time as registering the birth, but did not. Parents, after all, must have some rights.

The name is followed by the sex of the child, and these are followed by the name and surname of the father, then the name, surname and maiden name of the mother. This all directly reflects expectations about sex roles in society. The priority of the male is indicated twice in the entry, by his coming first, the practical justification for this being that the child will naturally take his name, and by the mother being doubly classified, with surname and maiden name. The assumption clearly is that the parents are married, and that the father is the socially significant parent. So it is his occupation which gives the social class of the infant, and is the only entry which allows such classification.

If any of these expectations is not met – if the parents are not married, or the father is not known, or unemployed or a professional criminal, for instance – it is possible to fill out the form, but the result is to be forced to declare the aberration, and to make this aberration a permanent, official part of the very identity of the child. This constitutes a pressure on the parents to conform to their prescribed roles, to be normal for their child's sake if not their own.

The certificate is a precise and effective ideological instrument. It coercively transmits a model of family relationships, and represents the individuals associated with the particular birth as stereotypes with predetermined roles and functions. It presents a world in which the only person apparently capable of acting is the registrar, though he is a social individual who is replicated throughout the British Isles. It is a world in which the main activity seems to be administrative, consisting essentially of acts of classification and certification. What is being classified is a human being with basic human needs and feelings, the product of human sexuality and dependent on others to feed and support it. But these needs and feelings and the activities that are associated with them are only present in this world in a transformed guise, as the basis of classification rather than activities as such. The exclusion of this whole side of the process at issue is systematic and thorough, though not total. Sexuality enters through the categories of father and mother, who are the biological parents, and work enters through the category of occupation – of the father. The occupation of the mother, presumably, is too obvious to be asked: she is a mother.

Registration is obligatory for all children born in Britain, the contemporary secular equivalent of rituals of incorporation in tribal societies. Parents can also have their child baptized. Another more secular option is to publish a birth notice in a paper, either in the local paper or in a national paper like *The Times*. Not every parent will want to do this, since its function is presumably to mediate a relationship with a manageable community who would be likely to be included within the readership of the paper concerned: either a local community or a supra-community united by all its members taking *The Times*.

Although the parents may seem to have complete freedom of choice as to whether a notice is put into the paper or not, once they do so the form of the notice is fairly strictly determined. Here to illustrate is a typical set of Birth notices from the Norfolk *Eastern Evening News* for Saturday, 7 February 1976.

MINNS – February 5th to JANE (née Stolworthy) and Paul, a daughter, (Emma Jane). Thanks to Nurse Woods and all in attendance.
ROWLES – February 4th to JANE and Stuart, a daughter (Sarah Jane), a sister for Jonathan. Thanking all in attendance at Norfolk and Norwich Maternity Unit.

Birth notices in a paper follow basic conventions, though these are not as inflexible or impersonal as the birth certificate. The surname leads, the common surname which refers to the family unit and to individual members of it. In this example the Minns follow the birth-certificate format in giving Jane's maiden name. The function of this in this instance is to communicate the news to people who knew her before she was married and for whom her pre-married identity is still significant. Jane Rowles has been more fully absorbed into the Rowles family and name. Neither notice gives a self-classification according to occupation or class, and it would be unthinkable for this to happen. It could be called ungrammatical for this form, since it breaks basic rules of the genre. 'To Jane, and Paul (an accountant with Norwich Union) a daughter' would sound very odd. As with the birth certificate, the sex of the child is a more important fact than the name, this being indicated by the name being in brackets. Again we could call any departure from this ungrammatical, since it would be extremely odd and strained to have 'to Jane and Paul, Emma Jane (a daughter)'.

The notice has a simple and stylized form of syntax. Each of these examples consists of two sentences. The first of these is virtually obligatory. It is a highly compressed and conventionalized form, reminiscent of what Orwell called 'duckspeak', where a short-hand ready-made formulaic expression neutralizes real content and significance. In this case, the full form is difficult to recover, since the formula has been used for so long, with new names slotted in, much as in the case of birth certificates. The surface form is 'surname, to [female] (plus maiden name optionally) and [male], a son/daughter'. The order of the sexes differs from the normal order in English, and in the birth certificate, where males precede females, indicating their superior status. The female name in this paper is always in capitals, again indicating the superior status of the woman. This reversed order is an ideological inversion, providing a version of reality where women are more important than man.

If we try to guess at the sentence form that underlies this surface form, we might suggest:

A son/daughter has been born to Jane and Paul.
A son/daughter has been given to Jane and Paul.

The child is thus either the sole participant relating to an intransitive verb, or it is the object of a deed of gift, with the parents as beneficiaries. In the first case, birth is presented as an event which happens, not something which Jane and Paul do. In the second case, it is reasonable to ask who is the giver. The most likely candidate for this unknown giver is God. The vague 'to Jane' form certainly allows this as a possible interpretation, and behind it could lie a commonplace pious euphemism, in terms of which children come from God, not as a result of the sexual activity of two adults. Both these possible deep structures refer to the act of conception and birth, but in a mystified way. The other prepositions in the two notices also describe benefactive relationships, 'a sister for Jonathan' and 'thanks to Nurse Woods'. So the physical processes and relationships involved are neutralized and presented more comfortably as relations between goods or gifts which have been exchanged.

The main activity in this first sentence is naming, which fixes identities and relationships, and attaches this new individual to society. The predominant activity in the second sentence on the surface is the expression of gratitude to people associated with the birth, but in a transformed euphemistic form there is also a recognition of actions specific to the birth. Both have the formula 'all in attendance', which must be interpreted as coming from an underlying sentence 'All attend [at the birth? on the mother?]'. Even in this form the event is vague. The verb does not distinguish between what doctors, nurses, midwives or husbands might contribute, and 'all' encourages a vague image of all these people merging in a single celebratory group around the miracle of birth.

Birth certificates originate from a government department, and present a structure which is hard and clear and impersonal, making no concessions to the desires and experiences of the individuals concerned. Birth notices follow a set form, but they are paid for by individuals who decide to do so. The ideology that underlies them assumes the same model for the family unit, a married couple, but it is not specific about the relation of this family unit to society as a whole, and as we have seen, the relation of dominance between the sexes which is recorded accurately in the birth certificate is subverted in the birth notice. Behind their apparently bare forms, the birth notices mystify both physical and social realities, where birth certificates declare the second and are simply indifferent to the first.

The birth notice announces the happy event to the indeterminate circle of friends, relations and acquaintances of the family concerned, scattered amongst the readers of the paper. These people might respond by sending a congratulations card. These are commercially produced, available from newsagents, where cards for all occasions that are socially recognized are displayed: births, comings-of-age, engagements, marriages, bereavements, etc. There is a greater choice of cards than there is of birth notices, but even here there are certain formulae, and it is interesting that people prefer to choose a complete card, and simply add their own name and that of the recipient, rather than compose a card of their own.

The illustration shows a typical such card. In the original the colours are pastels, pinks and yellows and blues. It is clearly a feminine card, to be sent to a woman, probably by a woman. The words are interesting in comparison to the other records of birth that we have looked at. 'Congratulations' is a nominalization from 'I congratulate', but the 'I' has been effaced by the transformation, unlike the registrar in the birth certificate. The object of the congratulations is interesting too. The order is 'baby' then 'you', implying that the baby has done something even more worthy of congratulations than 'you'. If 'you' refers to the mother, then the

Congratulations
To BABY and YOU

father has been discreetly eliminated from the event, and the mother has been downgraded in her importance. The process is similar to ideological inversion we observed in the birth notice, but it is taken one stage further. There the mother was represented as more powerful than the father. Here the baby is seen as more potent than both.

The verse overleaf develops this theme further.

> Welcome, Little Darling,
> Bet you're glad you're here,
> 'Cause you've found yourself a family
> That's as nice as you are dear!

The infant here is addressed as though it were a fully intelligent and articulate being, who has been the sole agent in the process. 'You've found yourself a family' has the baby doing the finding, and 'yourself' is a reflexive benefactive. This is not 'a sister for Jonathan' but 'a family for Baby, found by Baby'. The baby is a discriminating egoist, with total control in this world.

At one level, of course, this is a joke which is readily translated. Everyone knows that Baby couldn't read the card, so that mother will overhear the compliments. And the cute pretence that Baby found the family is reminiscent of the euphemisms about reproduction which are used with children, which any one who has had a child must have outgrown. But this is only a decoding, it is not an explanation of the ideological function of the card. Why is the transposition made, and what is the appeal of the images it presents?

Turning to the picture again, we see that at the centre of it is the baby, with a toy in its pram, and three winged babies floating around. This is a world from which all adults have been eliminated, including the mother. Instead of the mother attended by doctors, nurses and others, here we have a baby with cherubic attendants. There is no need for adults in this world. The pram is floating, the baby is happy and self-sufficient, and the attendant cherubs are self-absorbed. No one in the picture looks at anyone else. It is an image of total irresponsibility, and it absolves the mother of all responsibility. It glamourizes the relationship, removing all the smells and sounds and dirty tasks of motherhood, removing all need for a mother. It is a seductively subversive vision, of a world of weightless prams and babies who are fully effective agents, where birth involves no effort and no labour. The mother's role has been given to the three cherubs, babies even smaller than the baby in the pram. The mother has become a baby, escaping from the responsibilities of motherhood into an infantile fantasy.

So the card even more strongly than the birth notice offers an anti-ideology. If the implications of these two forms were to be acted on, they would involve a revolution in social relations, a repudiation of male supremacy and the whole ideology of motherhood. But of course, they are not acted on or intended to be acted on. Just as ritual allows the controlled expression of anti-social and forbidden feelings, so these forms allow a safe expression of an ideology in terms that are felt to be, and fundamentally are, an affirmation of the prevailing social relations. A naive reading of the two extremes, birth certificates and greetings cards, might lead an analyst to suppose that these are records from different societies, with different views of sexual relationships. In fact these are products of the same society, and they enshrine the same ideology, in functionally different forms.

10 · Critical linguistics

ROGER FOWLER and GUNTHER KRESS

I

The language materials analysed in this book suggest that there are
strong and pervasive connections between linguistic structure and
social structure. These connections go far beyond, in importance
and in provocativeness, the correlations between social groupings in
a population and styles of speech which have been described in
traditional sociolinguistics.[1] Our studies demonstrate that social
groupings and relationships influence the linguistic behaviour of
speakers and writers, and moreover, that these socially determined
patterns of language influence non-linguistic behaviour including,
crucially, cognitive activity. Syntax can code a world-view without
any conscious choice on the part of a writer or speaker. We argue
that the world-view comes to language-users from their relation to
the institutions and the socio-economic structure of their society. It
is facilitated and confirmed for them by a language use which has
society's ideological impress. Similarly, ideology is linguistically
mediated and habitual for an acquiescent, uncritical reader who has
already been socialized into sensitivity to the significance of patterns
of language.

Any text, then, embodies interpretations of its subject, and evaluations based on the relationship between source and addressee.
These interpretative meanings are not created uniquely for the
occasion; the systematic use of these linguistic structures is connected with the text's place in the socio-economic system, and hence
they exist in advance of the production of the text and our reception
of it. To generalize further, there are social meanings in a natural
language which are precisely distinguished in its lexical and syntactic structure and which are articulated when we write or speak.
There is no discourse which does not embody such meanings. Our
'organized selections' from among these meanings are responses to
our practical theories of the nature of the communicative events in
which we participate; we have been socialized into holding these

theories and our judgments are largely automatic. It is important to stress the automatic nature of this process. Much of the commentary in this book suggests the processes 'X manipulates Y through language' and 'X pulls the wool over Y's eyes through language'. But these processes tend to be unconscious for most members of the speech community, for much of the time. If they were not, they would not work.

One centrally influential system of assessments that language-users draw upon concerns the differences of power and status between themselves and their interlocutors. We saw the workings of this system very clearly in the interviews and the rules, but it is influential in other discourses. Once we become conscious of the ways in which interpersonal structures encode power relationships, it is easy to see spoken interactions as enactments of or negotiations about status – contrary to the 'commonsense' view of, say, the research interviewer or the job interviewer that their discourses are neutral, designed merely to elicit information. The lack of immediate two-party interaction tends to obscure such classifications and negotiations in written discourse, but they are present none the less.

If linguistic meaning is inseparable from ideology, and both depend on social structure, then linguistic analysis ought to be a powerful tool for the study of ideological processes which mediate relationships of power and control. But linguistics is an academic discipline, and like all academic disciplines it rests on a number of assumptions which constitute an ideology of the subject. It is not a neutral instrument for the study of ideology, it is one that has been neutralized. The need then is for a linguistics which is critical, which is aware of the assumptions on which it is based and prepared to reflect critically about the underlying causes of the phenomena it studies, and the nature of the society whose language it is.

There are two prevalent and related dualisms in current linguistic theory which we feel have to be challenged. One is the belief that 'meaning' can be separated from 'style' or 'expression'.[2] Our analyses suggest on the contrary that lexical items, linguistic forms and linguistic processes carry specific meanings. When they are realized in a coherent discourse, systematic options from sets of alternatives are exercised, and the total and interacting effect of these carries a meaning over and above that of the items and processes in isolation.

The second dualism which we challenge is that between 'linguistic' and 'sociolinguistic' patterning in texts and utterances. This posits that a fundamental distinction is to be drawn between the structures provided by the grammar of a language, and the ways in which these are deployed in actual instances of linguistic communication. According to this theory, the specific language – English or French or whichever – is basically a set of structures, or a system of rules for generating structures, which have been acquired or facilitated or elicited through primary socialization but which are not 'social' in character – they are formal constructs, a selection from the possibilities afforded by the biological character of human beings. They may therefore be described – a grammar may be written – without any reference to social function, to the needs of use in communicative context. Social use, or social meaning, according to this view, is a secondary or superadded factor: sociological or sociolinguistic processes operate on the output of the grammar by the selection of 'appropriate' structures.

This dissociation of language structure from language use – most provocatively expressed in Chomsky's 'idealized' competence versus 'degenerate' performance – has been vigorously attacked in recent years. One line of criticism, best represented by the writings of Dell Hymes,[3] argues that any realistic theory of language ability should be a theory of *communicative* competence. So a grammar should account not only for the ability to produce and comprehend sentences (in Chomsky's terms, the pairing of sounds and meanings through the mediation of syntax) but also for the production of contextually appropriate utterances, the perception of inappropriateness, etc. We may add to these criteria various pragmatic criteria that have been proposed recently, such as the performance of illocutionary acts, and the recovery of the implicatures of a discourse. This enriched 'communicative competence' will clearly vary from person to person rather than, as in Chomsky's idealization, being the same for all members of a linguistic population.

However, over and above this we speak of the individual as socialized, not as unique. People's roles, status and position in the class system, properties which link them with and divide them from others, bear on this communicative ability so that their total language ability is a product of social structure. The claim that 'language ability is a product of social structure' is made in strong terms by 'functionalist' linguists, notably M. A. K. Halliday.[4] We follow Halliday in requiring that social meanings and their textual realizations be included within the scope of a grammatical description. The stronger claim made by Halliday is that, since language is learned in contexts of interaction, and since the structure of language in use is responsive to the communicative needs of these interactions (of course reflecting wider social patternings), the structure of a language should generally be seen as having been formed in response to the structure of the society that uses it.

Three basic assumptions underlie this kind of claim: 1 that language serves a number of specific functions, and that *all* linguistic forms and processes express one or all these functions; 2 that the selections which speakers make from among the total inventory of forms and processes are principled and systematic; and 3 that the relation between form and content is not arbitrary or conventional, but that form signifies content. The first two of these assumptions are taken over from the work of Halliday,[5] though in an adapted form. Halliday posits that language serves three major functions: to communicate about events and processes in the world, and the entities involved in these ('ideational function'); to express a speaker's attitude to these propositions, and to express a speaker's perceived relation with an interlocutor ('interpersonal function'); and to present these in coherent, adequate and appropriate texts ('textual function'). Distinct areas of the overall grammar of a language are organized in systems to realize these functions. Speakers make appropriate selection from these systems, so that choice of a linguistic form is always choice from among a specific range of options. The choice itself is thus highly significant and its reason can be traced to contingencies experienced by the speaker in a given speech (and social) situation. The larger needs and purposes of a speaker in a given situation ensure that the selections which are made are not random but unified.

Speakers, as members of specific social and speech groups, tend to find themselves in recurring situations, making similar demands. This fact accounts very readily for the emergence of codes (or speech-styles), and for the fact that the 'meanings' of such codes are readily recognized. However, it is our third assumption – coupled with the preceding two – which fully enables us to complete the link between social reality and linguistic form. The meaningfulness of choice from a system alone is not enough, if one regards the items in the system as arbitrary and conventional representations of their referents. It is only when we acknowledge the meaning carried by the items themselves, that linguistic form can be demonstrated to be a realization of social (and other) meaning. The selection of one form over another points to the speaker's articulation of one kind of meaning rather than another. In Saussure's system a term has meaning by virtue of its opposition to other terms, though in itself the term is without content. In our theory terms in systems have meaning by opposition, but they also have content in their own right. We hope that our analyses have provided an informal demonstration of the validity of this principle, since to discuss it in greater detail would take us far beyond our present brief.[6]

The three assumptions give us a powerful counter to the dualisms we mentioned, and enable us to link linguistic form, realized in discourse, to the social world of the users of discourse. It will be clear that the link we make is very different from that posited by traditional structural linguistics or from Chomskyan linguistics. Both of those movements are concerned with an idealized grammar quite abstracted from social forces. Chomskyan linguistics posits biological universals as the source of language. This model would have to grant some social influence on the acquisition of a language (since children brought up in England learn English rather than French, obviously an outcome of their being nurtured in an English-speaking community). But in Chomsky's linguistics this is a weak social influence: what the child learns as a consequence of being brought up in a particular linguistic community are simply the forms of that language, forms without any social content.

Conventional sociolinguistics, which we shall consider in the next section, does not assume any more intimate relationship between (what it separates as) social structure and linguistic structure than Chomsky's linguistics does. Sociolinguists seem to assume that there is for each language-community a given grammar which pre-exists social processes. There is language, and there is the use of language (competence and performance again); social structure has its effects at the level, or stage, of 'use'. To rephrase the position in terms of the development of language in the individual, the child first acquires the language and then learns to use the language(s) he has acquired within social contexts of communication according to norms of appropriateness. According to sociolinguists, these appropriate links between society and language are accidental, arbitrary; and it is the task of sociolinguistics to discover and document these links.

There is a problem for us in discussing established sociolinguistics, which is that the concepts 'language' and 'society' are divided by the sociolinguists, so that one is forced to talk of 'links between the two', whereas for us language is an integral part of social process.

However, adopting this separation of terms for the sake of exposition, we must find fault with sociolinguistics on the grounds that it fails to acknowledge the two-way relationship between language and society. Sociolinguistics speaks only of the influence of social structure on (the use of) language. Our analyses suggest that the influence works in the other direction as well. Language serves to confirm and consolidate the organizations which shape it, being used to manipulate people, to establish and maintain them in economically convenient roles and statuses, to maintain the power of state agencies, corporations and other institutions. As we have seen, this is effected partly by direct and indirect speech acts, partly by more generalized processes in which the theory or ideology of a culture or a group is linguistically encoded, articulated and tacitly affirmed. Thus in a very basic way language is a part of, as well as a result of, social process. In the next section we take issue with sociolinguists for failing to recognize this. We show that this failure is a product of the ideology embodied in the language and practice of sociolinguistics itself.

2

The predominant and most respected type of argument in sociolinguistics may be called correlational. It claims – with massive and plausible research documentation – that in given communicative contexts appropriate forms of speech and writing occur regularly. Thus variables in linguistic structure correlate with variables in type of situation, speaker, subject-matter, class-context, etc., in a rule-governed fashion.[7] The linguistic variables may be situated in any area of linguistic structure – phonology, morphology, vocabulary, syntax. In some cases they may be quite minute, as for instance the phoneme /r/ which Labov discovered correlated with social stratification in the Lower East Side of New York City, elsewhere they may be major and obvious, as in the choice between 'tu' and 'vous' in French; they may even involve a choice between two quite distinct languages – Spanish and English in the New York Puerto Rican community, Spanish and Guaraní in Paraguay.

Interestingly from our point of view, one factor which recurs in many studies of sociolinguistic variation is power or status, and difference of power. This is explicit in Brown and Gilman's famous paper 'The Pronouns of Power and Solidarity'. Many languages offer a choice between two second-person pronoun forms which Brown and Gilman designate T and V: French 'tu' and 'vous', German 'du' and 'Sie', Russian 'ty' and 'vy', etc. Practice varies somewhat between communities, but in general someone who is of superior status through age, generation, property, occupation, social role(s) is allowed to address someone who is subordinate on relevant criteria as T; the subordinate must return V. T/V encodes a relationship in which power is unequal; T has acquired the social meaning of authority, condescension, V subservience, deference. Brown and Gilman call this the 'power semantic'. It interacts with a second and somewhat conflicting set of usages. People who do not know each other very well make the 'safe' choice V, encoding respect, distance, formality. However, people in an intimate relationship, or people whose social roles suggest parity of status, address one another as T: children, lovers, members of the same family, close colleagues, particularly those who work low down in an institutional hierarchy. This is, according to Brown and Gilman, the 'solidarity semantic'.

Brown and Gilman's study is an important and stimulating work in sociolinguistics; it proceeds with a boldness of analysis and generalization which is unfortunately lacking in other sociolinguistic studies. Rather than merely cataloguing the various particular contextual factors to which the T/V alternation responds, Brown and Gilman have looked for general and powerful sociological regularities underlying them. They have also attempted to place the power and solidarity dimensions in the contexts of history and ideology.[8] We believe their historical analysis is incorrect (see below), but this kind of contextualization is nevertheless vital for giving substance to the bare correlational facts. Finally, Brown and Gilman have had the courage to call the power and solidarity dimensions 'semantic', suggesting that social facts directly determine categories of linguistic structure (as we have claimed).

We must now ask whether correlational studies such as Brown and Gilman's, or Labov's, or Ferguson's, are normative as well as descriptive. Sociolinguistic research in general seems to claim only that certain linguistic forms, or certain quantities of linguistic forms, occur in specified social environments, being replaced by others in other environments. The two variables which correlate, social context and linguistic form, are specified in terms of the theoretical categories of the relevant academic disciplines: role, status, class, etc., for sociology; phoneme, transformation, etc., for linguistics. It seems therefore that correlational sociolinguistics does no more than describe linguistic variation and its circumstances objectively and scientifically, without evaluation of the phenomena described.

The supposed objectivity of 'mainstream' American sociolinguistics of the 1960s has been vigorously challenged by Norbert Dittmar in his excellent book *Sociolinguistics: A Critical Survey of Theory and Application*.[9] Dittmar argues that the sociolinguistic research programmes of the 1960s were developed in response to the economic needs of American society. Of compensatory education programmes growing out of this research, he writes

Their avowed aim is to get the 'social dynamite' . . . under control and to adapt the Blacks (and other minorities) to the requirements of a highly-industrialized capitalist society engaged in international competition, i.e. to eliminate illiteracy and to satisfy the need for qualified workers (technicians, etc) (p. 242).

If sociolinguistics is the product of a particular model of social structure, we would expect the theoretical concepts of the discipline to be geared to the pragmatic requirements of the society that devised the model. Dittmar points out that this is the case with the notion of 'upward social mobility' which is central to Labov's work. An important observation in Labov's research is that those individuals who are anxious to move upward in a stratified class system engage in linguistic hypercorrection, e.g. they use more post-vocalic /r/s than do the classes above them. Why is 'upward social mobility' important? Dittmar suggests that it embodies an ethos of individualistic economic competitiveness which was highly useful for the American industrial economy. He also points out that the principle of upward social mobility is antagonistic to the principles of equality of opportunity and equality of benefit: it makes the poor individually responsible for striving for those benefits on their own behalf. Thus the term 'upward social mobility' is extremely tendentious and should be regarded not as a generally applicable concept in sociological theory but as a product of the academic ideology of a particular society.

This kind of sceptical analysis ought to be applied to other allegedly scientific terms in the social theory underpinning sociolinguistics. Where descriptions proceed in terms of an ideologically conservative sociological theory whose categories correspond closely with the society's official categories, sociolinguistics is unable to perceive or criticize the official vision.[10] To the extent that such work cannot offer a critique of the social system in which linguistic interaction takes place, it is normative. In sociolinguistics, inequality is neutralized as variety. As Dittmar says, 'Society is considered as a social system which is stable and permanent, and which functions by means of the interaction of its parts – an example of this interaction is the adaptation of the individual to social norms (his socialization)' (p. 249). In verbal deficit theory the speech of the verbally deprived is to be nurtured up to middle-class norms; in variety theory the communicative repertoire will accommodate a range of class languages each appropriate to the roles of the relevant workers within the economic system.

Words like 'appropriate', 'typical', 'normal' are used liberally throughout the literature. Though the overt claim is merely that form *a*, or variety *a*, tends to appear in or correlate with situation *x*, it is typically expressed in terms such as 'form *a* is appropriate to, normal in, situation *x*'. Consider this extract from Ferguson's classic article on diglossia:[11]

The importance of using the right variety in the right situation can hardly be overestimated. An outsider who learns to speak fluent, accurate L and then uses it in a formal speech is an object of ridicule. A member of the speech community who uses H in a purely conversational situation or in an informal activity like shopping is equally an object of ridicule.

This is typical in two ways. First, it couches statements of usage in the style of statements of propriety. Second, it concerns a linguistic distinction which differentiates situations and speakers from the point of view of formality and prestige. (L and H refer to 'Low' and 'High' varieties of a language, e.g. Egyptian and Classical Arabic, Haitian Creole and French. H is the formal variety, associated with power and prestige, L is the informal vernacular.) Thus a value-judgment is being passed about the necessity of behaving appropriately in situations which directly reflect the divisions of socio-economic structure and the authority of institutions. No explanatory analysis is given of the institutions which require speakers to make this selection between H and L. Sociolinguists might well say that this is not their business; but the point is that, in failing to analyze the meanings which underlie a sociolinguistic system while writing positively about the smoothness and regularity with which it works, sociolinguists may unwittingly give the impression that they endorse the values that it expresses. At the very least, a satisfactory description of the efficiency of sociolinguistic correlations may lead to a reluctance to disturb the processes which make them work, and so to a tacit acquiescence in their material bases.

Another doubtful implication of such work lies in the suggestion that forms of language are *freely chosen* by language-users. According to both our theory and correlational sociolinguistics, language is a system of alternatives among which selection is made according to circumstances. Words like 'select' and 'choose' seem inevitable in expounding or exemplifying this theory, and occur frequently in the literature. They are not, however, used in the absolute sense of acting freely without constraints. 'Select' means 'select what is appropriate'. Appropriateness is established by socio-economic factors outside the control of the language-user, and the abilities he draws upon when 'choosing' are available to him through socialization. That is to say, sociolinguistic competence is an ability which society has imposed on language-users whether they like it or not. When they exercise this competence (as they do each time they speak or write, and continuously as they speak or write) their linguistic performance is under the sanction of social norms. The process is deterministic. It is also, presumably, more or less unconscious. Spontaneous speech is too fast for planned choices of words and constructions; planning slows down and inhibits verbal production, and that is itself sociolinguistically functional, so that deliberate planning produces discourse which is formal and serious. Even when choice is conscious, it may still be totally determined.

Writing allows time for planning and opportunity for revision, but these privileges by no means turn writers into free agents. They work towards specific models which have their social functions; they are likely to use certain forms and structures not by consciously analysing the structure of sentences but by aiming at the model in a generalized, intuitive fashion. The rightness of the syntactic and the lexical choice for the particular meaning is a gift of the writer's society, not a creation of his own.

When we look in this way at the relationship between society and language, 'correlation' ceases to be a neutral facet of sociolinguistic description, and emerges as a fact about social organization which invites critical scrutiny. To recapitulate:

1 Forms of social organization influence linguistic structure and linguistic usage.
2 This influence operates in a deterministic fashion: social structure x demands linguistic variety a.

3 The process may be unconscious or, if a speaker does know what is going on, he or she is under great pressure not to resist it.

4 Social structure bears on all parts of language, not merely those parts that are 'about' personal and group relationships such as personal pronouns or the labels for classes or roles.

5 Different forms of language should not be regarded as cognitively equivalent. They are not 'merely stylistic' in effect, but affect the potential expression of concepts, and thus the availability of concepts, too.

The above set of causal links is by itself interesting enough to anyone concerned with the way social structures operate. If we add the following, the arguments become very provocative:

6 Prominent among the social structures which influence linguistic structures is inequality of power.

7 Language not only encodes power differences but is also instrumental in enforcing them.

3

The linguistic analyses in this book differ from conventional linguistics and sociolinguistics in taking as their subjects real, socially situated and usually complete texts. These texts are not mined for structures which exemplify the general construction of language, or of English, or the characteristic expression of some social group (although we use linguistic terminology which would figure in any of those three projects, and offer hypotheses which relate this work to the third of them). The texts are not appropriated as sources of data, but are treated as independent subjects for critical *interpretation.*[12]

Texts are the linguistic part of complicated communicative interactions. These, in turn, are implicated in social processes in complex ways. The structure of discourse and of texts reflects and expresses the purposes and roles of its participants, these in turn being products of the prevailing forms of economic and social organization. But communication (thus language) is not just a *reflex* of social processes and structures. In the expression of these processes and structures they are affirmed, and so contribute instrumentally to the consolidation of existing social structures and material conditions. Interpretation is the process of recovering the social meanings expressed in discourse by analysing the linguistic structures in the light of their interactional and wider social contexts.

The *critical* nature of this linguistic interpretation has its motive in the fact that so much of social meaning is implicit: not contained in the statements of the texts, and often not in the speech acts ostensibly offered by the language structures (e.g. declaratives or questions turn out to be commands).[13] An activity of unveiling is necessary in this interpretation, or, to put it in stronger terms, an activity of demystification. We do not say that authors and speakers deliberately obscure or mystify their aims, or that language is generally an instrument of conscious conspiracy to conceal and distort. We suspect that often people do not consciously recognize the purposes they encode in language, and that the aims which they mediate in their 'professional capacities' may not coincide with their beliefs and sympathies. Furthermore, it is unnecessary to assume that a speaker or writer analytically chooses or constructs a syntax of mystification (e.g. decides to delete agents); the 'regulations' style, for instance, will be guaranteed by the sociolinguistic principle of appropriateness of style to context and will be automatically used once that 'style' has come into existence (in the manner we outlined above) and if speaker or writer (or committee, etc.) has the 'appropriate' style in his repertoire. Social structure provides the resources, individuals mediate their realization. So the resistance which critical linguistics offers to mystificatory tendencies in language is not resistance to language itself, nor to individual users of language, but to the social processes which make language work in communication as it does. It is a critique of the structures and goals of a society which has impregnated its language with social meanings many of which we regard as negative, dehumanizing and restrictive in their effects.

4

Critical analysis should also be practical analysis. The critic ought not to be content just to display his own virtuosity (which is the case with most of what passes for *literary* criticism) but ought to be committed to making a technique of analysis available to other would-be practitioners; if the critic does not attempt this, his sincerity must be doubted.[14] Although this book was never designed as an instruction manual in critical linguistics, it certainly seeks to offer, by exemplification and discussion, an analytic method that can be applied to texts and discourse. Applied, we believe, without an advanced knowledge of linguistic theory. In fact, many of the critical analyses published here were originally worked out in undergraduate seminars which did not presuppose an advanced knowledge of linguistics.

Our students quickly came to appreciate, however, that there is no analytic routine through which a text can be run, with a critical description issuing automatically at the end. In each case, the critical analyst starts out with the hypothesis that the text has some specific signification in social structure. At this point a procedural problem intervenes. Although the structure of English has received extensive description, there is no process of step-by-step analysis which is guaranteed to reveal what constructions characterize the text, still less, which ones relate significantly to the hypothesis being investigated. The inexperienced critic faced with a new text may well find it as complex and apparently structureless as does someone confronted with speech in a language he does not know.

Here the three assumptions which we offered earlier in place of the dualism in linguistic theory come into play. The first assumption asserts that language has three predominant functions (Halliday's 'ideational', 'interpersonal' and 'textual', cf. note 4 above); as a consequence the analyst is entitled to attempt to relate each linguistic item and each linguistic process to one or more of the three functions. The second assumption asserts that choices are made from systems, and in a systematically guided manner, the guidance deriving from the social contingencies and the purposes of the participants in the discourse. This systematic selection ensures the unity or congruence of the items, structures and processes realized in the text (though we are well aware that speakers may act in confusion or with complex and even contradictory purposes). The third assumption states that the meanings are carried and expressed in the syntactic forms and processes, that is, that the analyst can 'read off' meaning from the syntax.

On this basis we can offer some help to the aspirant in critical linguistics. To our students doing fieldwork in sociolinguistics we said 'we cannot tell you in advance what constructions are going to be significant in the texts you collect; but we have found that the following are very often worth looking at'. Our experience has shown us that certain structures are particularly likely to be revealing, and can be the basis for a checklist. The remainder of this chapter is, in fact, an annotated checklist of linguistic features which have frequently proved revealing in the kind of critical linguistics we have been doing.

A final caution: there is no predictable one-to-one association between any one linguistic form and any specific social meaning. Speakers make systematic selections to construct new discourse, on the basis of systems of ideas – ideologies – and complex purposes of all kinds. To isolate specific forms, to focus on one structure, to select one process, in fact to lift components of a discourse out of their context and consider them in isolation would be the very anti-thesis of our approach. Different features and processes must be related to one another.

We offer our checklist under five main headings: 1 Events, states, processes, and their associated entities: the grammar of transitivity; 2 the interpersonal relations of speaker and hearer: the grammar of modality; 3 the manipulation of linguistic material: transformations; 4 linguistic ordering: the grammar of classification; 5 coherence, order and unity of the discourse. As we have pointed out above, any one linguistic form or process may (and nearly invariably does) serve several functions, so that our divisions introduce some falsification. We hope, however, that, read in conjunction with our insistence on the multi-functional use of linguistic form and our emphasis on the systematic nature of selections, the headings will provide some initial help in analysing language.

1 The grammar of transitivity. Among the deeper semantic features of a text, it is always revealing to see what kinds of predi-cates occur: these are words for actions ('run', 'raise'), states ('tall', 'red'), processes ('widen', 'open'), mental processes ('understand', 'sad'), usually appearing as verbs and adjectives in the text, some-times as nouns derived from underlying verbs or adjectives ('com-pletion', 'sincerity'). Predicates (and their associated participants) carry the main responsibility for representing the events and situations to which the text refers. They are studied in relation to the roles of the nouns which accompany them. Here is a sentence which highlights the agent-action (-affected) semantic structure: 'Mrs Loppenthien pickles, bottles, preserves her own homegrown fruit and vegetables, gives dinner parties with typical French cuisine, and keeps an eye on her 21-year-old son's studies.'[15] This is in the context of a newspaper article on women living or working in more than one country. Clearly the semantics of participant and process focus on the role of the subject as actor and the action-nature of the events. By contrast, an article on the Mull of Kintyre stresses the mental processes and states of the people who live and visit there; these people, unlike Mrs Loppenthien, take the more passive role of 'affected participant': 'The relaxed outlook of the natives combined with the general lack of amenities may dismay younger tourists. At present most annual migrants tend to be middle-aged with an interest in walking, golfing, bird-watching or archaeology. A younger generation might not be as easily entertained.'

Within the grammar of transitivity there is a small number of highly significant alternative 'models' for the presentation of events. Some questions to ask are:

1 Does the action affect one or more entities? E.g. 'Snow fell (in parts of Scotland)' compared to 'A whirlwind smashed £100,000-worth of greenhouses'.

2 Does the action produce a new entity? E.g. 'A local foundry . . . made up a new mould and bell'.

3 Is the action performed by the agent on him or herself? E.g. 'The British . . . understand themselves better when they look at themselves through French eyes'.

4 Is the action initiated by the actor or by another participant? E.g. '. . . making sure that air is flowing all the time', where 'the air' moves (i.e. is actor) but does so because of the action of a controlling and initiating agent; here the initiator and actor appear in two different clauses. In '. . . begonias and gloxinias can be started in cool houses' the initiator (here the deleted subject of the passive) and the actor (the 'begonias' and 'gloxinias') are in the same clause.

These questions will reveal differing linguistic 'dispositions' of events. Over and above these it is fruitful to ask who, if anyone, benefits from the action, what other circumstances attend on the event and how they are connected to it, spatially or temporally, instrumentally or causally.

What kinds of entities perform actions? The most straightforward type of agent would seem to be animate, either human (Mrs Loppenthien) or animal (the Grand National winner Red Rum): 'Teachers call off meals boycott'; 'Tens of thousands of sea-birds are about to pass through the area . . .'. But there are other alternatives, and it is always necessary to look for inanimates, abstractions and names of organizations apparently performing actions: 'Mushrooms and their hallucinogenic properties are creating a legal tangle in magistrates' courts'; 'yellow buses brushing past'; 'The Observer has chosen . . . a special winner'; '. . . the bigger body does provide reasonable accommodation for four adults . . .'. In some discourse all the agentive participants are abstract nouns, often complex nouns which are derived from sentences or parts of sentences by nominalization: 'In the cinema vast resources are more likely to inhibit the imagination than to release it . . .'. (Try the effect of reading these sentences literally!)

A subject + verb + object syntax ('Egypt + will continue + its peaceful efforts') suggests agency and transitivity; often this is an illusion, as we saw with Brian Gentle's syntax. Among the scores of examples of pseudo-actions found in the one newspaper we scanned are: 'I take the trans-Europe to Paris'; 'We know a great deal'; 'But the locals had the last laugh'; 'We make a rapid reconnaissance'; 'an equipment list which matches or beats anything in its class'. The many apparent actions suggested by the syntax turn out to be states or mental processes, or things which happen to rather than are done by the participant referred to in the subject noun. Here the interest for the analyst lies in the fact that an event of one type (involving just one participant) is presented in the surface form of another event (involving two participants, one the actor, the other the affected).

2 *The grammar of modality.* This covers linguistic constructions which may be called 'pragmatic' and 'interpersonal'. They express speakers' and writers' attitudes towards themselves, towards their interlocutors, and towards their subject-matter; their social and economic relationships with the people they address; and the actions which are performed via language (ordering, accusing, promising, pleading).

Let us begin with a very simple feature: naming conventions.[16] An individual may be addressed, or referred to, by any one of a range of choices comprising various parts of his name (Gunther, Gunther Kress, Kress), abbreviations (G. Kress, G. R. Kress, G. R. K.) combined with a title (Mr Kress, Mr G. R. Kress, G. R. Kress, Esq.) or without. The different possibilities signify different assessments by the speaker/writer of his or her relationship with the person referred to or spoken to, and of the formality or intimacy of the situation. One extreme of formality is illustrated by the *Obser-*

ver's 'Foreign Minister Mohammed Ibrahim Kamel' (distinguished foreign politician: title plus complete, unabbreviated name); but status may still be combined with familiarity, as in our own 'Prince Charles'. A neutral form for the *Observer* seems to be title plus first name plus last name: 'Mr Stanley Clinton Davis', 'M. Marc Bécam'; but note how a group of trade unionists are referred to using the familiar forms of their first names: 'Mr Fred Jarvis', 'Mr Jim Murphy', 'Mr Dick North'. Very well-known public figures are referred to by title plus last name: 'Mr Callaghan', 'Mrs Thatcher'; or, less formally, 'Willie Whitelaw'. Wives and children get first name only: 'Sonia', 'Paul', 'Keith'. Footballers are referred to by last name only, a form traditionally associated with servants and social inferiors: 'Brady', 'Hudson', 'Cunningham'.

Personal pronouns always deserve notice. Starting with 'I', it is worth reminding ourselves that every utterance has implicitly an 'I' or 'we' as a source, but this is usually not present in the surface structure: 'Personal pronouns always deserve notice' has the deep structure 'I [R.F., writing on 29 March 1978 endorsed by G.K. 30 May 1978] tell you [future readers] that personal pronouns . . .'. Removal of the pronoun associated with personal speech is felt to be appropriate to the impersonal, generalizing tone of newspapers, textbooks, scientific articles. In the *Observer*, the 'I' of action (as opposed to speech) is also rare, limited to self-centred articles by people not on the newspaper's staff: it is extremely frequent in a long article by President Sadat of Egypt – *The Story of My Life*, 'extracted from "In Search of Identity" by Anwar el-Sadat': 'Immediately before I made my speech, President Hafez Assad sent word reminding me of a promise I had made to visit him. I left for Syria shortly after speaking to the Assembly.' The 'I' of action is also a regular (but less foregrounded) feature of signed investigative and eye-witness reporting, where it seems to suggest exclusivity and authenticity: 'A former Inland Revenue man told me last week . . .'; 'One defence lawyer showed me three communiqués . . .'.

The plural form 'we' displays the added complexity that the source claims to speak of and for himself and on behalf of someone other than himself. The simplest 'we' form is 'exclusive' 'we': the writer refers to himself and some other person(s) not including his addressees. Brian Jackson describes how he and his wife set out to walk along Hadrian's Wall, and in his article 'we', 'us' and 'our' consistently refer to those two individuals, excluding the readers of the article and any other individuals encountered during their travels. An extension of this usage is what might be called the 'corporate "we"': the text speaks on behalf of an organization, differentiating it from the addressee but still personalizing the source. A Mercedes-Benz advertisement insists on this usage in almost every sentence: 'At Mercedes-Benz we build cars that find the perfect balance between . . .' and so on. This corporate 'we' is suspect, since the individuals it refers to cannot be identified (not as suspect, however, as the generalized inclusive 'we' mentioned below). And its effect is often alienating: if 'we' excludes the addressee, it can be transformed into the institutional 'they': 'We know what's best for you' is readily perceived as 'They think they can push us around'.

The second meaning of 'we', 'inclusive "we"', implicates the addressee in the content of the discourse and is therefore, ostensibly, more intimate and solidary; but unless the persons involved are all known and the actions overt and verifiable, it is potentially dangerous. A person can say to the members of her family 'we had a Chinese take-away last Saturday evening' and the utterance may be quite sincere and authoritative. Matters of judgment, feeling or prediction receive inclusive 'we' less happily. A lover who says to her partner 'We'll be so happy together' may very well be indulging in precarious wishful thinking, or in the indirect speech act of pleading. Inclusive 'we' in written discourse is even more hazardous because the included other is not known. Newspaper editorials use the form; from the *Observer*: 'What we have, then, is the reality of a coloured population that is likely to grow . . .', 'the children's integration into our education system . . .'; 'our obligations under human rights conventions'; 'once we acknowledge to ourselves that . . .'. The superficial impression is one of solidarity and involvement – the liberal *Observer* and its liberal readers sharing generous and humane motives towards the black population in England. But the 'we' and 'our' are not wholly sincere. The obligations spoken of (not to keep a register of immigrants) are the obligations of the government, not the newspaper or its individual readers. Similarly, in 'once we acknowledge to ourselves that . . . there will be no significant reduction in the number of coloured people who are going to live in Britain . . . we can get on with the building of a decent multiracial society', the referents of 'we' are mystified: the critical reader may well ask who is being asked to do what and who is capable of doing it. We (R.F. and G.K.) as individuals, in nearly twenty years of university teaching, have taught only a handful of 'coloured' students in

England and it is clear to us that our goodwill towards these people can do little to help build a decent multiracial society, since our personal opportunities to do so are quite out of scale with the enormity of the problem: the responsibility lies with the government to create conditions which will bring larger numbers of blacks into higher education. It is no use the *Observer* using the comfortable, reassuring 'we' form when the goal of 'we' is outside our control.[17]

One other 'we' which makes even stronger assumptions, is the 'we' used by a superior partner in an interaction, and which confidently, unquestioningly and unchallengeably includes the other, inferior partner. 'How are we feeling this morning?' (doctor-patient); 'We're going to eat it all up' (parent-young child); 'We're going to be very nice to Aunt Maisie' (mother-rest of family). This 'we' is akin to the *Observer*'s, except that in the examples above the power-difference between speaker and addressee is large (which it is not in the case of the *Observer*). The most threatening form of this 'we' occurs when a newspaper's 'we' (single voice speaking for a large group) is fused with the power-laden 'we' (the doctor-patient relation) in the pronouncements of those with state-power: 'We will all have to make sacrifices in the coming weeks and months'. (These are 'invented' examples.)

'You' is, as might be expected, complementary in meaning and usage to 'I/we'; as every piece of language has an explicit or implicit source, so does it have an implicit or explicit addressee. In spoken language, addressed to a present person or persons, it may or may not appear in the discourse. Its occurrence, and its frequency of occurrence, are measures of the speaker's consciousness of, care for, or, most often, desire to manipulate, the addressee. ('You' needs to be discussed in the context of speech acts performed upon an addressee: see the chapters on Interviews and Rules and Regulations above, and the discussion of speech acts, below.) Written texts such as personal letters may address, and name, a known individual 'you', but public language (the main interest in this book) is by definition addressed to a multitude of unidentifiable 'you's'.

The newspaper we studied shows wide and fairly predictable variation in the usage of 'you' forms. 'You' is largely absent from reporting sections, frequent in features sections directed to the individual's[18] actions and his/her reflections on his/her own actions: 'Cummerbunds are back . . . You can wear them several ways . . .'; '[Gardening] tools are expensive, but a good purchase should last you a lifetime.' Predictably, 'you' forms claiming intensely parti-cularized personal reference are most insistently used in advertise-ments: 'At Mercedes-Benz we build cars with one object in mind: to improve life for you as a driver and for your passengers. . . . Your seat is firm to give you support . . .'. At the other extreme from individual reference, 'you' sometimes means 'anyone' (as in proverbs and the like: 'You can lead a horse to water, but you can't make him drink'): 'Because in a car, you can't afford to leave anything to chance.' This generalized 'you' is close in meaning to the generalized 'we' noted above. As a general point, when two items seem virtually identical in meaning, an attempt to understand why the speaker/writer has used one form rather than another needs to be made. In this case, 'you' addresses someone, an individual or a group, who is or are different from the speaker. The addressee is being *told* some-thing. The collective 'we' on the other hand addresses the group, ostensibly from inside the group, coercively eliminating any poten-tial antagonism between speaker and addressee. Finally, there is a good deal of third-person reference to classes of implied individuals, often in overt or implied command structures: 'Savers who can't afford to take risks with their money have little to complain about just now'; 'Businessmen who want to shake up their travel habits should talk with their travel agents . . .'. Such constructions are akin to the mystified commands noted in the swimming club rules (pp. 27–32 above) and deserve careful analysis.

Governing the use of the personal pronouns are factors which we can, in a general way, describe as proximity and distance, directness and indirectness. Specific but varying social factors underlie these general categories. It is an immensely nuanced system; a metaphor to describe its function might be the court of a feudal oriental potentate. The distance from the throne which any individual has to observe is precisely regulated depending on his place in the social hierarchy. Some may look directly at the ruler, others must look to the side or down. These things are precisely coded and observed verbally by speakers of English. Terms of address and the pronoun-system are obvious areas in the language to look for these meanings: but most of the linguistic system is in fact responsive to these factors and expresses these meanings.

One area of critically interesting interpersonal structure is the topic of speech acts. The theory holds that every utterance, besides communicating content (ideas, information, propositions, etc.) constitutes an action performed by the speaker in relation to his addressee. To give the classic example: if I say 'I promise to pay you £5.00', my saying that *is* the act of promising.[19] Our interest in the language of control naturally leads us to pay particular attention to the explicitly manipulative acts of commanding (often called 'directives') and requesting. We have discussed these acts, and the syntactic structures which express them, at length in chapters 2 and 4, and there is no need for further detailed discussion here. As might be expected, the most explicitly directive structures are found in the newspaper's advertisements: 'Browse through the many books shown here . . .'; 'Fill in the coupon right now'; 'Make your relaxation richer . . .'. One point that needs to be emphasized can be made by contrasting the overt imperatives in the advertisements and the veiled forms in the club rules. Something in the social conventions which relate to advertising – perhaps an assumption of the honest directness of 'straight talk', perhaps the consumer's feeling that he is not threatened by the imperatives because he can opt not to obey them – allows the advertiser to use forms of directive which in other contexts would be extremely coercive. The most direct forms of speech acts are generally legitimized only when the power-differential between participants is extremely great and can be openly acknowledged – parents and children are (regrettably) the most familiar example.

Where the power-differential is less, or cannot be openly acknowledged, indirectness and distance appear again. Hence most commands (using this as a term to describe the intention of the speaker) do not appear in their direct syntactic form, the imperative. Instead declaratives and interrogatives are used (with modalizers of different kinds); and the indirectness of the speech-act, its linguistic distance from the intended act, signals the social distance and the social indirectness. Again, the kind of surface-form which is selected gives direct insight into the meaning which is expressed; as before, the relation between intention and surface expression is not conventional or arbitrary.

In speech-acts the major meanings are concerned with establishing linguistic role-relations between speaker and hearer (as commander, informer, questioner, and commanded, informed, questioned) and the consequent control of the addressee's behaviour. Degrees of distance and directness are signalled – necessarily, but incidentally. There is, however, a range of linguistic forms which are crucially concerned with the expression of proximity and directness either between speaker and hearer, or between speaker and message (though the latter most often has the former function – indirectly). Prominent among these forms and frequently discussed are modal auxiliaries:[20] 'trust your old auntie, you will'; 'He must have realized this when I met him in Washington'; 'I should point out . . .'; 'If the Union of the Left can ever be put together again . . .'. Here one needs to ask what meaning the modal verb expresses (obligation, ability, possibility, necessity, expectation, etc.) and whose authority is invoked. Closely allied to these auxiliaries are modal adverbs: 'possibly', 'certainly', 'necessarily'. These often occur with the modal auxiliaries, and the meaning of the full construction has to be established as a compound of the meanings of the adverbial and the modal auxiliary, and of their joint effect. In '. . . the figure that might conceivably satisfy the Liberals' the meaning of 'might' is (conditional) possibility, ostensibly part of the proposition, though with the speaker as its source. 'Conceivably' has an unspecified agent or agents: the commentator, the Liberals, politicians generally; and its meaning points to a mental process in this unspecified agent. Allied to modal adverbs are the so-called sentence adverbs: 'Unfortunately the hobbies of some groups conflict . . .'; '. . . and farmers, rightly, are demanding . . .'. Here the speaker provides modal 'glosses' on the proposition, without declaring the authority for these judgments.

Related to these linguistic items in function, but distinct in structure, are utterances such as 'You look tired'; 'France's defeated left-wing alliance seemed to have lost more than . . .'. A paraphrase reveals the functional contiguity of 'look', 'seem', with those discussed above: 'You could/might be tired'; 'France's defeated left-wing alliance may have lost more than. . . .'. There is a vast range of verbs to which propositions can be attached to convey different stances by the speaker towards what he is saying, and through this, towards his addressee. Verbs like 'think', 'feel', 'want', 'wish', 'try', 'like', 'seem', 'understand', all have distancing effects, though all of different kinds. In each case, the meaning of the verb must be examined to understand what kind of distance or indirectness is suggested. In the case of 'think', for instance, the proposition which follows that verb is offered as part of a mental process of the speaker, with whatever degree of seriousness the hearer then wishes to attach to the speaker's mental process. 'Seem', on the other hand, is an effect produced in the speaker by external events of which he is merely an interpreter: 'I think they have lost . . .' as against 'they seem to have lost'.

Finally, two other major linguistic distancing devices: time and place.[21] Without going into detail, consider the modal effect of 'translating' the following into the present tense: 'Concorde test rig failed' (headline). 'A Civil Aviation Authority Spokesman said: "There are a number of theories at present being investigated to find out why this was so".' Presumably the inability of the test rig to reveal the effects of stress accurately still continues, so that the 'accurate' tense should be '. . . to find out why this is so'. Anyone engaged in analysing the modal function of language will need to pay the closest attention to tense: what is the effect of choosing one tense over another, in conjunction with modal verbs or full verbs. In many cases the explanation is other than time-reference. In such analyses it is important to realize that 'present tense' is not a modally neutral form: it is one term among others in this system, if anything a particularly powerful term which signals certainty, unquestionableness, continuity, universality. Temporal 'distance' nearly always conveys modal 'distance'. Similarly with locative expressions, especially the so-called demonstrative pronouns, 'this', 'that', 'these', 'those', 'here', 'there'. Again, in many cases the spatial 'distance' indicated points to conceptual or modal distance.

3 *Transformations.*   Among syntactic transformations, two types have been particularly rewarding in our studies: nominalizations and passivizations. They have various, and overlapping, sets of consequences. To take nominalizations first: here we mean nominals which (whether or not they are listed in dictionaries as nouns) are derived from sentences or parts of sentences – to put it another way, nominal expressions of concepts for which an expression involving a verb or an adjective would have been available to the writer or speaker. The 'stylistic' effects of persistent nominalization are well known: in impressionistic terms, it attenuates any feeling of activity in the language. It is generally discouraged by writing handbooks which advocate a 'direct' style; it is particularly disfavoured for narrative. It makes for 'impersonality' in style; this is an effect of the deletions of participants, often the actor or the affected, which are possible with nominalization. Personal participants in a nominalized process may be preserved, marked with possessives and prepositions: in 'Giscard's sure-footed leadership of the majority', 'Giscard' is clearly agent and 'the majority' affected. More often, in complex sentences in written language, participants disappear completely and have to be 'understood' from the context. For instance, the first part

of the following sentence requires a considerable degree of reconstruction: 'There was much criticism of the negotiations, which Mr Jarvis described as a mixture of melodrama, pantomime and high farce.' The article is about the National Union of Teachers' response, at their annual conference, to a pay award. To some extent the piece allows the reader to determine who was criticizing whom, who had negotiated with whom about what, but one could not be absolutely sure without a detailed knowledge of who spoke at the conference – 'much' indicates more than Mr Jarvis – and of the constitutional machinery for negotiating teachers' pay and how it operated on this occasion.

Modality and tense disappear in nominalizations. In the middle of a report of the wreck of the oil supertanker *Amoco Cadiz*, which happened towards the end of March 1978 – the wrecked ship was in the process of breaking up, and oil spilling, at the time this newspaper went to press – the *Observer* gives the information 'French moves to slap drastic restrictions on supertanker movements have been dropped after British intervention.' The nominalizations 'moves' and 'intervention' have the effect of obscuring the times at which these actions took place, and the newspaper's attitude to them. Some explanation and judgment follows; however, it remains unclear whether the French 'moves' were a consequence of this particular disaster, or had been made before the *Amoco Cadiz* was wrecked.

Two further effects of nominalization may be mentioned briefly. The first is objectification, the rendering of a process as an object: 'We still need lots of *contributions* to the jumble sale'; 'our new *development*, the "Interference Absorption Circuit"'; 'Now that you've had your first *look* at the new Record Saloon'. (Our italics in the last three examples.) This in turn affects lexicalization, the provision of words and phrases to code new concepts or consolidate existing ones: 'strict segregation', 'basic approach', 'school dinner services', 'people's trial', 'illegal detention'. Lexicalization fixes the object-as-process as a single habitualized entity.

The passive transformation has a similar range of consequences to those of nominalizations, e.g. deletion of participants (see 'associated' and 'treated' in the sentences below); lexicalization ('heavily-mortared suburban wall', 'expected problems'). An additional function, sometimes achieved by nominalization as well, is thematization; shifting a noun-phrase into the informationally significant first place in the sentence. Passivization allows a noun denoting an affected participant, a non-agent, to be placed in the subject position in the sentence, the left-hand noun-phrase slot which is convention-ally regarded as the theme or topic of the sentence (our italics again):

Salt has long been associated with high blood pressure.
The Pill, particularly, is treated with caution.

This device allows a writer or speaker to emphasize his thematic priorities, to emphasize what a text is 'about' even when the entities of the theme are, strictly speaking, semantically subordinate (affected rather than agentive). A further development is available, through the implicit connotation of agency which the subject position carries: passivized objects may seem to be agents, despite their real function as affected rather than affecting roles. The first of the two sentences above may easily be read to mean 'Salt causes high blood pressure'. Compare, from the report on the grounding of the *Amoco Cadiz*, 'The captain of the tanker is charged with pollu-ting the high seas'.

A very large number of transformations have been discussed by the advocates of transformational generative grammar. Most of them correspond to 'real' linguistic processes and all of these carry specific meaning and would need to be taken into account.[22] Here we briefly draw attention to three so-called 'movement' transforma-tions: negative-raising, raising of noun-phrases, and extraposition. Raising is a process by which a constituent in a subordinate clause is 'lifted' from the subordinate clause to be a constituent in the main clause. Negative-raising can be illustrated by a sentence cited above, 'We do not want to say more at present'. Without raising, this would take the form 'We want to say no more at present'; the negating constituent limits the amount of information the speaker is prepared to release. Raised, the negative modifies the verb, the mental process: 'not want'. The two sentences mean the same propositionally, but the emphasis is very different. Raising of noun-phrases is illustrated from a brief notice on the front page of the *Observer*: 'US coalminers are expected to return to work tomorrow'. The underlying sentence is '(Someone) expects that the US coalminers will return to work tomorrow': here the noun-phrase 'US coalminers' is subject of a subordinate clause. Raising lifts it to become the direct object of 'expects'; 'Someone expects US coalminers to return to work tomorrow'. This is then passivized – 'US coalminers are expected by someone to return to work tomorrow' – and finally the agent is deleted. 'US coalminers' has been 'promoted' to a position at the front of the sentence where it is the focus of attention. A slightly different example (similar to Chomsky's famous 'John is easy to please') is 'The identical moulded boats are very difficult to steer in wind'. In the underlying form 'For someone to steer the . . . boats is very difficult', 'boats' is the direct object of 'steer'; after the raising-transformation it is subject of 'difficult'. Lastly, extraposition is illustrated by 'It is now clear that the French government had decided to go it alone', or 'It was the fifth time that there had been a sinking in the race'. In each case the 'it' nas taken the place of a subject-noun-phrase which has been moved ('extra-posed') behind the verb and its complement. So in the first example, the under-lying form would have been ['The French government had decided to go it alone] is now clear': the transformation has moved the bracketed subject-noun-phrase from the front to behind 'is now clear'. 'It' remains as a marker of this process.

In all three cases what happens is that chunks of the utterance are moved about so as to focus our attention, and to direct our percep-tion, in certain ways. In the use of the negative, to regard one item as negated rather than the other; in the case of object- or subject-raising to re-orient our perception of the syntactic relations in the utterance; in the case of extraposition to bring the verbal or predi-cate element – 'is clear', 'was the fifth time' – nearer to the percep-tually crucial front position. Our attention and the sequence in which we decode are here being directed, manipulated, in complex ways; and any analysis of discourse needs to be responsive to these processes.

4 Classification. Turning now to classification, the linguistic ordering of the world, we look first at lexical features of texts – the words available to and chosen by writers and speakers. We have found the processes of relexicalization[23] and overlexicalization generally revealing. Relexicalization is relabelling, the provision of a new set of terms, either for the whole language or for a significant area of the language; it promotes a new perspective for speakers, often in specialized areas which are distinct from those of the larger social group. One form of relexicalization is neologism, the inven-tion of new lexical items which, by being visibly new, force the reader to work out the new concepts they signify: 'sputnik', 'skate-board'. An advertisement in the *Sunday Times Magazine*, 30 April 1978, contains the prominent slogan 'WE FAX IT ON OUR INFOTEC 6000' which was incomprehensible when first read. The

Infotec 6000 turns out to be a machine which sends copies of documents over telephone lines; 'Fax' is an invented term for this new process: it denotes a specialized process which is neither telex nor telephone nor xerox. The word is a linguistic challenge and it codes an apparently new concept. But not all relexicalizations are so unfamiliar. Sometimes they involve reorientations of the meanings of existing words; pointed, ostentatious inversions of meaning. Slang provides many examples, e.g. American 'bad' = 'good'. Political language involving confrontations of factions, particularly confrontation of an establishment culture with a deviant sub-group, provides excellent illustrations of the process. See, for example, the *Observer*'s report of the kidnapping of the former Italian Prime Minister Aldo Moro. Moro was kidnapped early in March 1978 at the time of the trial in Turin of fifteen members of the 'Red Brigades'. The Red Brigades on trial are present 'purely as "observers" of the trial, since they do not recognize the court'. Their relexicalization ' "observers" ' signifies their rejection of the role of accused; the newspaper's quotation marks signify that it, organ of the establishment, does not accept this relexicalization. At the same time, the Red Brigades who had captured Moro issued a series of communiqués stating that they had put him on trial: the paper speaks of a ' "people's trial" ' in a ' "people's court" '. The kidnappers appropriate the role of the judiciary, offering an ironic parody of the official events in Turin; the establishment rejects this appropriation, hence the quotation marks. As March and April went on, the system of relexicalization became increasingly productive, 'people's trial' generating a very considerable set of quasi-legal terms widely reported in dissociating quotes in the English language media. At the time of writing (30 April 1978) the latest seemed to be 'people's prison', a phrase quoted on BBC television news. In all these cases familiar words are used to convey deviant, parodic, values.

Overlexicalization is the provision of a large number of synonymous or near-synonymous terms for communication of some specialized area of experience. A striking example was found in an article on financing car purchase in the *Observer* of 26 March 1978. The following is only a selection of the phrases designating 'loan' in one brief article: 'credit deal', 'credit bargains', 'low-interest finance', 'low-interest-rate schemes', 'special credit scheme', 'overdraft', 'personal loan', 'credit alternatives', 'finance house loans', 'hire purchase', 'bank loans'. The importance for critical linguistics of overlexicalization is that it points to areas of intense preoccupation in the experience and values of the group which generates it, allowing the linguist to identify peculiarities in the ideology of that group.

In classification we find the positioning of adjectives and other modifiers highly revealing. The major distinction is between 'predicative' and 'prenominal' positions for adjectives (and other modifiers).[24] Predicative adjectives are separated from the noun they qualify by 'is' or some other variant of the copula: 'The commentary, as usual, was informative and literate'; 'Most of the world's television is significantly worse than Britain's'; 'They are all equally impressive'. By contrast, the prenominal position incorporates the adjective into the noun-phrase which it modifies: 'a totally new approach': 'an intelligent and sophisticated mood'; 'impeccable effects'; 'the greasy conditions'; 'a beautiful midfield through-pass'. Predicative positioning, in English, necessitates preservation of a copulative verb between the noun and the adjective, and this must express the writer's/speaker's commitment to the evaluation he makes: when Clive James writes 'is . . . worse' or 'was . . . literate', his 'is' and 'was' declare 'this is my judgment'. That element of modality is less overt when the modifier is incorporated within the noun-phrase. Prenominal modification tends to indicate classification rather than evaluation – the referent of the noun becomes simply an instance of the category of 'totally new approaches', 'beautiful midfield through-passes', etc. Noun-phrases incorporating modifiers seem to be whole lexical items, unitary rather than analysed concepts; 'through' in 'through-pass' seems to be part of a compound lexical item rather than a modifier of 'pass', and similarly, progressively, 'midfield' and 'beautiful' may be absorbed.

5 Coherence, order and unity. The last topic on our checklist, coherence, order and unity of the discourse, opens a whole new area of linguistic investigation. We do not have the space to enter into this here, but point our readers to an excellent work dealing with this topic, M. A. K. Halliday and R. Hasan's *Cohesion in English* (London: Longman, 1976). In the construction of a coherent discourse, the speaker or writer implements his conception of the inner order of the materials which he is presenting. The interrelation of events, their respective sequence, importance, interdependence are indicated in the structure of the discourse as a whole. We have pointed to forms and processes which are used in this overall construction of a discourse. We would ask the prospective analyst of language to consider how the different linguistic features which we have pointed to interrelate: transitivity with modality, types of classifications with modality, transformations and transitivity, transformations and the processes of foregrounding in all areas of the text, and so on. The major notion always is that of the predominant unity or congruence of all the linguistic units as it defines the ideological basis of the discourse itself.

Notes

Chapter 1 Orwellian linguistics

1 *The Collected Essays, Journalism and Letters of George Orwell*, edited by Sonia Orwell and Ian Angus, 4 vols (first published London: Secker & Warburg, 1968; our page references are to the Penguin edition, Harmondsworth, 1970).

2 C. K. Ogden and I. A. Richards, *The Meaning of Meaning* (London: Routledge & Kegan Paul, 1923); C. K. Ogden, *Basic English* (numerous publications from 1930); A. Korzybski, *Science and Sanity* (Lancaster: Science Press, 1933); S. Chase, *The Tyranny of Words* (New York: Harcourt, Brace, 1937).

3 C. K. Ogden, ed. E. C. Graham, *Basic English: International Second Language* (New York: Harcourt, Brace & World, 1968), pp. 60–1.

4 B. Bernstein, *Class, Codes and Control*, vol. I (London: Routledge & Kegan Paul, 1976), esp. ch. 9.

5 *Collected Essays*, vol. IV.

6 On the BBC, see S. Hood, *A Survey on Television* (London: Heinemann, 1967). See also P. Golding, *The Mass Media* (London: Longmans, 1974), ch. 4.

7 See B. L. Whorf, *Language, Thought, and Reality* (Cambridge, Mass.: MIT Press, 1956).

8 See N. Chomsky, *American Power and the new Mandarins* (Harmondsworth: Penguin, 1969), for an up-to-date study of how academics can falsify history in the name of objective scholarship. Chomsky uses Orwell's *Homage to Catalonia*, as a sufficiently reliable version of events in the Spanish Civil War, to bring out the suppressions and distortions of academic historians' accounts of the period.

9 'Terminology in Air War', *New York Times*, 16 June 1972, p. 3. See Haigh A. Bosmajian, *The Language of Oppression* (Washington D.C.: Public Affairs Press, 1974), ch. 6 and especially p. 127; also Edward and Onora Nell, 'War Words', *College English* (May, 1967), pp. 603–6.

Chapter 2 Rules and regulations

1 On speech acts and their integration in situations see J. R. Searle, *Speech Acts* (Cambridge University Press, 1968) and 'What is a Speech Act?', in P. P. Giglioli (ed.), *Language and Social Context* (Harmondsworth: Penguin, 1972), pp. 136–56.
2 See M. A. K. Halliday, 'Anti-Languages', *UEA Papers in Linguistics*, vol. 1 (April, 1976), pp. 15–45.
3 On the resistance of states to commands, cf. G. Lakoff, 'Stative adjectives and verbs in English', *Harvard Computational Laboratory Report NSF-17* (1966).
4 Not, of course, *literally* a relationship between persons. We have in mind M. A. K. Halliday's 'interpersonal' function of language: see 'Language Structure and Language Function', in J. Lyons (ed.), *New Horizons in Linguistics* (Harmondsworth: Penguin, 1970), pp. 140–65.
5 Only one example in our extract, but many more as the text continues.
6 These modal usages are general and conventional, and you will find plenty of examples in ordinary domestic documents; e.g. the 'Extract from the Rules of the [Halifax Building] Society' printed at the end of the passbook uses 'shall' and 'may' in a manner entirely compatible with UEA usage. Their origin is the language of legal institutions and legal documents.
7 All language (not just 'rules') serves the analysis of reality. The world-view-constructing properties of language are crucial in literature which, not having any 'real' practical context, must compose a new world for its readers: see R. Fowler, *Linguistics and the Novel* (London: Methuen, 1977); G. Kress, 'Poetry as Anti-Language', *Poetics and the Theory of Literature*, 3 (1978).
8 Compare M. A. K. Halliday, 'Linguistic Function and Literary Style: An Enquiry into the Language of William Golding's *The Inheritors*', in *Explorations in the Functions of Language* (London: Edward Arnold, 1973), pp. 103–43.

Chapter 3 The social values of speech and writing

1 Peter Trudgill, *The Social Differentiation of English in Norwich* (Cambridge University Press, 1974).
2 The classic statement of this position is in N. Chomsky's *Aspects of the Theory of Syntax* (Cambridge, Mass.: M.I.T. Press, 1965).
3 For an illuminating survey essay on the neurological aspects of speech see J. Laver's 'The Production of Speech' in J. Lyons (ed.), *New Horizons in Linguistics* (Harmondsworth: Penguin, 1970), pp. 53–75.

4 See M. A. K. Halliday, 'Notes on Transitivity and Theme in English', *Journal of Linguistics*, 3 (1967), 37–81.

5 M. A. K. Halliday, 'Language Structure and Language Function', in J. Lyons, op. cit.; and chapters 12 and 14 in G. R. Kress (ed.), *Halliday: System and Function in Language* (London: Oxford University Press, 1976).

6 See W. Labov's 'The logic of non-standard English', in P. P. Giglioli (ed.), *Language and Social Context* (Harmondsworth: Penguin, 1972) on the effect of intimidating interview situations.

7 For a discussion of tense from this point of view see G. R. Kress, 'Tense as Modality', *UEA Papers in Linguistics*, 5 (1977), 40–52.

8 For a fuller discussion see A. C. Gimson, *An Introduction to the Pronunciation of English* (London: Edward Arnold, 1962).

Chapter 4 Interviews

1 See R. Brown and M. Ford, 'Address in American English', in John Laver and Sandy Hutcheson (eds), *Communication in Face to Face Interaction* (Harmondsworth: Penguin, 1972), pp. 128–45; S. M. Ervin-Tripp, 'Sociolinguistic Rules of Address', in J. B. Pride and J. Holmes (eds), *Sociolinguistics* (Harmondsworth: Penguin, 1972), pp. 225–40.

2 See M. A. K. Halliday, 'Modality and Modulation in English', in G. R. Kress (ed.), *Halliday: System and Function in Language* (London: Oxford University Press, 1976), pp. 189–213.

3 See G. Kress, 'Tense as Modality', *UEA Papers in Linguistics*, 5 (1977), 40–52.

4 See Frieda Goldman-Eisler, 'Hesitation and Information in Speech', in C. Cherry (ed.), *Information Theory* (London: Butterworth, 1961); Basil Bernstein, 'Linguistic Codes, Hesitation Phenomena and Intelligence', (1962), in *Class, Codes and Control*, vol. I (London: Routledge & Kegan Paul, 1971), ch. 5.

Chapter 5 The ideology of middle management

1 Names used here, as elsewhere, are fictitious.

2 See M. A. K. Halliday, 'Modality and Modulation in English', in G. R. Kress (ed.), *Halliday: System and Function in Language* (London: Oxford University Press, 1976), pp. 189–213.

3 On intonation and information structure in speech, see M. A. K. Halliday, 'Notes on Transitivity and Theme in English', *Journal of Linguistics*, 3 (1967), 199–244.

4 See G. R. Kress, 'Tense as Modality', *UEA Papers in Linguistics*, 5 (September, 1977), 40–52.

Chapter 6 Theory and ideology at work

1 The terms that might have been used are either too unsettled, too much involved with unacceptable notions, or too firmly integrated in a different language to be readily taken into English without a major piece of work. (And this study is too short for the amount of work needed to introduce a new term.) Examples of such terms are 'paradigm' as used by T. Kuhn, *'The Structure of Scientific Revolution'* (Chicago University Press, 1962), and by many others since, or 'savoir' in M. Foucault, *Archaeology of Knowledge* (London: Tavistock, 1972). This last book and L. Althusser 'Ideology and Ideological State Apparatuses', in *Lenin and Philosophy* (London: New Left Books, 1971) are amongst the ones I have found useful on this issue.

2 See for example, R. Harré, *An Introduction to the Logic of the Sciences* (London: Macmillan, 1967).

3 This has been the subject of much work in the history of science in the last thirty years or so, from various positions. The most familiar examples to English readers are T. Kuhn, op. cit.; P. Feyerabend, *Against Method* (London: New Left Books, 1975); I. Lakatos, *Criticism and the Growth of Knowledge* (Cambridge University Press, 1970). A different, and on the whole more satisfactory tradition of work is accessible through translations such as M. Foucault, op. cit., or D. Lecourt, *Marxism and Epistemology: Bachelard, Canguilhem and Foucault* (London: New Left Books, 1975). The last book has a preface discussing relations between the two traditions of work.

4 For a discussion of this see F. Burton and P. Carlen, 'Official Discourse', *Paper for the 1977 Annual Conference of the British Sociological Association*.

5 For an explanation of this, see M. A. K. Halliday, 'Language Structure and Language Function' in J. Lyons (ed.), *New Horizons in Linguistics* (Harmondsworth: Penguin 1970), pp. 140–65.

6 An introduction to modality can be found either in Halliday's 'Language Structure and Language Function', J. Lyons, op. cit., or in 'Modality and Modulation in English' in G. R. Kress (ed.), *Halliday: System and Function in Language* (London: Oxford University Press, 1976).

7 For a discussion of the departure in this chapter from the more familiar notion of transformation, see below, and also G. Kress and T. Trew, 'Transformations and Discourse: a Study in Conceptual Change', *Journal of Literary Semantics*, 7 (1978).

8 There are related, though significantly different, concepts of 'African' in some of the varieties of the ideologies described as 'African populism' in J. Saul, 'On African Populism', in G. Arrighi and J. Saul, *Essays on the Political Economy of Africa* (New York: Monthly Review Press, 1973).

9 For extended accounts of this ideology and its relation to reality, see B. Davidson, *In the Eye of the Storm* (Harmondsworth: Penguin, 1975); and M. Loney, *White Racism and Imperial Response* (Harmondsworth: Penguin, 1975).

10 These terms and this distinction come from R. Hodge and G. Kress, *Language as Ideology* (London: Routledge & Kegan Paul, 1979). The distinction is based on those made by Halliday. The distinction is primarily one between clause types, and is used here derivatively and provisionally to apply to words.

11 This would not apply to recent, post-1965, Chomskyan theory, although related points would apply.

12 M. A. K. Halliday, 'Anti-languages', *UEA Papers in Linguistics*, 1 (1976), 15–45.

13 For a discussion of this, see G. Kress and T. Trew, 'Ideological Transformations of Discourse', *Sociological Review*, 26, 4 (1978).

14 S. A. Institute of Race Relations, *Annual Survey 1977 for the period July 1, 1976 to 30 June 1977*. This material, like much of the other material in this study, was made available to me by the research department of the International Defence and Aid Fund, London.

Chapter 7 'What the papers say': linguistic variation and ideological difference

1 G. Kress (ed.), *Halliday: System and Function in Language* (London: Oxford University Press, 1976), ch. II 'Types of Process', p. 159.

2 See p. 110, previous chapter.

3 'Yob' was originally a slang term for 'boy', from which it is derived by backward spelling (and 'yobbo' is an extension of it, as the Anglo-Irish 'boyo' is an extension of 'boy'). It means 'An arrogant and resentful loutish and violent Teddy boy', according to Eric Partridge's *Smaller Slang Dictionary* (London: Routledge & Kegan Paul, 1964).

4 In M. A. K. Halliday, 'Anti-languages', *UEA Papers in Linguistics*, (1976), 15–45.

5 This process of 'mediation' is discussed in Stuart Hall, Chas. Chritcher, John Clarke, Brian Roberts, *Policing the Crises: Mugging, the State, and Law and Order* (London: Macmillan, 1978). The book deals with many of the important aspects that go beyond the scope of this study of the linguistics of ideological process.

6 Again, see *Policing the Crises* (which is the source of the *Sun* editorial about 'muggers' quoted here).

7 This is from a National Front internal circular, reproduced in the *Socialist Worker*, 30 July 1977.

8 For a full discussion see Stuart Hall, 'The treatment of "football hooliganism" in the press', in *Football Hooliganism, the Wider Context* by Roger Ingham, Stuart Hall, John Clarke, Peter Marsh, Jim Donovan, (London: Inter-Action Inprint, 1978).

9 The clause describing 'Sunday's violence', the events of the previous day, has been left out of the analysis.

10 The *Guardian* with 'gangs' in its headline looks like an exception to the patterns. In fact its headline is less like a summary than a conclusion drawn from a long report which only mentions 'a gang' right at the end. The headline is something of a middleway compromise of the two perceptions.

11 See for example the 'Policing Carnival' editorial in *Race Today* (Sept./Oct. 1977), p. 123, and *The Black Liberator* (Dec. 1978), pp. 8–27.

12 Circulation figures are calculated from the certified average daily net sales for the half-year ended June 1977, published by the Audit Bureau of Circulations.

13 I have used the concept of discourse in these last two chapters without explicit discussion. The concept is central to the project of bringing linguistic theory to bear on the social. The word 'discourse' is itself an example of a focus of theoretical/ideological conflict expressed in discourse, in this case conflict in sociolinguistic practice. In the sociolinguistic writings that will be most familiar to readers of English, 'discourse analysis' is predominantly the analysis of structures of speech interactions between individuals, a position expressing an individualist, social-psychological approach in social theory. A selection of articles representative of this tradition can be seen in J. Laver and S. Hutchinson (eds), *Communication in Face-to-Face Interaction* (Harmondsworth: Penguin, 1972). The way I have been using 'discourse' is lodged within a quite different orientation in social theory. It is derived largely from writings such as those of Foucault already referred to (see p. 217), but draws also on a related concept of discourse present in an earlier phase of work in American linguistics, as represented, for example, by Zellig Harris's 'Discourse analysis', *Language*, 28 (1952), 1–30. (For further discussion, see also G. Kress and T. Trew, 'Transformations and Discourse: a Study in Conceptual Change', *Journal of Literary Semantics*, 7 (1978.)

Chapter 8 Newspapers and communities

1 Hence the value of 'hooligans', 'yobs', etc., young, working class and violent, a small minority in fact, constituting the image of the anti-community. This gives a function to the overlexicalization already noted in this area (see Ch. 7). So many groups of law-abiding adults

(strikers, pickets, demonstrators) have to be damned by association with juvenile delinquents so often that many synonyms are needed to avoid too obvious repetition.

Chapter 9 Birth and the community

1 See A. Van Gennep, *Rites of Passage* trans. M. B. Vizedom and G. L. Caffee (London: Routledge & Kegan Paul, 1960).

Chapter 10 Critical linguistics

1 See below, pp. 190–4, for further discussion. We refer to correlational work such as that of William Labov conveniently popularized in Peter Trudgill, *Sociolinguistics* (Harmondsworth: Penguin, 1974).
2 See R. Fowler, 'Style and the Concept of Deep Structure', *Journal of Literary Semantics*, 1 (1972), 5–14, attempting to maintain this dichotomy, and R. Fowler, 'Headlinese: A Counter-Example to the Ohmann Thesis', *UEA Papers in Linguistics*, 3 (1977), 36–48, abandoning it.
3 See his paper 'On Communicative Competence', in J. B. Pride and J. Holmes (eds), *Sociolinguistics* (Harmondsworth: Penguin, 1972), pp. 269–93; Dell Hymes, *Foundations in Sociolinguistics* (London: Tavistock Press, 1977).
4 M. A. K. Halliday, 'Language Structure and Language Function', in J. Lyons (ed.), *New Horizons in Linguistics* (Harmondsworth: Penguin, 1970), pp. 140–65; 'Towards a Sociological Semantics', in *Explorations in the Functions of Language* (London: Edward Arnold, 1973), pp. 72–102.
5 See G. R. Kress (ed.), *Halliday: System and Function in Language* (London: Oxford University Press, 1976).
6 For some relevant discussion, see Umberto Eco, *A Theory of Semiotics* (Bloomington: Indiana University Press, 1976; London: Macmillan, 1977); Rosalind Coward and John Ellis, *Language and Materialism* (London: Routledge & Kegan Paul, 1977).
7 Some well-known and representative correlational studies include W. Labov, *The Social Stratification of English in New York City* (Washington, D.C.: Center for Applied Linguistics, 1966); W. Labov, *Sociolinguistic Patterns* (Philadelphia: University of Pennsylvania Press, 1972); R. Brown and A. Gilman, 'The Pronouns of Power and Solidarity', in P. P. Giglioli (ed.), *Language and Social Context* (Harmondsworth: Penguin, 1972), pp. 252–82; C. A. Ferguson, 'Diglossia', in Giglioli, op. cit., pp. 232–51; S. M. Ervin-Tripp, Sociolinguistic Rules of Address', in J. B. Pride and J. Holmes (ed.),

Sociolinguistics (Harmondsworth: Penguin, 1972), pp. 225–40; and
J. J. Gumperz, 'Social Meaning in Linguistic Structures: Code-
Switching in Norway', in J. J. Gumperz and D. Hymes, (eds),
Directions in Sociolinguistics (New York: Holt, Rinehart & Winston,
1972), pp. 409–34.

8 'The third section proposes a connection between social structure,
group ideology, and the semantics of the pronoun' (Giglioli, op. cit.,
p. 252).

9 Trans. Peter Sand, Pieter A. M. Seuren and Kevin Whiteley
(London: Edward Arnold, 1976); see especially Ch. 7, concentrating
on American studies of Black English.

10 Both Labov and Trudgill, for instance, utilize models of social class
stratification which originate in government departments. Both
assume a finely graded hierarchy of four or more socio-economic
strata (Labov has ten grades potentially, but does not use them all).
It might be objected that this concept of a finely graded hierarchy
rather than, say, a dichotomy, is itself a pacificatory model disguising
divisions as differentiation.

11 Giglioli, op. cit., p. 236.

12 Much relevant discussion of criticism and interpretation is to be
found in the Introduction and texts reprinted in Paul Connerton,
(ed.), *Critical Sociology* (Harmondsworth: Penguin, 1976). There is
an interesting hint in Connerton's reference to Chomsky (pp. 19–20)
that he would agree with us in considering established linguistics as
normative.

13 J. R. Searle, 'Indirect Speech Acts', in P. Cole and J. L. Morgan
(eds), *Syntax and Semantics*, Vol. 3: *Speech Acts* (New York:
Academic Press, 1975), pp. 59–82.

14 For the application of the principles and methods of critical linguistics to *literary* texts, see R. Fowler, *Linguistic Criticism* (Oxford
University Press, forthcoming).

15 This sentence, and the majority of other examples in the remainder of
this chapter, are taken from the London *Observer* newspaper for
Sunday 26 March 1978.

16 For references to some classic articles on pronouns and naming, see
above, note 7. For sexism in reference to persons, see Robin Lakoff,
Language and Woman's Place (New York: Harper, 1975); Casey
Miller and Kate Swift, *Words and Women* (New York: Anchor
Books, 1977).

17 On the use of 'we' to mystify responsibility, see Richard Ohmann,
'Writing, Out in the World', in his *English in America: A Radical
View of the Profession* (New York: Oxford University Press, 1976),
especially pp. 175–6. The chapter contains a good deal of critical
linguistic analysis which is very compatible with the present book.
For a literary analysis based on inclusive *v.* exclusive 'we', see

R. Fowler, 'Literature as Discourse', in Godfrey Vesey (ed.), *Communication and Understanding* (Hassocks, Sussex: Harvester Press, 1977), pp. 174–94.

18 In features sections of newspapers, 'the individual' receives a very focused social-economic-sexual typing, with assumed tastes, actions and belief systems differing sharply from paper to paper.

19 J. L. Austin, *How to Do Things with Words* (New York and London: Oxford University Press, 1977); J. R. Searle, *Speech Acts* (Cambridge University Press, 1969); Searle, 'What is a Speech Act?', in P. P. Giglioli (ed.), *Language and Social Context* (Harmondsworth: Penguin, 1972), pp. 136–56; Searle, 'Indirect Speech Acts', in P. Cole and Jerry L. Morgan (eds), *Syntax and Semantics*, Vol. 3: *Speech Acts* (New York: Academic Press, 1975), pp. 59–82; Searle, 'A Classification of Illocutionary Acts', *Language in Society*, 5 (1976), 1–23.

20 An integrated discussion of this area is given in M. A. K. Halliday, 'Functional Diversity in Language as seen from a Consideration of Modality and Mood in English', in *Foundations of Language*, 6 (1970), 327–51 (reprinted as chapter 13 in G. R. Kress, (ed.), *Halliday: System and Function in Language* (London: Oxford University Press, 1976). A discussion linking modal verbs with speech act theory is J. Boyd and J. P. Thorne, 'The Semantics of Modal Verbs', in *Journal of Linguistics*, 5 (1969), 57–74.

21 For an extended discussion see G. R. Kress, 'Tense as Modality', *UEA Papers in Linguistics*, 5 (1977), 40–52; and R. I. V. Hodge and G. R. Kress, *Language as Ideology* (London: Routledge & Kegan Paul, 1979), especially chapters 5–7.

22 See A. Akmajian and F. Heny, *An Introduction to the Principles of Transformational Syntax* (Cambridge, Mass.: MIT Press, 1975).

23 We have taken this term from M. A. K. Halliday, 'Anti-languages', *UEA Papers in Linguistics*, 1 (1976), 15–45. Halliday gives three examples of this process. For other discussions which make use of this concept see R. I. V. Hodge and G. R. Kress, *Language as Ideology*, op. cit., chapter 4; and G. R. Kress, 'Poetry as Anti-language: a Reconsideration of Donne's "Nocturnall upon S. Lucies Day"', *PTL*, 3 (1978), 327–44.

24 These constructions have been much discussed in transformational generative grammar. The first article in this debate is C. Smith, 'A Class of Complex Modifiers in English', *Language*, 37 (1961), 342–65. The semantic import of the position of adjectives was discussed by B. L. Whorf, *Language, Thought and Reality* (Cambridge, Mass.: MIT Press, 1956). There is an extended discussion in Hodge and Kress, op. cit.

Index